(3)

English
Elements

*12 units
plus 4 revision units
and 12 homestudy units*

*Myriam Fischer Callus
Jackie Sykes*

Max Hueber Verlag

We would especially like to thank

- **Louise Bulloch**, Dozentin am Institut für Lehrerfortbildung in Hamburg und
  Kursleiterin an Institutionen in der Erwachsenenbildung

for advice and feedback on *English Elements 3*.

We would also like to thank the copyright owners for permission to reproduce
the material used. A list of sources appears on page 230.

6.	5.	4.			Die letzten Ziffern
2010	09	08	07	06	bezeichnen Zahl und Jahr des Druckes.

Alle Drucke dieser Auflage können, da unverändert,
nebeneinander benutzt werden.
1. Auflage
© 2001 Max Hueber Verlag, 85737 Ismaning, Deutschland
Verlagsredaktion: Rebecka Howe, München
Illustrationen: Reinhard Wendlinger, München
Herstellung: [HLM] Holger Latzel, München
Lithographie: Scan & Art, München
Druck und Bindung: Georg Appl, Wemding
Printed in Germany
ISBN 3-19-202496-8

English Elements 3
Introduction

English Elements 3 is aimed at students learning English at a pre-intermediate level. Whilst it is the natural progression after *English Elements 2*, it is additionally an independent coursebook equally suitable for students who have not yet worked with the *English Elements* series.

English Elements 3 creates a balance between consolidating the main structures, functions and lexis from *English Elements 2*, and introducing new language. Through a suitable mixture of listening, reading, writing and speaking activities, *English Elements 3* gives the learner the opportunity to practise the target language at a pre-intermediate level.

The **Note, Remember, Looking at Language, Functional Language** and **Grammar Reference Section** all help the student to focus on the language. The structures, functions and topics in *English Elements 3* will start to prepare the student for both the European Language Certificate in English B1 (Threshold Level – A Common European Framework / Council of Europe) and the University of Cambridge Preliminary English Test (PET).

English Elements 3 primarily promotes active student participation. The learner is presented with a multitude of opportunities to speak and write. Pair work, group work and whole class activities are designed to break down the fear of speaking in the target language and to encourage the learner to be creative. The creative writing activities give the learner a chance to experiment with the language. The cross-cultural activities allow the student not only to reflect on different behaviour, tradition and beliefs in other cultures, but also to voice their own experiences and opinions.

A focal point of *English Elements 3* is vocabulary building. The varied and progressive topics of each unit enable the learner to consolidate and extend their vocabulary fields. Students are encouraged to share their previous knowledge through brainstorming, word wheels and mind mapping activities. The **Word Bank** is a constant reminder to collect and learn new vocabulary.

Nevertheless, listening and reading skills are by no means neglected. Modern lively realistic texts have been chosen to give students meaningful and motivational practice. Reading and understanding extracts from books and newspapers can give students a feeling of achievement. Additionally, each main unit contains **Learning Tips**. These provide students with strategies on how to learn a foreign language – for example, how to cope with reading and listening texts without understanding every word.
They will also help the learners reflect on their language learning, inside and outside the classroom. *English Elements 3* helps learners become more responsible for their own learning. The autonomy, the responsibility and the creativity of the learner is an important factor in all the units of the book.

A key aspect of the *English Elements* series is to promote effective communication in English in both the private sphere and the workplace. The **Job Talk** section of each main unit gives the student meaningful language practice in the field of work. Activities include writing e-mails and faxes, telephoning with a business partner, or a presentation of a company.

The **Homestudy Section** for each unit and the four revision units interspersed after every three units, create a coursebook and a student workbook in one. The Homestudy Section provides plenty of opportunities to recycle the language features in the main units. Additionally, for reference, *English Elements 3* provides Tapescripts, a Key and Vocabulary lists at the back of the book.

As with all the books in the *English Elements* series, we hope that *English Elements 3* provides the learners with an enjoyable and valuable learning experience as their language skills progress.

Your English Elements Team

Your Language Biography

(European Language Portfolio based on the Common European Framework of Reference for Language, developed by the Council of Europe)

Before you start with Unit One, take a few minutes to answer the following questions. This section helps you to:
- evaluate and describe your language needs.
- reflect on the best way to learn English, inside and outside the classroom.
- set your personal objectives.
- plan further learning of English.

Why are you learning English?
- for your job?
- for travel?
- for study?
- for pleasure?

What do you want to achieve by the end of the course?
I want to be able to:
- listen and understand _____
- speak to _____
- read _____
- write _____

Which language skills are most important to you?
- speaking
- listening
- reading
- writing

How do you learn best?

_____
_____
_____
_____

What language activities do you enjoy doing?

_____
_____
_____
_____

How many hours a week are you prepared to learn at home?

_____

Is it important for you to prepare for an English exam/certificate?   ▢ Yes   ▢ No

If 'yes', which exam/certificate?

_____

Where did you learn English?

_____

For how long?

_____

What other foreign languages can you speak?

_____

Table of Contents

V   Vocabulary and Functional Language
G   Grammar
S   Skills
J   Job Talk
L   Learning tip

Language Learning

1 Saying hello

a Introduce yourself to as many people
as possible in five minutes.
Try to remember their names.
Example: Hello, my name's Jenny. Nice to meet you. –
Hi, I'm Katja. Nice to meet you, too.

Greet the people you already know.
Example: Hello, Paul. Nice to see you again. How are you? –
Hi, Monika. I'm fine, thanks. Good to see you, too.

b Finding out information

Look at the information about your teacher on the board. What are the
correct questions that fit to the information? Start your questions with
'what', 'where', 'how' etc.

Example:

| Sandra | What's your first name? |
| English, German | What languages do you speak? |

c What is important for you to find out
when meeting a new person?
Work in pairs and write five questions.

What ...   Do ...
        name?
Why ... nationality?   Are ...
        job?
Which ... hobbies?
        family?
Where ... shoe size?   Have ...
        pets?
When ...   anything else?   Is ...

How many ...

Remember

When you want more information than
'yes' or 'no', you use a question word
like 'what', 'where', 'how' etc.
Example: What do you do? –
I'm a sales manager.

1. _____ ?
2. _____ ?
3. _____ ?
4. _____ ?
5. _____ ?

d Now sit next to someone you don't know. Ask your questions and answer your partner's questions.
Make a note of your partner's answers. Tell the rest of the class one thing you now know about your partner.

2 Words to talk about yourself

a One way to remember words is to put them into word wheels. Can you complete the following word wheels? Work together in a group of three or four.

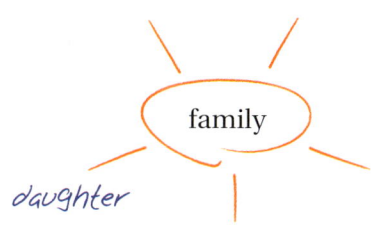

daughter · family

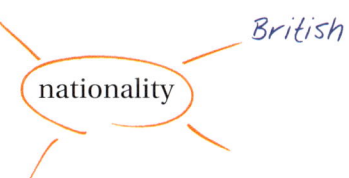

nationality · British

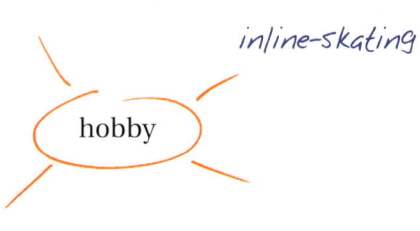

job · computer programmer

hobby · inline-skating

b Now write five sentences about yourself – some true, some false. Use the vocabulary above.

1. _____ .
2. _____ .
3. _____ .
4. _____ .
5. _____ .

Remember

Questions and short answers in simple present
Examples: Do you listen to English songs?
– Yes, I do. / No, I don't.
Are you German?
– Yes, I am. / No, I'm not.

c Work in pairs and try to find out which of your partner's five statements are false. Explain why.

3 Different cultures: standing in a queue

a The British always stand in a queue when waiting for a bus / taxi or at a bank. Make a queue in your classroom. Stand in the order of how long it takes you to get to the classroom.

Examples:
Where do you live? – I live in …
How long does it take you to get here ? – It takes me …

Now tell the rest of your class about the person behind you.
Example: This is Paul. It only takes him five minutes to get here.

b Do you stand in a queue for anything in your country?
How do you react if someone pushes in?
What do you say?

4 Why English?

a There are lots of reasons for learning English.
Make a list of why people want to learn English.

for holidays
for business
because of penfriends

b Now listen to an interviewer talking to students at a language school. Why are they learning English? Look at your list (**4a**) and tick (✔) the reasons you hear. Add any new reasons.

c Now look at the following questionnaire and answer the questions. Then ask the people in class and put down their names.

> ### Remember
> You use the **simple present** when you talk about something that is true in general.
> *Example:* I **need** English at work.

Do you …	you	people in class
● have friends in an English-speaking country?	■	_____
● like listening to English music?	■	_____
● need to phone in English?	■	_____
● need English at work?	■	_____
● want to speak English on holiday?	■	_____
● write letters/e-mails in English?	■	_____
● want to train your brain?	■	_____
● want to learn just for fun?	■	_____

d Tell the class one or two things you found out.
Example: Claudia is learning English because
she needs English at work.

e Listen to the song 'Tom's Diner'
and number the pictures accordingly.

 Listen again to check your order.

In this song Suzanne Vega describes a situation at a café.
She sings about scenes that are happening at the moment
of singing (or speaking).

Now look at the first two verses. Can you fill in the gaps
with verbs in the correct tense?

I _____
In the morning
At the diner
On the corner

I _____
At the counter
For the man
To pour the coffee

f Can you match the American words
from the song with the British
equivalent?

American	British
1. diner	pull
2. funnies	tights
3. hitch	café
4. stockings	cartoons

> **Remember your word bank.**

5 Writing a letter

a You would like to take an English course in the UK. You read about *The Park Language
Centre* in a magazine and now you would like to write a letter to the school.

Before you start, can you remember the correct start and finish?

1. Dear Jo		Best wishes
2. Dear Mr Green		Lots of love

Unit 1   **13**

5b Now write a short letter to *The Park Language Centre* and ask them to send you a brochure about their courses.

The Park Language Centre
141 West Street
Sheffield S1 4ES

Dear ...
I would like to ...
I'm interested in ...
Could you please send ...

6 Learning and leisure

a At *The Park Language Centre* in Sheffield you can learn English in the morning and do an activity in the afternoon. What leisure activities do you think the school offers?

_____

Programme

General English
Programme 1
   15 lessons per week
   Max 10 per group
   Minimum level: Elementary

Programme 2
   21 lessons per week
   Max 10 per group
   Minimum level: Elementary

Business English
   1 class per week
   6-8pm
   Max 10 per group

Cambridge First Certificate
   1 class per week
   6-8pm
   Max 10 per group

Academic English
   1 class per week
   6-8pm
   Max 10 per group

b Listen to the dialogue between a learner and the assistant at *The Park Language Centre* and complete the table with the correct information below.

Number of activities on offer: ☐ ☐

Number of English lessons in one week: ☐ ☐

Previous experience of the activities: ☐ Yes ☐ No

c Listen to the dialogue a second time and write down the answers to the following.

1. Which different activities are on offer? – _____

2. What types of clothing do you need to bring? – _____

d Which course combination would you like to do? What alternative combinations do you think the school should offer?

Note

Opinions
I would like to do ...
I think it's a good idea because ...
I think it's a good idea, but ...
In my opinion they should offer ...

Remember your word bank.

7 Accommodation at The Park Language Centre

a The texts on the next page explain the different types of accommodation available at *The Park Language Centre*. Work in pairs.
Can you match the correct heading to each paragraph?   1 ☐   2 ☐   3 ☐   4 ☐
Circle the words that helped you to find out.

Shared student houses **a**	Host families **b**	Hotels **c**	Self-catering **d**
1	**2**	**3**	**4**
Our families will provide you with a comfortable bedroom, full-board during the week, and half-board at the weekends. Facilities are available for your clothes laundry. There is new bed linen every week. The host family will encourage you to join in with their family life.	You can still stay with a family, but can cook for yourself. You will be responsible for your own shopping, cooking and cleaning, but your host will help you if you have any difficulties.	This is ideal for students wanting to make friends with students from local Universities and Colleges. Students have their own bedroom, but share the kitchen facilities, living room and bathroom with other students in the house.	We can send you a list of available hotels and can book your choice of hotel for you.

b Which accommodation would you choose and why?

Example: I would choose a shared student house
because I want to get to know other people.

c Now, in the texts above, find all the words for rooms in a house and words for different types of housework. Can you think of any more?

rooms	housework
bedroom	*cooking*
_____	_____
_____	_____
_____	_____

> **Remember your word bank.**

8 In English, please!

a Going to an English course is a great start to learn English. However, you can improve faster if you also learn outside the classroom. Listen to the following 'eight hot tips' from English learners and fill in the missing words in the sentences below.

always ✓ • *every morning* ✔ • *never* • *in the evening* • *every night* • *usually* • *once a week* • *often*

Eight Hot Tips

1. Well, **every morning** on my way to work I look at the adverts for English words.

2. When I arrive at work, I _____ write down a list of what I want to do in English.

3. Let me think … I talk in English on the phone to a class member _____ .

4. I _____ send short e-mails in English to a colleague.

5. Oh, I know, I play my favourite English CD _____ .

6. Well, I _____ have an English conversation in a café with a friend.

7. Oh, I _____ forget to take my English word bank with me.

8. _____ I choose one word in English that I want to remember before I go to sleep.

Why don't you make it a habit to learn English outside of the classroom!

8b Look back at the text in **8a** and write down the words and phrases for definite and indefinite time.

definite	indefinite
1. every morning	1. _____
2. _____	2. _____
3. _____	3. _____
4. _____	4. _____

c Write down five sentences about your English learning habits using the words in **8b**.

1. _____
2. _____
3. _____
4. _____
5. _____

d Now work in groups of four and share your learning habits with the others. Make a note of the ideas that you like.

Example: Well, I always learn English vocabulary
on the bus.
– That's a good idea.
– I can't do that because …

> **Remember**
>
> **Adverbs of frequency**
> You normally put words like **always**, **often** etc. before the main verb (but after the verb **be**).
> *Example:* I **always** learn English vocabulary on the bus.
>
> **Time phrases**
> You can put phrases like **every day**, **once a week** etc. at the very beginning of the sentence or at the end.
> *Example:* **Every day** I choose five English words to learn. / I choose five English words to learn **every day**.

9 What is a language?

English has many words from other languages like 'yoghurt' from Greek or 'faux pas' from French. Can you think of any German words in the English language?

a Did you know that the following German words are used in the English language?

rucksack (in BE) • *kitschy (in BE)* • *gesundheit (in AE)* • *to abseil (in BE and Aus)* •
schadenfreude (in BE) • *kindergarten (in BE, AE, Aus)*

Can you complete the sentences below?

1. We're going on a long walk. Don't forget to take your _____ .
2. In Great Britain people usually say 'Bless you' instead of _____ .
3. I enjoyed a strange feeling of _____ when my ex-boyfriend got divorced.
4. There are two or three _____s in the area where we now live.
5. Their house is full of _____ ornaments.
6. Lisa _____ed down the rock-face.

b Work in pairs. Can you now think of ten English words which are often used in the German language?

1. computer
2. _____
3. _____
4. _____
5. _____

6. _____
7. _____
8. _____
9. _____
10. _____

Asking for information / Giving information about yourself

What's your name? – My name's Katja.
Where are you from? – I'm from Germany.
What are your hobbies? – I like swimming, sailing and reading.
Where do you work? – I work for an international company.
Have you got any children? – Yes, I've got one daughter.

Giving an opinion

I would like to do a combination course.
I think it is good because I can do lots of things.
In my opinion you can learn more this way.

Simple present

You use the **simple present** to talk about facts and habits.
Examples: I **like** English songs.
She **phones** her friend once a week.
We sometimes **eat** snacks.

Present progressive

You can use the **present progressive** to talk about actions which are true for a certain time and you also use it to talk about something which is happening at the moment of speaking.
Examples: **I'm attending** an English course.
He**'s eating** a sandwich at the moment.

Adverbs of frequency

With adverbs of frequency you can say 'how often' something happens. You normally put these adverbs, 'always', 'usually', 'never' etc., before the main verb.
Examples: I **usually** get up earlier in the summer.
He **never** eats snacks.

Time phrases

You put phrases like 'every day', 'once a week' etc. at the beginning of a sentence or at the very end.
Example: **Every day** I listen to the news in English. / I listen to the news in English **every day**.

Memory Box

Fitness

1 Paying compliments

a When you meet someone, paying a compliment is a nice way to start off the conversation. Listen to the dialogues and complete each compliment.

that haircut • *really fit* • *great flat* • *nice jacket*

1. That's a _____ !
2. What a _____ !
3. _____ really suits you !
4. You look _____ !

b Get together in groups of three or four. Greet each other and pay each other a compliment using one of the expressions in **1a**.
Don't forget to use their name and to thank someone if they pay you a compliment too!

2 Jog, hop, skip

a To feel good or to look good many people do sports. In your group find five sports for the following headings. See if your group can finish first!

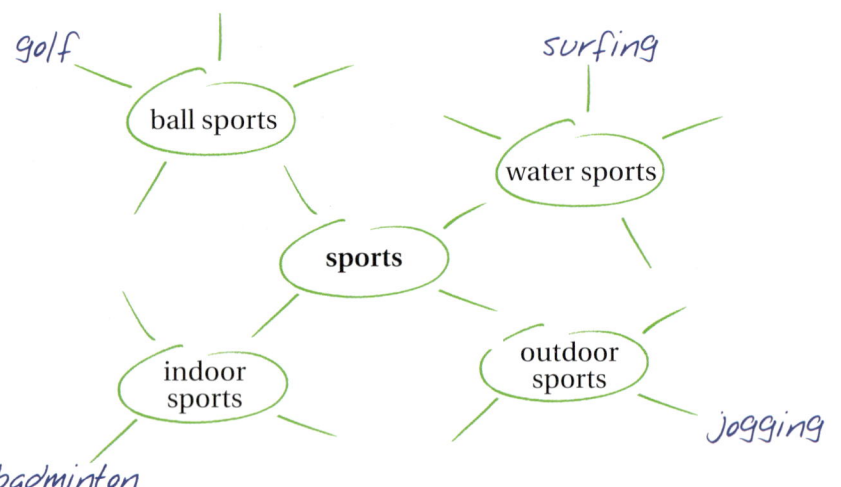

golf
ball sports

surfing
water sports

sports

indoor sports

outdoor sports

jogging

badminton

> **Learning Tip – Vocabulary**
> When a word field (e.g. sports) becomes too big it helps to break it down into sub-headings.

b Tell your group which sports you prefer and why.
Examples: I prefer jogging because I want to be outdoors.
I don't like doing any sports …

Remember your word bank.

3 The fitness test

a 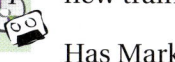 Have you ever been to a gym? Listen to Mark talking to his new trainer at the Fast Track Gym and fill in the table below.

Has Mark ever …	Yes	Never
1. been to a gym?	☐	☐
2. done any sports?	☐	☐
3. smoked?	☐	☐

> **Remember**
>
> You often use **ever** and **never** with the **present perfect**.

b **How fit are you?**

Work in pairs and find out how fit your partner is with this fun questionnaire. Remember to use the present perfect.

Example: spend all day walking
Have you **ever spent** all day walking? – Yes, I have. / No, I haven't. / No, never.

Partner A looks at this page.
Partner B looks at **page 114**.

Ask your partner the following questions starting with 'Have you ever …?'

Partner A
Have you ever …?
1. swim in the sea for one hour non-stop
2. ride a bike the whole day
3. do aerobics
4. run in a race
5. abseil down a mountain

Results for partner B
Less than 3 'yes' answers:
    It's time to find the right track!
More than 3 'yes' answers:
    You're on the right track – don't lose it!

> **Remember**
>
> In sentences with **no definite time signals** for the past you use the present perfect.
> *Examples:* **Have** you **ever done** aerobics?
>   – Yes, I have. / No, I haven't.
>   Pat **has never watched** TV all day.

▷ For a list of irregular verbs see **page 183**.

c Report back to the class.

Examples: Hannah has never spent a lazy weekend.
        Joe has abseiled in France.

4 Days for charity

Have you ever done anything for charity? – On certain days in the year people in Britain do 'strange' things to raise money for charity.
Can you imagine what people do for charity?

a Listen to the following people and fill in the table below to match the speaker and the activity with the title of the charity day.

Title	Speaker	Activity
The Red Nose Day	_____	_____
The Boxing Day Dip	1	_____
Hit the Roof Day	_____	abseil down a mountain

> ### Remember
> You use the **simple past** to talk about something completed in the past at a definite time.

b First read the notes below.

1. Anthony / swim / on Christmas Day
2. He / run / to the river
3. Jenny / wear / a blue plastic nose
4. She / collect / £100 for charity
5. Gill / abseil / down a mountain
6. It / take / her 10 hours

True ☐ ☐ False
☐ ☐
☐ ☐
☐ ☐
☐ ☐
☐ ☐

Then listen to the speakers again and decide if the notes are true or false.

c Now complete the notes from **4b** in the simple past giving the correct information.

1. Anthony didn't swim on Christmas Day. He swam on Boxing Day.
2. _____
3. _____
4. _____
5. _____
6. _____

> ### Remember
> In the **simple past** you write positive sentences with the past tense verb.
> *Example:* He **swam** on Boxing Day.
>
> For negative sentences you need to use 'didn't' + the infinitive of the verb.
> *Example:* He **didn't swim** on Christmas Day.

d Work with a partner and ask her/him about a special festivity (e.g. Christmas, Easter, Valentine's Day, Halloween) in her/his country or a special personal day (e.g. birthday, wedding day).

Use the questions below to find out what she/he did on that day last year.

1. When was it?
2. What did you do?
3. What did you eat?
4. What did you wear?
5. How was it (good, interesting, fun)?

Remember

In questions in the **simple past** you use 'did' + infinitive with any verb except 'be'.
Examples: **Did** you **swim** in the sea? – Yes, I did. / No, I didn't.
How long **did** you **stay** in the sea? – I stayed in for five minutes.

But you use **was/were** with the verb **be**.
Examples: **Was** Anthony in the sea on Christmas Day? – Yes, he was. / No, he wasn't.
Were his daughters on the beach? – Yes, they were. / No, they weren't.

---

e Simple past or present perfect?

Use the correct tense to complete these sentences.

1. Yesterday I _____ (want) to go to town.
2. _____ you ever _____ (be) to Italy?
3. Ten years ago Mauro _____ (do) a parachute jump for charity.
4. They _____ never _____ (run) in a marathon.
5. _____ you _____ (watch) the Olympics on TV last night?
6. George _____ _____ (swim) at the weekend
   because he _____ (have) a cold.
7. I _____ _____ (fly) in a helicopter before.
8. _____ Enzo _____ (live) here five years ago?
9. When _____ (be) Boxing Day last year?
10. I _____ (decide) to stay at home last weekend.

Note

to raise money for
to spend money on
to give money to
to donate money to

f Different cultures: charities

Discuss with the rest of the class.
What do people do for charities in your country?

5 Sounds

Put the following regular verbs in the simple past together under the following 'sound' headings.

abseiled • collected • looked • agreed • wanted •
walked • smoked • decided • stayed

[ɪd]	[d]	[t]
1. _____	_____	_____
2. _____	_____	_____
3. _____	_____	_____

Then listen to check.

> **Learning Tip – Sounds**
> Although regular verbs in the simple past end with 'ed' they are not all spoken the same. To help you to remember the pronunciation, group together words which sound the same.

6 Find someone who …

a Go round the class and ask the correct questions to find someone who has done / who did the following. Be careful with the tenses!

Examples:
do an English course last month
Did you **do** an English course **last month**? – Yes, I did. / No, I didn't.

drive a car
Have you **ever driven** a car? – Yes, I have. / No, I haven't. / No, I've never driven a car.

1. … live in a different flat 5 years ago
2. … go to the US last year
3. … work in an international company
4. … have a hectic time last month
5. … eat an Indian meal last night
6. … eat oysters
7. … ride a motorbike
8. … buy a CD / mini disc / DVD last weekend
9. … be to a Greek island
10. … learn English vocabulary yesterday

> **Remember**
> Sentences in the **simple past** often have signal words such as **yesterday**, **ago**, **last year** etc.

b Report back to the class.

Examples: Francis did an English course last month.
Isabelle has driven a car.

7 Down at the gym

a The four people below are looking for a class to do at the gym.
Read the class descriptions and decide which course is the best for each person.

1. Martia gets up early every day and wants to do a class before work. _____
2. Steve has never done any sports but now wants to try. _____
3. Melanie loves riding her bike but hates going out in the rain. _____
4. Colin is looking for a sport which will also help him to relax. _____

THE SUNDERLAND HEALTH & RACQUET CLUB

SPECIAL MILLENNIUM MEMBERSHIP OFFER*
1ST MONTH FREE*

RELAXATION IN A HECTIC WORLD

Health & Fitness Studio Programme

Starter Step / Starter Aerobics
If you've never been into an aerobics studio before, these are the classes for you. They are an introduction to the basic techniques and focus on general fitness.

Over 50s
A class for members over 50 who feel they have specific exercise needs. There is a combination of specific exercise routines with a lot of supervision and personal care.

Early Bird Workout
The best time of the day to workout! A constantly changing session which brings every part of your sleepy body to life. For people who can function at 7 am!

Yoga
Yoga is a sport which is for breathing and relaxation. It harmonises the mind and the body. It will increase flexibility and help to relieve stress.

Aqua Aerobics
Aqua aerobics are safe and effective exercise routines which use the resistance of the water. All-round fitness is the main point of these sessions.

Spinning
For people with power who want to ride a bike whatever the weather. These stationary bikes let you ride up and down hills to music with the support of a trained supervisor. Not for lazy people!

Which course would you like to do?

> ### Remember
>
> **Who** and **which** are used to link two sentences together.
> You use 'who' when you talk about people.
> *Example:* A class for members over 50 **who** feel they have specific exercise needs.
>
> You use 'which' when you talk about things.
> *Example:* Yoga is a gentle sport **which** exercises breathing.

b In groups describe a sport / a sportsman / a sportswoman / something you need for a particular sport and the rest of the group should guess what it is.

Examples: It's something which you need to play squash. *(a squash ball)*
It's a sport which you play outside. *(football)*
It's a sportsman who is in the water a lot. *(a swimmer)*

8 Telephone expressions

The Training Department of DCD wants to send their marketing and sales managers on a 4-day 'Fitness Power Course' to test their team skills in a different environment than the workplace.

a Look at the following phrases Elena Taffy uses when she phones 'Power Courses'. Can you guess what the missing words are?

1. *Starting the call:*   T_____ i_____ Miss Taffy f_____ DCD.

2. *Asking:*   I w_____ l_____ s_____ information.

3. *Offering:*   W_____ you l_____ me t_____ send …

4. *Checking:*   Sorry, c_____ you r_____ that, p_____?

5. *Thanking:*   Thank you v_____ m_____ for your h_____ .

6. *Finishing:*   Thank you for c_____ . B_____ .

 Now listen to check your answers.

> Remember your word bank.

b Work in pairs. Sit back to back. Practise phone conversations using the above expressions.

Partner A looks at this page and partner B looks at **page 114**.

Partner A
1. You work for Euro-chain. You would like some information about balloon rides for an incentive day for your marketing department. Your address is 12 Brunton Street, Edinburgh EH9 5EQ, Scotland. Phone your partner.

2. You have downloaded some information about trekking in Nepal that you want to give to your colleague. Your partner phones you and you answer the call. Ask her / him for their e-mail address.

9 Making suggestions

Work in groups of three.
Student A looks at **page 115**,
student B at **page 119**
and student C at **page 118**.

Explain your situation, your group makes suggestions and you reply.

Examples: I'm always tired. –
Why don't you drink a hot drink?
Have you thought of jogging?
Have you tried taking a cold shower?

That's a good idea.
I don't like …
That sounds interesting (but) …
Maybe I'll try that …
Well, I don't know …

Memory Box

Paying compliments

That's a nice coat.
What a great car!
That colour suits you.
You look great!

Relative clauses

Relative clauses can be used to define words.
The relative pronoun **who** is used to define
people and **which** is used to define things.
Examples: Spinning is for people **who** want
to cycle whatever the weather.
Yoga is a sport **which** is for
breathing and relaxation.

Making suggestions and replying

Why don't you do some sports?
Have you thought of jogging?
Have you tried swimming?

That's a good idea.
Well, I don't know …
That sounds interesting (but) …
Maybe I'll try that …
I don't like …

Simple past

You use the **simple past** to talk about
something that happened in the past and
which is over. You say when it happened
(yesterday, last month, in March).

Example: Last Boxing Day Anthony **swam** in
the sea.

In questions and negatives you use **did/didn't**.
Examples: How long **did** you **stay** in the sea?
I **didn't see** the race.

In questions with **be** you use **was** or **were**.
Examples: **Were** you at the gym last night?
Was Fred in the office yesterday?

Present perfect

In sentences with **no definite time signals**
you use the **present perfect**.
Examples: I**'ve been** to the new gym.
Have you **ever done** any sports?

The present perfect contains two parts:
have/has + past participle in positive
statements and questions
haven't/hasn't + past participle in negative
statements and questions

ever and **never** are often used with the
present perfect.
Examples: **Have** you **ever been** to a gym? –
Yes, I have, but Phil **hasn't been**
there.
They **have never run** in a race.

Moving On

1 The traveller's companion

a Choose from the list below
and put the words for the car parts
in the correct place on the pictures.

*petrol tank • bonnet • windscreen •
headlights • tyre • indicators •
wheel • wing • rear lights •
steering wheel • boot • mirror*

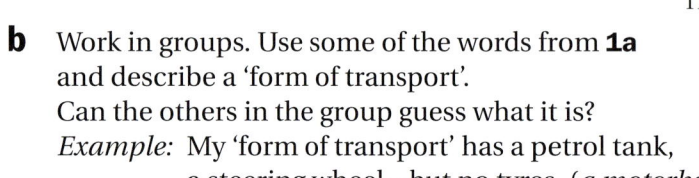

b Work in groups. Use some of the words from **1a**
and describe a 'form of transport'.
Can the others in the group guess what it is?
Example: My 'form of transport' has a petrol tank,
a steering wheel – but no tyres. (*a motorboat*)

> ### Note
>
> | AE: gas | BE: petrol |
> | AE: hood | BE: bonnet |
> | AE: trunk | BE: boot |

Hippie trail led to riches for Lonely Planet

c Before you read the article about a different way of travelling, look at the title
and decide whether the following statements are true or false.

1. Hippies find gold   **True** ☐ ☐ **False**
2. A hippie plans to build on the moon   ☐ ☐
3. An ex-hippie couple write successful guide books
   about the world   ☐ ☐

Now read this article to find out.

In the early 1970s Tony Wheeler and his wife, Maureen, travelled from London across Europe, the Middle East and Asia to Australia. They left England in a £100 mini-van and drove across Europe, Turkey and Iran into Afghanistan. They made a £3 profit on the van and went on by bus and train through Pakistan and India. They trekked in Nepal, hitchhiked through Malaysia and took boats to Java and then on to Sydney.

People were fascinated by the Wheeler's 11,000-mile journey.

'People asked us about our route and where we stayed. So we decided to put what we knew into a small book.' Maureen brought her typewriter home from work at weekends to write up the book and Tony drew all the maps and diagrams. They spent all their savings on printing 'Asia on the Cheap'. When the book was sold in Asia, America and Europe, Wheeler realised he could build a travel guide business.

Since 1970 the Wheelers have produced more than 400 travel books. For over 30 years they have written guide books for every continent. Their company 'Lonely Planet' has become well-known for its well-researched and up-to-date guide books. For the last 20 years independent travellers have come to think of the guide books as bibles. Since 1990 they have also produced phrase books for travellers.

(adapted from The Sunday Times)

d In the text there are lots of words for printed material.
Can you find words in the text to match the following definitions?

1. A piece of paper showing pictures of different countries. _____
2. A piece of paper describing where to find something with lines, arrows etc. _____
3. A book with useful sentences in a foreign language. _____
4. A book explaining about a foreign country. _____
5. A very holy book. _____

e Read the last paragraph again and underline
the phrases with 'since' and 'for'.

Present perfect with 'since' and 'for'
You also use the **present perfect** when you talk about an action that has started
in the past and is still going on today.
Examples: The Wheelers **have written** guide books **since 1970**.
They **have written** guide books **for over thirty years**. *(They started
writing guide books in the early seventies and are still writing today.)*

You use both 'since' and 'for' to say 'how long' something has been happening.
You use 'since' when you say the beginning of the period, e.g. 'since 1970'.
You use 'for' when you say the period of time, e.g. 'for over thirty years'.

Learning Tip – Grammar
When learning the present perfect verbs divide them into three categories:
– regular verbs (-ed), e.g. has lived
– irregular verbs same as the past tense, e.g. has learnt
– new irregular verbs, e.g. has ridden

f Put in either 'since' or 'for'.

- _____ over 30 years
- _____ 1973
- _____ the last 20 years
- _____ 1986
- _____ 1990

Now check your answers in the sentences 1.-5. below
and put the verb in the present perfect.

1. The Wheelers _have written_ (write) about their travels for over 30 years.
2. Since 1973 'Asia on the Cheap' _____ (sell) over half a million
copies.
3. For the last 20 years the 'Lonely Planet' books _____ (become)
very popular with independent travellers.
4. Since 1986 'The Lonely Planet Publications' _____ (donate)
a percentage of the income from each book to Third World Projects.
5. Since 1990 the Wheelers _____ (produce) phrase books.

2 Life changes

a People change over the years. Work in pairs.
Which of the following adjectives match which picture
below to describe how the triplets have changed?

*fit • successful • lazy • motivated • rich • busy • healthy •
big • tall • dissatisfied • boring • fascinating • smart • serious*

b Can you write sentences to describe how the triplets have changed over the years?
Example: Mike has become fitter, healthier and more motivated.

1. Mike has become _____ .
2. Martin has become _____ .
3. Martia _____ .

> **Comparison of adjectives**
> When you compare people or things you add **-er** to most short adjectives.
> *Example:* Mike has become **richer**.
>
> You use **more + adjective** for most two-syllable and longer adjectives.
> *Example:* Mike has become **more motivated**.

c How has your life changed since you were a child / a teenager?
Work in groups. For the next five minutes find out about the
changes from the other students.
Example: How has your life changed since you were a
teenager? – I've become richer / fitter / lazier.

d Report back to the class.
Example: Jo has become richer and lazier.

3 Enquiring about cottages

a Elena Taffy phones 'Exclusive Cottages' to find out about their accommodation.

Listen to the dialogue and fill in the table on the right by putting a tick (✔) in the correct box.

		all	some	none
1.	standard kitchen facilities	☐	☐	☐
2.	dishwasher	☐	☐	☐
3.	shower & bath	☐	☐	☐
4.	jacuzzi	☐	☐	☐
5.	fireplace	☐	☐	☐
6.	swimming pool	☐	☐	☐

b Put 'some' or 'any' into the following sentences.

> Remember your word bank.

1. Could you send me _____ information about self-catering accommodation, please?
2. Have you got _____ accommodation with jacuzzis?
3. I'm sorry, we haven't got _____ rooms with a balcony.
4. We've got _____ cottages near the sea.
5. We didn't have _____ bookings last week.

> ### Remember
> **Some** is used in positive sentences and polite requests.
> **Any** is used in negative sentences and general questions.

c Elena Taffy, personal assistant at the DCD company, writes a fax to 'Exclusive Cottages'. Complete the fax using the following words.

send • advance • confirmation • wishes • booking • Mr • deposit

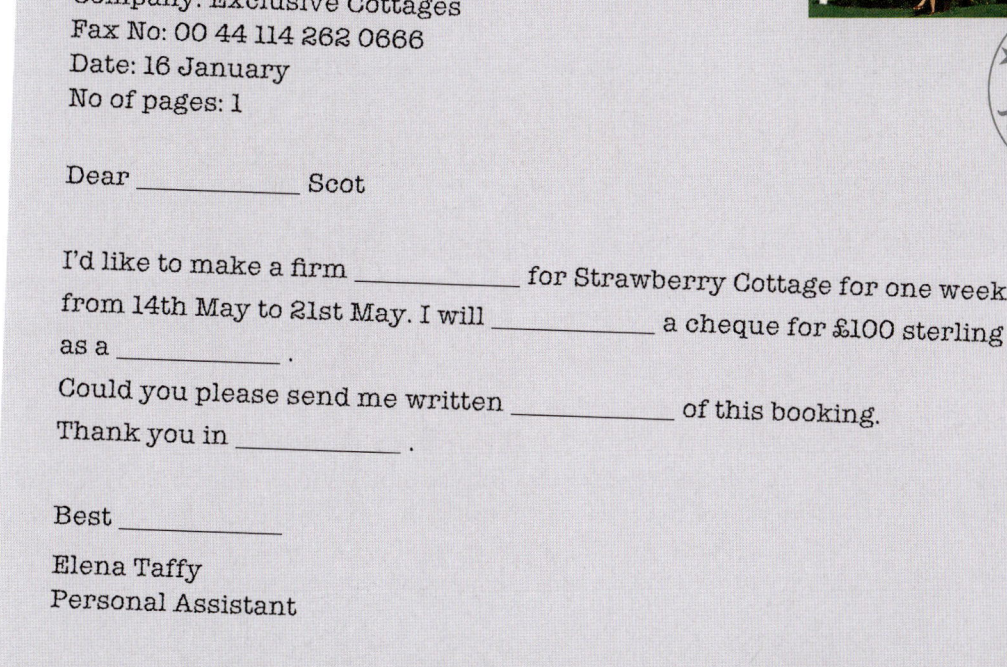

FAX
To: Gordon Scot
Company: Exclusive Cottages
Fax No: 00 44 114 262 0666
Date: 16 January
No of pages: 1

Dear _____ Scot

I'd like to make a firm _____ for Strawberry Cottage for one week from 14th May to 21st May. I will _____ a cheque for £100 sterling as a _____ .

Could you please send me written _____ of this booking.
Thank you in _____ .

Best _____

Elena Taffy
Personal Assistant

4 Accommodation

a With a partner draw a word wheel of the different kinds of places you can stay when you are on holiday.

Which accommodation would you choose and why?

cottage

holiday accommodation

Remember your word bank.

b Read the following information from these two holiday accommodation brochures. Then fill in the missing words.

*single • bath • check (2) • breakfast •
deposit (2) • balcony • cancel*

ELAINE'S
A BED AND BREAKFAST

Elaine's offers three bedrooms; two with king-size beds, private _____ and a private _____ outside. The third room has a queen-size bed, private bath with a jacuzzi tub. Room rates are based on _____ or double rooms. Prices include a full _____ in the morning.
_____ -in is at 4.00 p.m. and _____ -out is at 12.00 noon.
A first night _____ is required on an advance reservation. Cancellation must be 7 days before arrival. Failure to _____ may result in loss of your _____ .

*fridge • utensils • fireplaces • furniture •
deposit • stove • pillows*

RUIDOSO LODGE CABINS

All our lodge cabins offer fantastic views of the countryside. The cabins vary in theme and colour scheme. Wood and fire starters are provided for the _____ . Kitchens include a _____ , a microwave, a _____ , a toaster, a coffee machine and all the basic cooking and eating _____ . All cabins have king-size beds with bed linen and _____ . The lodge cabins provide a mountain cabin feeling, with lots of wooden _____ (chairs, tables etc.).
One half of the reservation is payable in advance. We allow 4 working days for receipt of the _____ . The balance is payable on arrival.

Learning Tip – Reading
Compare reading in a foreign language to detective work. You won't understand everything the first time so you have to look for clues in the text. Read the text quickly and then go back to areas that were not clear the first time. Sometimes it's possible to guess the meaning of a word from its context.

c In groups of four choose one of these unusual types of accommodation in the pictures and write a short text about it. Use as much vocabulary as you can from **4b**.

Now read your description to the other groups so that they can guess which type of accommodation / picture your group has chosen.

> **Learning Tip – Writing**
> With writing tasks always concentrate on using the knowledge that you know NOT what you don't know.

5 Different cultures: The concept of personal space

"You're breathing down my neck."

"You're standing on my toe."

In Britain and the US personal space – the accepted distance between two people standing next to each other – is about 45 cm. In Japan it is 25 cm and in Brazil it is 20 cm.

How much personal space is typical in your country when talking to each other?
How much do you personally feel comfortable with?
What's your experience of other countries?

6 Sounds

When saying the English 'v' as in 'van' make sure not to say it like an 'f' as in 'fan' as this can lead to misunderstandings.

The English 'v' sounds very much like the German 'w' sound (e.g. 'wie').

 Look at the following pairs of words first. Then listen to five words and underline the ones you hear.

1. van — fan   4. view — few
2. vary — fairy   5. vast — fast
3. very — ferry

7 Vocabulary quiz

a In **3** you have looked at the use of 'some' and 'any' again.
Now look at the following word combinations with 'some' and 'any'.

somewhere • *anybody* • *something* • *anything* • *somebody* • *anywhere*

Which of these combinations have to do with

■ places? _____
■ people? _____
■ things? _____

b In pairs, now change the words in brackets in this vocabulary quiz
using 'somewhere', 'anywhere', 'something' (2x), 'anything' or 'somebody'.
The first sentence has been done for you.

1. It's *somewhere* (a place) you can swim.   *swimming pool*
2. It's _____ (a book) which gives you information about another country.
3. It's _____ (any food) you eat in the morning when you get up.
4. It's _____ (a person) who likes to travel without using a tourist agency.
5. It's _____ (a small amount) you pay in advance when you book a Bed & Breakfast.
6. This is an 'umbrella word' for _____ (any place) you can stay on holiday.

> You use **something**, **somebody**, **somewhere** in positive sentences.
> *Example:* **Somebody** has sent us a letter.
>
> You use **anything**, **anybody**, **anywhere** in negative sentences and general questions.
> *Examples:* You don't have to pay **anything**.
>   Do you know **anybody** who can help?
>
> And in positive sentences where a certain person, thing or place is not important, you also use **anything**, **anybody**, **anywhere**.
> *Example:* You can bring **anybody** you want to the party.

c Now guess the vocabulary from the clues in **7b**.

d In pairs, can you now make up three clues for words in this unit / first three units using 'somebody', 'something' or 'somewhere' for the rest of the class to guess.

1. _____
2. _____
3. _____

Present perfect with 'since' and 'for'

You can also use the **present perfect** to talk about an action that has started in the past and is still going on today.

Example: The Wheelers **have written** guide books **since 1970**.
(They started writing guide books in 1970 and are still writing today.)

'since' and 'for'

You use both **since** and **for** to say *how long* something has been happening.
You use **since** when you say the beginning of the period, e.g. 'since 1970'.
You use **for** when you say the period of time, e.g. 'for over thirty years'.

since 1970 ——————— for over 30 years ————————→ now
(beginning *(period)*
of period)

Examples: She**'s lived** in Cologne **for 10 years**.
They**'ve worked** at the same company for years.
I**'ve driven** a car **since 1990**.
We**'ve had** a cat since **last month**.

since	for
8 o'clock	two hours
Monday	ten minutes
April	six months
1990	five years
we arrived	a long time
breakfast	a week

Comparison of adjectives

You add **-er** to most short adjectives.
Example: Martin has become **smarter**.

For most two-syllable and longer adjectives you add **more + adjective**.
Example: Petrol has become **more expensive**.

'Some' and 'any'

You use **some** in positive sentences when you do not say the exact amount.
Example: We've got **some** cottages near the sea.

You use **some** in questions when you expect the answer to be 'yes'.
Example: Would you like **some** brochures about our cottages?

You normally use **any** in questions when you don't know if the answer will be 'yes' or 'no'.
Example: Have you got **any** accommodation with jacuzzis?

You also use **any** in negative sentences.
Example: I'm sorry we haven't got **any** rooms free.

Compounds with 'some' and 'any'

You use **something, somebody, somewhere** in positive sentences.
Example: **Somebody** has sent us a letter.

You use **anything, anybody, anywhere** in negative sentences and general questions.
Examples: You don't have to pay **anything**.
I don't know **anybody** who doesn't like summer.

(Revision 1)

1 Umbrella words

a Work in pairs to find 'umbrella words' for the following groups of words.

1. chair, table, bed,

   _____ , _____ , _____   *furniture*

2. dishwasher, fridge, microwave,

   _____ , _____ , _____   *k   f*

3. aqua aerobics, abseiling, jogging,

   _____ , _____ , _____   *s*

4. cottage, hotel, lodge cabin,

   _____ , _____ , _____   *a*

5. train, ferry, van,

   _____ , _____ , _____   *t*

6. Turkish, Italian, Dutch,

   _____ , _____ , _____   *n*

b Can you add three more items to each group in **1a**?

c Complete the following clues to find the words. The missing word (vertical) describes the time we have when we don't work. – _____

1. An area of water
2. A type of accommodation
3. A new indoor sport
4. You can have a bath or a …
5. You stand in this when you wait for a bus
6. UNICEF is a …
7. The money you pay in advance for accommodation

2 Mix and match

Can you match the following statements/questions with the correct answer?

1. What about going to the cinema tonight?	a. Yes, you are right.
2. Thanks for your help.	b. Oh, thanks.
3. Why don't you see a doctor?	c. Nice to meet you, too.
4. That really suits you.	d. That's a good idea.
5. Have you tried going to bed earlier?	e. That's OK.
6. Nice to meet you.	f. No, I haven't.

3 Information exchange

Work in pairs. Ask your partner questions in the simple past to find the missing information in the text below.

Example: 'In the early _____ Tony Wheeler and his wife, Maureen, travelled from ...' –
When did the Wheelers travel?

Partner A looks at this page.
Partner B looks at **page 115**.

Partner A

In the early _____ Tony Wheeler and his wife, Maureen, travelled from London across Europe, the Middle East and Asia to Australia. They left England in a £100 mini-van and drove across Europe, _____ and _____ into Afghanistan. They made a £_____ profit on the van and went on by bus and train through _____ and _____ .
They trekked in Nepal, hitchhiked through Malaysia and took boats to _____ and then on to Sydney.
'People asked us our route and where we stayed. We decided to put what we knew into a small book.' Maureen brought her _____ home from work at weekends to write up the book and Tony drew all maps and diagrams. They spent all their savings on printing '_____'.

4 Questions and answers

Fill in the correct words to complete the questions and answers.

1. Q: Have you got _____ (some / any) lodge cabins available in June?
   A: No, I'm sorry, we haven't got _____ (some / any) available in June.

2. Q: Have you _____ (never / ever) been to Japan?
   A: No, I've _____ (never / ever) been there.

3. Q: _____ (Do / Did) you go to work yesterday?
   A: No, I _____ (don't / didn't).

4. Q: Did you _____ (bought / buy) it at the market?
   A: Yes, I _____ (bought / did).

5. Q: _____ (Are / Do) you learning English?
   A: Yes, I _____ (do / am).

The Working World

1 The hurry sickness quiz

More and more people can't find enough time in a day. Are you suffering from 'hurry sickness'?
Try this quiz to see whether you are suffering from the same problem.
First answer the questions yourself and then ask your partner.

	you	your partner
1. Are you forever excusing yourself for being late?	▮	▮
2. Do you find you are always the last one to arrive?	▮	▮
3. Do you forget to write 'to do' lists for the next day?	▮	▮
4. Do you forget to use your time-planner?	▮	▮
5. Do you try and fit more and more into your day?	▮	▮

▷ Look at **page 116** to find out whether you are suffering from hurry sickness.

2 Hurry sickness

a James Gleick did a survey on the working habits of Americans. Look at the following statements and guess which are true and which are false.

1. Americans work shorter hours than in the past. **True** ▮ ▮ **False**
2. Doing nothing has become a terrifying concept.
3. Americans are lazy.
4. More people are doing time-management courses.

Read the article below to see if you were right.

A NEW BOOK BY THE American writer James Gleick showed the growth of 'hurry sickness' in the United States: People working longer hours and fighting to fit more and more into every day.

Technology is helping to speed up the world: laptops, mobile phones, pagers, remote controls. We live in an instant world. Adverts for energy boosting drinks read: 'Having difficulty keeping up with yourself?'

We want lazy afternoons but instead we do classes in e-mail services, language classes, even time-management courses. The idea of doing nothing has become terrifying for many people. 'When the time comes to be alone, we want a cellular phone.'

Surveys show that working couples see less of each other than ever before. Workers and bosses fight over time.

More and more people are doing time-management courses. On these courses groups learn to make priority lists in their diaries; 'A' is for vital, 'B' is for important, 'C' is for optional. They have pages for 'personal mission statements' and 'goal planning' pages. These kind of diaries show our fear of time ...

b Can you find words in the text that have opposite meanings to the following words?

1. hard-working _____
2. unemployed _____
3. to slow down _____
4. to co-operate _____
5. everything _____
6. health _____

Remember your word bank.

c In groups of three or four read the following suggestions.
Decide which of the three headings to put them under.
Can you add three more ideas?

	vital	important	optional
do overtime until the work is finished	▮	▮	▮
have a break every day	▮	▮	▮
meet your boss to discuss flexitime	▮	▮	▮
go to the canteen every day	▮	▮	▮
take a day off every month	▮	▮	▮
_____	▮	▮	▮
_____	▮	▮	▮
_____	▮	▮	▮

d Compare your lists with another group
to see whether you have the same.
Do you think you manage your time well?

3 The do's and don'ts of time-management

a Listen to the dialogue and match up the activity
on the left with the advice on the right.

activity		advice
want to change your lifestyle		mustn't
do everything on your list		must
forget your list completely		don't have to

Do you agree with the
tips that Dr Walter gives?

You use 'must' when you talk about something that is necessary.
Example: You **must** be at work no later than 9.00 a.m.

You use 'don't have to' when you talk about something
that isn't necessary.
Example: You **don't have** to eat in the canteen.

You use 'mustn't' when you talk about something
that isn't allowed.
Example: You **mustn't** smoke in the office.

Learning Tip – Vocabulary
Be careful not to translate directly as it is not always correct, e.g.
'mustn't' and the German 'muss nicht' do not mean the same.
Examples: You mustn't smoke in here. *(darfst nicht)*
You don't have to do everything on your list. *(musst nicht)*

3b Put the correct verb into the following sentences.

mustn't • don't have to • must

1. You _____ travel on a tram without a ticket.
2. You _____ translate every word to understand an English text.
3. You _____ have a driving licence if you want to drive a car.
4. You _____ do sports but it is better for you!
5. If you go to the US on holiday, you _____ take your passport with you.

4 Company regulations

a In pairs exchange information to complete the memo on the right.

Example: What are the regulations for overtime? – When you do overtime you **must** leave the office before 8.00 p.m.

Partner A looks at this page. Partner B looks at **page 116**.

Partner A
Use the prompts below to make up the company regulations using 'must', 'don't have to' and 'mustn't' in your answer. Then answer your partner's questions.

1. **Must**
   overtime – When you do overtime you must leave the office before 8.00 p.m.
   private phone calls – …
2. **Don't have to**
   clothing – …
   flexitime – …
3. **Mustn't**
   smoking – …
   travel expenses – …

Internal Memorandum

To: **all colleagues**
From: **Gerald Sighs** (Personnel Manager)
Date: **25 July**
Re: **Company regulations**

Just a quick note to remind you all of the company regulations:

1. **Overtime**
   When you do overtime you must leave the office before 8.00 p.m.
   _____

2. **Flexitime**
   _____
   _____

3. **Meetings**
   _____
   _____

4. **Travel expenses**
   _____
   _____

5. **Holiday entitlement**
   _____
   _____

6. **Smoking**
   _____
   _____

7. **Private phone calls**
   _____
   _____

8. **Clothing**
   _____
   _____

Thank you for your co-operation.

b Read the e-mail from a new colleague below and write a short reply to describe your company or workplace regulations with 'must' / 'mustn't' / 'don't have to'.

From: paula-marsden@dcd.de
Subject: Hello

Dear …
My name's Paula Marsden and I'm your new colleague! I'm starting next week and I would be very happy if you could give me some information about our company regulations. What are the do's and don'ts in our department for example?

Hope to hear from you soon.
Best wishes
Paula

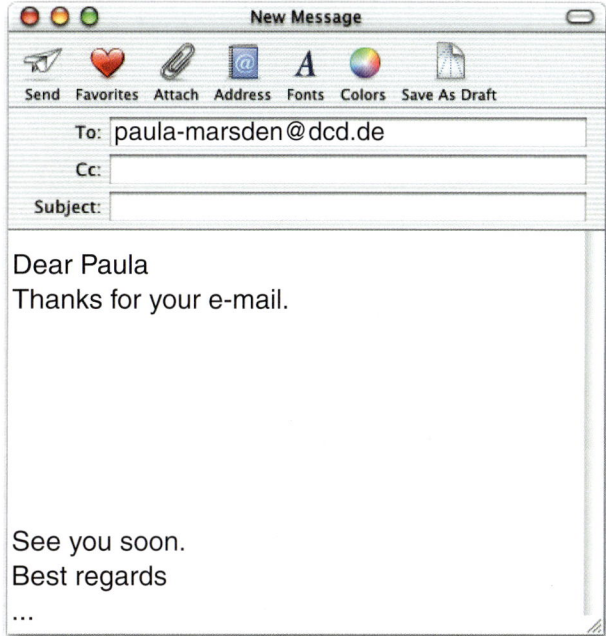

To: paula-marsden@dcd.de
Cc:
Subject:

Dear Paula
Thanks for your e-mail.

See you soon.
Best regards
…

5 Different cultures: British English versus American English

a Although the Americans and the British both speak English there are lots of different words, e.g. the Americans say 'vacation' but the British say 'holiday'.

Can you match the following words?

British	American
mobile (phone)	enterprise
colleagues	résumé
company	president
personnel department	co-workers
curriculum vitae	human resources
managing director	cell(ular) phone

> **Remember your word bank.**

Although there are these differences you can often hear the American vocabulary in Britain used by the British but you will not hear the British words in the United States.

b Are there any 'American English words' in your language?

6 You and your job

a What is the most important thing for you in your job?
Listen to the following people talking about their jobs
and fill in the reason why they are so happy with their jobs.

1. the _____ salary
2. the _____ colleagues
3. the _____ job
4. the _____ opportunities

b Look at this ad for the best job in town. Underline all the adjectives
in the superlative form.

The Best Job Ever

Looking for the most interesting job with the best opportunities for promotion?

You will enjoy the highest salary you've ever had and the most secure position in our biggest branch office.

You will work for the most interesting boss with the friendliest of colleagues and the nicest working atmosphere you can imagine.

Please apply in writing to:
The Best Company in Town
Fortune Avenue
Richmond, CA 94805

We offer the best chances of developing your own ideas and trying the latest work tools on the market.

---

c Now work with a partner and change this ad into
'The Worst Job Ever' using the opposites of all the adjectives.

Example: the most interesting job → the most boring job

> **Remember**
>
> good – better – best
> bad – worse – worst

d Work in pairs. Find out from your partner about her/his present
job or a past job. Use as many superlatives as possible.

Example: What was the best/the worst/the most interesting part
of your job? – Well, the best/worst part is/was …

7 The work desk and the snack counter

a Work with a partner. Make a list of as many things
that you can find in a typical top drawer of a work
desk and the things you can find on the snack
counter in a supermarket.

top drawer	snack counter
pen	*chocolate*

Learning Tip – Vocabulary
Strange or bizarre associations can also help you
to remember vocabulary.
Examples: types of snacks in a desk drawer, different
kinds of fruit in the bath, office utensils in a bus

---

b Compare your list from **7a** with the text below.

POST'S DONE – TIME FOR A CHOCOLATE BAR AND SUSHI

Your top drawer at work is for diaries, pens, pencils and Tippex – but the study of the UK office top drawers by *'Office Angels'* shows that the desk has the best part of a supermarket snack counter. Food ranges from chocolate and crisps to yoghurt and ready-made meals.

Although 42% had fruit on their desk, it was found that 57% preferred chocolate or biscuits in their desk drawer. In the drinks department, one in ten of us stores herbal teas but the most popular drink is coffee.

So why do so many of us keep a snack drawer? Hunger is one explanation. However, the survey showed it was also boredom, stress relief and using food to boost concentration.

One in ten of us also keep food at work which is past its sell-by date. Office drawers contain rotting bananas, unrefrigerated yoghurt, soft rice cakes and mouldy chocolate.

Odd eating habits? Chocolate and cheese and onion crisp sandwiches, eating yoghurt with their fingers, eating three chocolate bars one after the other …

(adapted from The Sunday Times)

Do you keep anything like this in your desk drawer?

c Read the text again and find four linking words which are used in the sentences to make a contrast.

b_____ , a_____ , o_____ , h_____

d Put the correct words from the list in **7c** into the following sentences.

1. _____ it was raining, he decided to go for a walk.
2. You should try to do some sports every day.
   _____, most people don't find the time.
3. Will you arrive on Saturday _____ Sunday?
4. It's a nice area _____ I wouldn't like to live there.

Linking words
When making a contrast of two ideas in the same sentence you can use 'although', 'but' and 'or'.
When you make a contrast where the ideas are in two different sentences you can use 'however' to link both sentences.

e Now make up four sentences of your own using the linking words in **7c**.

8 Secret eating habits

a Look at these words/expressions and put them on a 'love/hate scale'.

enjoy • dislike • hate • love • can't stand • like

love   hate

b Now find out your partner's secret eating habits at work / at home.
In your answers use one of the words from the scale above.

Example: Do you like eating cheese and jam sandwiches? –
No, I can't stand them! / Yes, I love them!

Partner A looks at this page. Partner B looks at **page 117**.

Partner A
1. eating ice-cream for a late breakfast in your office/home office
2. drinking sparkling wine at three o'clock to boost your energy levels
3. eating cake while writing e-mails
4. dunking your biscuit in your cup during a department meeting
5. …
6. …

> When you use a verb after 'love', 'enjoy', 'like',
> 'dislike', 'can't stand', 'hate' you use the
> **-ing form** of the verb.
> *Examples:* I **can't stand eating** sauerkraut.
> I **like eating** sandwiches.

c Below you find the beginning of a 'secret diary'.
Write down on a piece of paper five sentences to say
what you love, hate etc. about your habits.

> SECRET DIARY - LOVES AND HATES
>
> I LIKE TALKING TO OTHER PEOPLE ON THE PHONE.
> I CAN'T STAND DOING PAPERWORK.
>
> …

d Mix all the diaries together,
redistribute them and guess
who the writer is.

9 Sounds: Silent letters

a Sometimes the 'b' and the 'k' in words are 'silent'. Underline the word where there is a 'silent' letter below.

Example: k<u>nee</u>

battle	knee	thumb	snack
knowledge	job	sickness	lamb
bomb	sparkling	comb	knife
horrible	know	habit	keep

b Now listen to check your answers and circle the 'silent' letters.

Modal verbs – 'must', 'mustn't', 'don't have to'

You use **must** when you talk about something that is necessary.
Example: You **must** be at work no later than 9.00 a.m.

You use **don't have to** when talking about something that isn't necessary.
Example: You **don't have to** eat in the canteen.

You use **mustn't** when talking about something that isn't allowed.
Example: You **mustn't** smoke in the office.

Superlative form of adjectives

The superlative form of many short adjectives is **-est**.
Example: This is **the lowest** salary I've ever had.

When you use short adjectives ending in **-y**, you drop the -y and add **-iest** to the adjective.
Example: She is **the friendliest** boss that I've known.

When you use long adjectives you use **most** + **adjective**.
Example: What was **the most exciting** job you've ever had?

Note the irregular superlatives **best** and **worse**.
good – better – best
bad – worse – worst

-ing form of verbs

When you use a verb after 'love', 'enjoy', 'like', 'dislike', 'can't stand', 'hate' you use the -ing form of the verb.
Example: I **love eating** chocolate.

Linking words

When making a contrast of two ideas in the same sentence you can use **although, but** and **or**.
Examples: **Although** it was a Sunday, he was at the office.
You can take a tram to the airport, **but** the bus is quicker.
Would you prefer red **or** white wine?

When you make a contrast where the ideas are in two different sentences you can use **however** to link both sentences.
Example: They work in the city. **However**, they prefer to live in the country.

The E-World

1 Commuting

a Today many people commute to work, often by car or by train. Look at the adjectives below and decide which form of commuting you would associate them with.

comfortable • convenient • efficient • reliable • expensive • time-consuming

Examples:
For me, commuting by car is time-consuming because there are a lot of traffic jams.
Well, personally, commuting by train is more efficient for me as I can work on the train.

b Now you're going to read a text about 'telecommuting'. Before you read, can you guess what 'telecommuting' is? Read the text to see if you were right.

Telecommuting

Betsy Englesson gets up every morning at 5 am, takes her dogs for a run, showers, and goes to the office. Because she works at home as a telecommuter, her time-saving commute takes all of 10 seconds. By 7.30 am, she's hard at work.

Betsy is a global account manager for a company in Pennsylvania. Her boss is in California and her colleagues are a team in Germany. This proved to be an extremely inefficient way to work as she had to go on numerous business trips to Europe. Telecommuting is perfect as it means most of her meetings can now take place over the phone or on-line.

Working from home three to four days a week Englesson saw her productivity level skyrocket and her stress level drop. She no longer had to worry about getting to work on snowy streets. Additionally, she no longer has to feel uncomfortable with office politics.

"I'm not unreliable, in fact I'm very disciplined, so telecommuting works well for me," Englesson says. She also likes working with her 'colleagues' – her two dogs and her husband, a lawyer, who also works at home. "We have lunch together all the time," she admits.

There are also disadvantages of working at home. She can have problems with office equipment. "It can be really inconvenient when my computer breaks down and I have to hire someone to come to my house to help – which is not inexpensive I can tell you!" Englesson also has to fight feelings of isolation.

(adapted from www.workforceonline.com)

> **Note**
> AE: the commute
> BE: the journey

Now look at the adjectives in **1a** again and underline the opposites in the text.

> **Learning Tip – Reading**
> Let the context and your own background knowledge help you to guess the meaning of new words. *Example:* 'Englesson saw her productivity level skyrocket.' From your background knowledge of 'sky' and 'rocket' and from the context of working from home we can guess that 'productivity levels' must go up.

c **Skyrocket & drop**
Work with a partner. Mark the verbs below
with a (↑) for an upward movement
and (↓) for a downward movement.

↑ to skyrocket ☐ to increase

☐ to drop ☐ to grow

☐ to fall ☐ to decrease

d In groups make a list of the advantages and disadvantages
of working from home? Use the text in **1b** and think of other ideas.

advantages	disadvantages
no stress	no colleagues
_____	_____
_____	_____
_____	_____

What does working from home mean to you personally?

Example: Well, personally, working from home means
no stress, no colleagues, no …

2 The Digital Dream

a Digital technology is here to stay.
Can you match the following beginnings
and endings about digital technology?

Example: If you use a digital camera, you can easily
transfer pictures to your computer.

> For situations that are generally true you
> can use **if** and then the **simple present** in
> both parts of the sentences.
> *Example:* **If** you **listen** to a Dolby
> surround system, you **have**
> perfect sound effects.

If you use a digital camera,   you can download songs from the internet.

If you play a digital versatile disc (DVD),   you can easily transfer pictures to your computer.

If you have an ISDN line,   your message arrives in a few seconds.

If you use the text message service on your mobile,   you can surf the net and phone at the same time.

If you have an MP3 file on your computer,   you have a perfect sound and a perfect picture.

b Can you now complete the following sentences.

1. If I get up too late, I _____

2. If you don't check the oil in your car, _____

3. If it rains all summer, people _____

4. If there is a power cut, _____

5. If you lose weight too quickly on a crash diet, you _____

3 Plans to keep up with the Electronic Age

a Read the ideas of how to keep up with the electronic world. Decide which ones are the most important for you.

b Listen to the dialogue and tick the ideas in **3a** that the speaker says she is going to do.

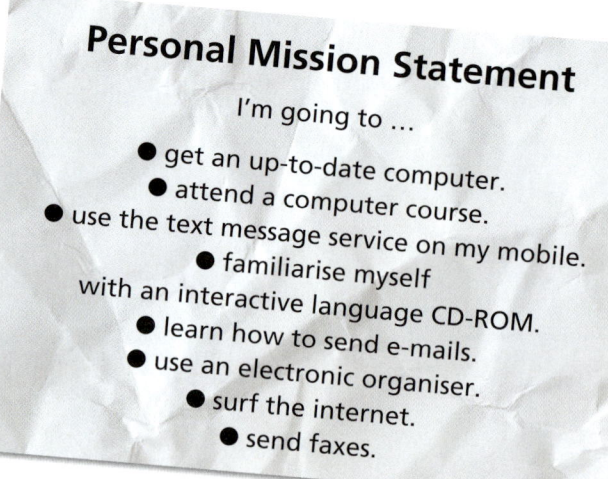

Personal Mission Statement

I'm going to …

- get an up-to-date computer.
- attend a computer course.
- use the text message service on my mobile.
- familiarise myself with an interactive language CD-ROM.
- learn how to send e-mails.
- use an electronic organiser.
- surf the internet.
- send faxes.

c Write down a 'Personal Mission Statement' for yourself. Write your sentences on a piece of paper. Start with 'I'm going to …'

Redistribute the pieces of paper and try to find the owner.
Example: Are you going to …? – Yes, I am. *or:* No, I'm not.

> ### Remember
>
> You use the **going to** future when you talk about your plans in the future (but you haven't made the final arrangements).
>
> *Examples:* **I'm going to** attend a computer course.
> She**'s going to** learn Spanish.
> They**'re going to** visit the new art exhibition.

4 Asking for information

a Here are two short e-mails which are mixed up. Decide which sentences belong to Sandra's mail and which to James' mail. Put the letters **a.–j.** in the correct order before you write down the mails on a separate piece of paper.

a. I look forward to hearing from you in the near future.
b. Thank you for your interest in our products.
c. Best regards
   Sandra Smith
d. Dear Ms Smith
e. With reference to your advert on the 'Computer World' web page I'm interested in buying one of your computers.
f. Could you please send me your brochure and price list.
g. Dear Sir / Madam
h. If you have any questions please contact me as soon as possible.
i. Best wishes
   James Jordan
j. I'm happy to send you our brochure and price list.

Sandra's mail

g

James' mail

d

> **Learning Tip**
> Look for clues to help you.
> Do the beginning of each mail
> and the ending first.

b Can you find phrases in the two e-mails to complete the table below.

opening	requesting	closing
1. _____	1. _____	1. _____
2. _____		2. _____

c Write an e-mail to Computer World for some information about an electronic product. Use as many phrases from **4a** as possible. Exchange mails with a partner and write a reply.

d E-tiquette
In the working world many employees prefer to send e-mails rather than to phone clients. In the world of leisure many people prefer to send text messages on their mobiles rather than to phone a friend.
Is it the same in your country? What do you feel about this change in communication from speaking to writing?

5 Predictions for the Third Millennium

a Do you agree or disagree with the following statements about this millennium?

In twenty years' time …
1. every household will have a computer.
2. most people will shop via internet.
3. you will have only one electronic system which will be a computer, a TV, a radio, and a music centre.
4. nobody will write letters.
5. mobiles will be the only form of phone.

Remember

You use the **will-future** to express what you think will happen in the future. It's only an idea, not a plan.

Example: I think that many people **will shop** via internet.

Use the following phrases in your answer.

I agree because …   I disagree because …
I think so because …   I don't agree because …
That could be true because …   I'm not so sure because …

b In groups write down five predictions about the third millennium and then ask the rest of the class if they agree or disagree with your statements.

Learning Tip – Speaking
Learn to live with errors. Don't be afraid of speaking because you could make a mistake. Ask your teacher to write down your main errors and correct you after a discussion and not during it.

6 Computer hazards

a Although computers can make life easier, things can go horribly wrong. What will happen in the following situations? Can you complete the sentences?

1. If you work too long at the computer, _____
2. If you turn off the computer without saving first, _____
3. If you don't have any paper in your printer, _____
4. If you forget your e-mail password, _____

b **Trouble shooting**
Ask your partner what she/he will do in the following situations.

What will you do if …
1. your computer crashes?
2. you lose your disc?
3. your mouse doesn't work?
4. you can't switch off the computer?
5. you want to up-date your computer skills?
6. …
7. …

Example: If the computer crashes,
I'll call the computer hot line.

> ### Remember
> You use **if-sentences type** 1 when you talk about situations in the future which can happen.
> You use: If + simple present, will + infinitive
>
> *Example:* **If** the computer **crashes**,
> **I'll** call the computer hot line.

7 Websites

a Match the website with the contents. What does the abbreviation 'www' mean?

www.visitbritain.com   **www.hueber.de**   **www.amazon.com**   **www.travelclub.de**

buying all kinds of books

booking cheap flights and hiring cars

buying language books

tourism in Great Britain

b Abbreviations are often used when writing text messages or e-mails. Work with a partner and guess what these abbreviations mean.

1. ASAP
2. CU
3. EZ
4. IC
5. L8ER
6. OIC
7. PLS / PLZ
8. THX
9. WWWWW?
10. W/B or WB

c Do you like sending e-mails and text messages?
What is your favourite website?
What do you think are the advantages and disadvantages of buying products or booking holidays on the internet?

8 Asking for permission

a Listen to three dialogues. Tick the dialogue in which the speaker gets permission.

Dialogue 1	■
Dialogue 2	■
Dialogue 3	■

b Listen to the dialogues again. Which three words do the speakers use to ask permission?

Asking for permission: m_____ , c_____ , c_____

c Work in groups of three. Using the situations in the File Section ask someone in your group for permission to do something. Another person in the group should give permission or refuse, giving a reason why.

Examples: May/can/could I borrow your car? – Of course.
– I'm afraid not because …
– I'm sorry, but …
– That's fine by me.

A looks at **page 116**.
B looks at **page 118**.
C looks at **page 119**.

> ### Note
> **May/can/could** are used for asking permission, but don't use **want**.

9 Word stress

a How many syllables have these words got? Where is the stress?
Put the words in the columns below.

develop ✔	important	connect	internet
mobile	office	computer	commerce
moment	reply ✔	chocolate	commuter
colleague ✔	salary	atmosphere ✔	résumé

●·	·●	·●·	●··
colleague	reply	develop	atmosphere

b Listen to the words to check your answers in **9a**.

10 The Modern Day Little Red Riding Hood

a You are going to hear a modern version of 'Little Red Riding Hood'.
Below are the titles for each verse.
Can you number the titles 1.-5. as you listen to the verses?

The small pistol ☐
A big face ☐
The new coat ☐
The wrong lines ☐
As sweet as caviar ☐

b Can you remember the original story
of 'Little Red Riding Hood'? How is this
story different from the original?

c Can you remember the parts of the
body that were mentioned in the story?
Can you add to this list?

parts of the body

_____

_____

d In pairs describe one of the following pictures for your partner to guess which picture you are describing.
Example: She /he has got short blond hair.
She/he is wearing …

Memory Box

Asking for permission and responding

May I borrow your car?	I'm afraid that's not possible.
Can I open the window?	Yes, of course. / That's fine by me.
Could I use your phone?	I'm sorry, I can't help you.

Agreeing / Disagreeing

I agree with you.	I disagree.
I think so too.	I don't agree.
That could be true.	I'm not so sure.

'Going to' as a future tense

You use **going to** when you talk about a plan in the future, but you haven't made final arrangements.
Examples: I**'m going to** buy a computer.
We**'re going to** do a computer course.

Will-future

When you predict what you think will happen in the future, you use the will-future.
Examples: In the future everybody **will have** a mobile.
In the next 20 years you **won't write** letters, you **will send** e-mails.

If-sentences

When you talk about something in the future which can happen, you use **if** and **will**.
If-sentences are made up of two parts: the if-clause and the main clause.
You use the following combination of tenses in **if-sentences type 1**:
If + present tense, will + infinitive
Examples: **If** the computer **crashes**, I**'ll call** the computer hot line.
I**'ll risk** losing the data **if** I don't **save** it regularly.

For situations that are generally true, you can use the **simple present in both parts** of the sentence.
Examples: **If** I **get** up too late, I **have** to hurry.
If my car **breaks** down, I **ring** the AA/ADAC.

Feeling Good

1 Sounds and feelings

a Listen to the sounds and tick whether they give you a good or a bad feeling.

	good feeling	bad feeling
1.		
2.		
3.		
4.		
5.		
6.		

b Now look at the following phrases and decide whether they give you a good or a bad feeling.

	good feeling	bad feeling
to rush from place to place		
to switch off		
to cope with stress		
to be calm		
to get tension headaches		
to get backache		
to relax your mind and body		
to feel exhausted		
to feel dizzy		
to let off steam		

c Below are two stories about two people and their stressful lives. However, the texts are mixed up. Can you put the paragraphs in the correct order?

Revitalise

a Lindsey works long hours in a bank in Brooklyn, New York. She works from 8 am to 6 pm, with an hour commute each way. 'I'm always rushing from one place to the next. Exercise helps me to cope with some of the stress: I go swimming twice a week and I also do a couple of weekly sessions with an aerobics video.'

b And the result? 'It felt wonderful at the time but for the rest of the day I felt a bit dizzy. After that I felt great for about a week. It was a physical feeling of well-being and a mental feeling of tranquillity.'

*C*Nick is a school teacher and lives with his partner and two children in West Bloomfield, Michigan. Nick's stress builds up slowly from day to day. 'I have to be calm with my colleagues and then calm with my own family. I never really get the chance to let off steam. I start to get tension headaches and backaches and feel exhausted at the end of the day.'

*d*Did it work? 'I feel more relaxed when I do yoga, and I sleep much better which means I'm more refreshed the next day. I like the focus yoga gives me. It helps me to switch off from the pressures of the day. I'll definitely keep doing it.'

*e*As Lindsey is disciplined enough to do home videos we gave her 'Yoga Workout'. The exercises aim to relax the muscles and calm the mind. Because Yoga requires total concentration, it's a great way to focus the mind. We asked her to practice four times a week.

Lindsey	Nick
G	C

*f*To help Nick work out the tension, we gave him a head-to-toe body massage. It included reflexology – a kind of foot massage. Powerful treatments like this can cause side-effects such as dizziness and headaches.

(adapted from Top Santé)

> ### Note
> AE: to do a video
> BE: to watch a video
>
> AE: to practice
> BE: to practise

d In groups of four answer the following questions.

What happens to you when you feel stressed?
How do you cope with stress?

2 How to stop becoming old before your time!

a Put a tick (✔) next to the following tips which you find useful.

1. Plan to exercise three times a week.
2. Finish doing your housework by Friday to have the weekend free.
3. Decide to improve your diet.
4. Keep working on your brain – it should always be active.
5. Don't postpone booking a health & fitness weekend.
6. Stop eating after 8 p.m.
7. Imagine looking as good as you do now in 20 years' time!
8. Hope to stay healthy and you will.
9. Offer to help an older person once a week to see how different their lives are to your own now.
10. Continue being positive about yourself!

b Divide the verbs from **2a** under the following headings.

verb + infinitive	verb + -ing form of verb
plan to exercise	finish doing

c Take five verbs from the above list and write five tips for the class of how to stay young.

1. _____
2. _____
3. _____
4. _____
5. _____

You normally use the **-ing form** of the verb after the following verbs: 'continue', 'finish', 'stop', 'keep', 'imagine', 'postpone'.
Examples: She **continued** talk**ing**.
They **finished** clean**ing** their flat.

You normally use the **infinitive** after these verbs: 'decide', 'hope', 'offer', 'plan'.
Examples: I **decided to visit** my uncle.
I **hoped to leave** on Friday.

3 A health & fitness break

a Look at the advert for a health & fitness break. In groups plan a weekend at 'The Beach Club'. Write out a timetable for the weekend.

Travel & Holidays

Health & Fitness Breaks
Personal training right on the beach
3 or 5 day breaks with plenty of zest and a lot of focus.
Extensive use of our superb leisure facilities.
Prices start at just £ 239.00 per person.

Call Sarah at The Falmouth Beach Resort Hotel
Tel: 01326 318084 Fax: 01326 319147
Email: falbeach@aol.com

The Beach Club
HEALTH AND FITNESS
At The Falmouth Beach Resort Hotel

Saturday	Sunday
9:00 fitness breakfast	9:00
10:00	10:00 jog on the beach
11:00 stretching exercise	11:00
12:00	12:00
13:00	13:00
14:00	14:00
15:00	15:00
16:00	16:00
17:00	17:00

b Then present your timetable to the rest of the class.

Example: At 9:00 you have a fitness breakfast.

4 Weekend activities

a Listen to the three dialogues and write down what the people are doing this weekend.

	activity
Jenny	
Sue	
Sandra	
Mike	

What are you doing this weekend?

b **A week in the life of Hal Heckam**

You are in close contact with the famous football player Hal Heckam. A reporter has contacted you. He wants to write an article about a 'A week in the life of Hal Heckam'. He will pay you £1,000 if you find out about Hal's arrangements for next week. To get a good price for his article he wants to put into print what Hal is doing next week NOT what he did last week.

Student 1 looks at **page 121**.
Student 2 looks at **page 125**.
Student 3 looks at **page 120** *(top)*.
Student 4 looks at **page 123**.
Student 5 looks at **page 120** *(bottom)*.
Student 6 looks at **page 124**.
Student 7 looks at **page 118**.
Student 8 looks at **page 117**.
Student 9 looks at **page 114**.
Student 10 looks at **page 122**.

Interview everyone and ask the following:
● Who are you?
● When are you meeting Hal?
● What are you doing with him next week?

Example: who: hairdresser
time: on Friday at 3 o'clock
arrangements: is dyeing his hair

c Now look at the following sentences and fill in the correct verb in the correct future tense.

Examples: The train arrives at 19.30.
We're going on holiday next Saturday.

fly • take • leave • go • start • visit

1. Your boat to the islands _____ the harbour at 7.45.
2. We _____ our relatives this weekend.
3. The sales manager _____ his new sales team to Switzerland next week.
4. The language workshop in Düsseldorf _____ at 9.15 on Saturday.
5. I've just booked my holiday! I _____ to Cyprus in the first week of May.
6. As we have got free tickets we _____ to the opera tonight.

Can you now write two sentences about your timetable and two sentences about your definite arrangements for next week or month.

7. _____
8. _____
9. _____
10. _____

d Different cultures: Ironic humour

Laughing at yourself or making jokes is an integral part of British humour. The people don't have a low opinion of themselves; they are simply making fun!

How is it in your country?
Would you feel comfortable 'laughing' at yourself?

5 Feng Shui

a What have you heard about 'Feng Shui'? Look at the following statements and decide whether they are true or false.

1. Feng Shui is a Chinese man who lived 7000 years ago.   **True** ☐   ☐ **False**
2. The words 'Feng Shui' mean 'find followers'. ☐ ☐
3. You can have positive and negative energy. ☐ ☐
4. In your kitchen you should put the stove and the fridge next to each other. ☐ ☐
5. If you eat too much, you will definitely get miserable. ☐ ☐

b   Now read the text to check your answers.

'Feng Shui' is an age-old practice that welcomes the idea of living in harmony and balance with our environment. It is a combination of common sense and good taste, of intuition and logical thinking.

This Chinese art goes back over at least 7000 years. 'Feng Shui' literally means wind and water, two of the most positive and fundamental forms of life's energy. The principles of this art can make our living and working environments healthier. Recommendations are made to reduce the negative cycles of energy that enter your home or workplace.

To prevent chances of bad 'Feng Shui' in the kitchen, you should follow a few simple rules. Your sink and fridge shouldn't be next to the stove. This can give a conflict between fire and water. You ought to put your dishwasher next to your sink instead.
If the fridge is the first thing you see when walking into the kitchen, you will always go to it. You will eat more, put on weight and then, probably become miserable …

(adapted from websiteconcepts.com.au)

c   Find words in the text which have similar meaning to the following.

Remember your word bank.

1. basic   _____
2. suggestions   _____
3. surrounding   _____
4. mixture   _____
5. stop   _____

d   In groups take each room in the house and list as many different pieces of furniture for each room. You can look at the text again to find examples of kitchen furniture.

kitchen	living room	study	bedroom	bathroom
_____	_____	_____	_____	_____
_____	_____	_____	_____	_____
_____	_____	_____	_____	_____

e   In groups think about your own 'Feng Shui' tips and give advice for one or two rooms. Report to the class.

Examples: You should …
You shouldn't …
You ought to …

6 Sounds

a Put these words under the correct sound [s] as in 'place' and [z] as in 'sometimes'.

place ✔ • *sometimes* ✔ • *eyes* • *clothes* • *person* • *visit* •
sink • *message* • *sailing* • *symbolic* • *surprise* • *result*

[s]	[z]
Place	sometimes

b Listen to the words and check your answers.

7 Mobile messages

a Listen to Elena Taffy's mail box on her mobile and make any corrections to the appointments in the diary below.

Monday	Tuesday	Wednesday	1
10:25 Cath (canteen)	9:30 Paul (his office)	11:20 Sales meeting	
3:00 Brian (my office)	5:45 Elfie (AA Academy)	1:15 Jenny (Pomp restaurant)	

b Write a short text message to send to your partner's mobile phone to change an appointment and then reply to her/his message.

> **Learning Tip – Writing**
> Keep the message short and simple.
> Even though it is a business message, it is still
> written in quite an informal style.

Present progressive as future tense

You use the present progressive when you talk about definite arrangements in the future.

I	am	
he/she/it	is	+ -ing form of verb
we/you/they	are	

Remember these time indicators for the present progressive as future tense:
this weekend, tomorrow, on Friday.
Example: We**'re having** a party this weekend. (*We have already invited friends.*)

Present simple as future tense

You use the present simple when you talk about something in the future based on timetables (business/travelling/leisure time).
Example: At 9:00 you **have** a fitness breakfast.

The -ing form and the infinitive of verbs

You normally use the -ing form of the verb after the following verbs:
'continue', 'finish', 'stop', 'keep', 'imagine', 'postpone'.
Examples: She **continued** talk**ing**.
They **finished** clean**ing** their flat.

You normally use the infinitive after these verbs: 'decide', 'hope', 'offer', 'plan'.
Examples: I **decided to visit** my uncle.
I **hoped to leave** on Friday.

Giving advice

You **should** follow a few simple rules.
You **shouldn't** forget to exercise.
You **ought to** see a doctor
    if you get tension headaches very often.

my notes

1 The alphabet quiz

Look at this alphabet quiz and fill in the verbs and nouns.

The verbs

A: to **a**_____ a meeting

B: to **b**_____ calm

C: to **c**_____ from home to work (to travel)

D: to **d**_____ with an opinion

E: to **e**_____ a room (to come in)

F: to **f**_____ a letter (electronically)

G: to **g**_____ to the cinema

H: to **h**_____ when you are late

I: to **i**_____ money at the bank

J: to **j**_____ in the park

K: to **k**_____ working (not to stop)

L: to **l**_____ off steam

M: to **m**_____ friends at the weekend

The nouns

N: There's **n**_____ here yet. (no other people)

O: What's your **o**_____ on this subject?

P: With my **p**_____ I can type on the train.

Q: The **q**_____ is the head of Great Britain.

R: The longer word for 'fridge'. – **r**_____

S: I've got a **s**_____ – I ate too much.

T: My **t**_____ are on the end of my feet!

U: The **u**_____ in Paris is called the Metro.

V: The flowers look nice in that **v**_____.

W: A massage gives you a feeling of **w**_____.

X: Joker!

Y: **Y**_____ is a relaxing sport.

Z: A **z**_____ is an animal which has black and white stripes.

2 The four future forms

Put the correct future form of the verb in brackets in the blanks:
present simple, present progressive, 'will' or 'going to'.

1. The Eurotrain _____ (leave) at 6.45 tomorrow.

2. I don't think there _____ (be) a unified Europe in the future.

3. This weekend I'm just _____ (relax).

4. Are you _____ (attend) the meeting on Friday morning?

5. In ten years' time the mobile _____ (be) the only form of phone.

6. In my new job I _____ (not work) at the weekend.

7. In June I _____ (fly) to Jamaica.

8. _____ the Euro _____ (exist) in 20 years' time?

3 Mix and match

Match the following statements / questions to the correct answer.

1. Let's go for a drink tonight.
2. May I open the window?
3. You mustn't smoke in here.
4. I agree with John.
5. You don't have to start before 9.00 a.m.

a. Oh! I'm sorry.
b. That's good news!
c. Of course you can.
d. Great idea!
e. Well, I disagree.

4 Vocab quiz

Use the following clues to find the business vocabulary from units 1-6.
The missing word (vertical) is a business 'date'.

1. Another word for to 'telephone'.
2. Can you say it again, please?
3. Yet another word for to 'telephone'.
4. I look … to hearing from you.
5. An electronic message.
6. … for calling.
7. … regards.
8. A short internal letter.
9. A system where you choose when you start work.
10. Your 'work-free' days are your holiday …
11. A person who works from home is a …

5 Work, well-being and the world wide web

a Look at the text below and fill in the blanks with the correct vocabulary.

live (2x) • *working time* • *feng shui* • *telecommute* • *e-mails* • *stress* •
overtime • *internet*

In the not too distant future more and more people will _____ (work from
home in a home office). They will all have access to the _____ and their
main form of correspondence will be via _____ .
In their leisure time they will do courses to learn how to cope with _____ ,
for example yoga, relaxation courses or even _____ which will teach them
how to organise their home and office in a better way.
These employees will choose their own _____ ; they could start work at
5.00 am or at 5.00 pm. This means they will probably do less _____ as they
don't need to work extra hours to finish an important project.
This change in the working world with its new technology will allow people to 'work
to _____ ' and not '_____ to work'!

b Do you agree with this picture of the future working world?
Write 3-4 sentences.
- I think that …/ I agree that …
- I don't think that …/ I'm not so sure …

Stories

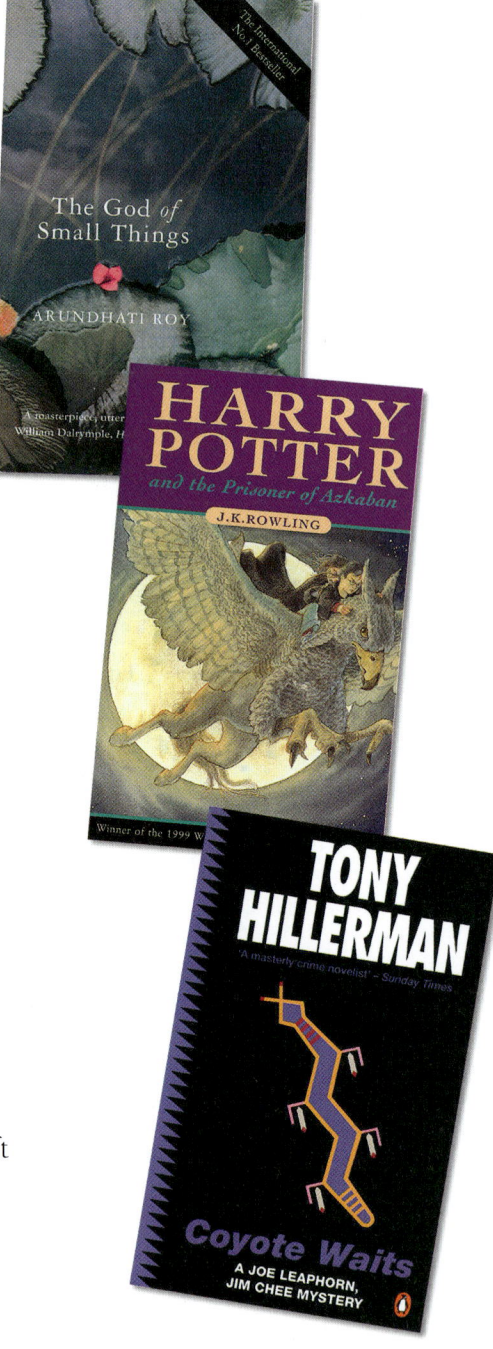

1 Reading Habits

a What do you prefer reading from the list below?
Compare your list with your partner.

	you	your partner
magazines	▦	▦
newspapers	▦	▦
comics	▦	▦
novels	▦	▦
short stories	▦	▦
poems	▦	▦
travel guidebooks	▦	▦
historical books	▦	▦
children's books	▦	▦
detective stories	▦	▦
others?	▦	▦

b What type of books from the list in **1a**
do you think the following extracts are from?

1. _____

They were nearly born on a bus, Estha and Rahel. Baba was
taking Ammu to the hospital when the car broke down. They left
the car and stopped a crowded State Transport bus from
Ayemenem to Delhi. If they'd been born on the bus, they'd have
got free bus rides for the rest of their lives …

2. _____

Chee didn't get all the way to the US Highway 666. When Chee
saw a man walking down the road, he braked and stared.
The man was walking down the center of the road while carrying
a whisky bottle in one hand. Chee saw he had something in the
back of his trousers. It looked like a pistol …

3. _____

Harry Potter was a very unusual boy in many ways. For one thing
he hated the school summer holidays with the Dursley family
in Leeds. For another, he really wanted to do his homework.
And he also happened to be a wizard. It was nearly midnight
and he was lying on his bed, a torch in one hand and a book
(*The History of Magic,* by Bathilda Bagshot) in the other …

Can you find key words that helped you decide
which type of book the extracts are taken from?

c Look at the extracts again. Can you find words which match the following definitions?

1. there are lots of people   _____
2. a trip on a bus   _____
3. to stop very quickly in the car   _____
4. to watch very intensively   _____
5. the opposite of normal   _____
6. at twelve o'clock   _____

> **Remember your word bank.**

2 Chain of events

a Look at the sentences below and decide if the actions happened one after the other, or if they happened at the same time.

1. Baba **was taking** Ammu to the hospital when the car **broke** down.

2. Chee **saw** a man **walking** down the road.

3. The man **was walking** down the center of the road while **carrying** a whisky bottle.

> You use the **past progressive**:
> 1. to describe two actions that were happening at the same time.
>   *Example:* The man **was walking** down the center of the road *while* **carrying** a whisky bottle in one hand.
>
> 2. to express a longer action that was in progress when a second (shorter) action began.
>   *Example:* Baba **was taking** Ammu to the hospital *when* the car broke down.
>
> 3. to describe the background action of a story.
>   *Example:* It was nearly midnight and he **was lying** on his bed, a torch in one hand and a book in the other ...

b Can you match the following parts of the sentences?

Example: Sandra was making the salad while Mauro was cooking the pasta.

1. Sandra was making the salad ✔
2. Pedro was steering the boat
3. The children were swimming in the sea
4. I was phoning on the mobile
5. We were having a party   *while*

a. our neighbours were trying to sleep.
b. Mauro was cooking the pasta. ✔
c. Phil was surfing the internet.
d. Rosa was holding the sails.
e. their mother was lying on the beach.

2c As a class make a chain story. Go round the class taking the last part of the sentence and making it the first with a new ending.

Examples:
1. Sandra was making the salad while Mauro was cooking the pasta.

2. Mauro was cooking the pasta while Jack was setting the table.

3. Jack was setting the table while Julian was dancing around the sofa.

> **Learning Tip – Speaking**
> Story-telling is a good way to practise
> connecting lots of sentences together which
> can increase your fluency and confidence.

d **When – Unusual moments in life**

Now work in pairs. Ask your partner what she / he was doing when the following events happened? If you can't remember make something up.

Example: What were you doing when the new millennium began? – I was dancing in the
                 street.

What were you doing …
1. … when the new millennium began?
2. … when you heard the news of Lady Diana's accident?
3. … when the Berlin Wall came down?
4. … when the alarm rang this morning?
5. … when the moon eclipsed the sun in 1999?
6. …
7. …

e  Listen to the beginning of this novel ('Enduring Love' by Ian McEwan) and fill in the gaps in the text. Be careful with the tenses.

The beginning is simple. We were _____ under a tree.

I was kneeling on the grass and Clarissa was _____ me the bottle –
a 1987 Daumas Gassac.

This was the moment, this was the pinprick on the time map:

I was _____ out my hand for the bottle when we _____
a man's shout.

We turned to _____ across the field and saw danger.

Next thing I was _____ towards it. I don't remember dropping the
bottle, or hearing Clarissa calling after me.

There was the shout again. I _____ faster.

And there, suddenly, from different points around the field,

four other men were _____ like me.

What was Clarissa _____ ? She said she walked quickly
to the centre of the field.

We were running towards a catastrophe. At the base of the balloon

was a basket in which there was a boy. Outside of the basket was a man
_____ on to a rope in need of help.

ENDURING LOVE
Ian McEwan
'I cannot remember the last time I read a novel
so beautifully written or utterly compelling from the very first page'
BILL BRYSON, *SUNDAY TIMES*

f What do you think happened next?
Can you write the next paragraph of the story?

3 Special Stories

Is there a special meeting in your life that you can remember very well?

a Listen to the following dialogues to see how and where the speaker met his/her partner.

1. _____
2. _____
3. _____

b Listen to the dialogues again to see how the speakers make the conversation more interesting.

Note down a) filler words and b) words to show interest.

Filler words	Words to show interest
1. Well, …	Really!
2. _____	_____
3. _____	_____
4. _____	_____

> **Learning Tip – Speaking**
> Filler words like 'well', 'hm' etc. prevent a
> conversation sounding 'flat'. Try to use them
> as often as possible to liven up a story.

c In pairs practise telling each other how you met someone important in your life (partner, friend etc.) and then act it out in front of the group. Don't forget to use the words from **3b** to make your dialogue sound more interesting.

> **Learning Tip – Intonation**
> If you want to sound interested you speak with feeling –
> your voice usually goes up and down.
> *Example:* Really? (↗) – Oh, no! (↘)

4 Couch potatoes

Which TV programme would you watch to find out the following? Try our quiz.

comedy • documentary • soap • children's • weather ✔ • chat • commercials • quiz • news • film

1. You want to know if it will be sunny tomorrow. weather report
2. You want to keep the kids happy for an hour. _____ programme
3. You want a cinema feeling at home. _____
4. You want to know what has happened in the world today. _____
5. You want to watch something funny. _____ programme
6. You want to know what new products are on the market. _____
7. You want to test your knowledge against other candidates. _____
8. You want to listen to interviews with famous people. _____ shows
9. You want detailed factual information. _____ programmes
10. You want to watch the lives of the same people every week. _____ operas

5 A TV star?

a Would you like to be on television? Look at the advertisement below and find out what kind of job it is.

We Need You!

Have you always wanted to be on TV?
Now is your big chance.
We are looking for candidates for our new show.
You needn't be a film star or a model.
You just need to be a bit of an exhibitionist and also enjoy being with people. You will stay in a house with 5 other candidates for 3 months and will have no contact with the outside world.
You simply have to agree that we can film and show on TV each evening everything that you do from the moment you get up to the moment you go to sleep. You have to give up your privacy for 3 months.
You also have to decide which candidate should leave the house so that after 3 months there is only one candidate left.

She or he will then receive **1 million dollars**.

Interested?
Please apply in writing to:
Fantasy Studios
PO Box 135 ST8
Richmond, CA 94805

You use **have to** when you must do an action.
Example: You **have to** pay your bills.

You use **need to** when an action is necessary.
Example: You **need to** eat food to stay alive.

You use **needn't** when an action is not necessary.
Example: You **needn't** eat chocolate to stay alive.

b Reread the text and then complete these sentences below using 'have to', 'need to', and 'needn't'.

Conditions of our Show

1. You _____ stay in the house.
2. You _____ be an actress or actor.
3. You _____ agree that the viewers can watch every moment of your life.
4. You _____ be a pop singer.
5. You _____ be an extrovert.
6. You _____ have lots of self-confidence.

c What kind of shows, series or daily soaps are popular in your country?
Do you think people in your country spend as much time reading as they do watching TV?
What types of books are popular at present?

6 Invitations

a Listen to the five dialogues and tick whether the people say 'yes' or 'no' to the invitations.

	yes	no
Dialogue 1	▪	▪
Dialogue 2	▪	▪
Dialogue 3	▪	▪
Dialogue 4	▪	▪
Dialogue 5	▪	▪

b Can you write in the missing words that the speakers use to make, accept or decline an invitation. Can you add to this list?

Inviting

Would you _____ to …?

Do you _____ …?

c Listen to the dialogues again to check your answers.

Declining

I'm _____ I can't, I …

I'm _____ , I'm …

Accepting

That'd _____ lovely.

I'd _____ .

d Now work in pairs. Use the expressions in **6b** to invite your partner and to accept or decline your partner's invitation. If you decline an invitation don't forget to give a reason why.

Partner A starts with the invitations on the next page. Partner B looks at **page 120**.

6d Partner A

Invite your partner to the following events.
1. a furniture trade fair
2. a bungee jump
3. a weekend shopping trip in London
4. a flea market
5. a house-warming party

Now it's your partner's turn to invite you.
Accept or decline your partner's invitations.

e Now look at these extracts from three different business letters. Work with a partner and try to fill in the spaces in the letters using the words below.

inform • attend • last • included • writing • invite • accept • details • provide • map • afraid • trip • hold

1.
... We would like to _____ you to our English workshop weekend on Saturday 26th June. The workshop will _____ two days and all meals and drinks will be _____ . Please let us know in _____ if you wish to _____ ...

2.
... I would like to _____ your invitation to the English workshop on Saturday 26th June. Could you _____ me of the costs of the workshop and if you could _____ accommodation. Would it be possible to send us a _____ and a description of how to get to the school? ...

3.
... I'm _____ I can't come to the English workshop on Saturday 26th June as I'm on a business _____ . However, if you _____ another workshop later on in the year, I will be very interested in receiving more _____ . ...

Which extract is
● an invitation?
● an acceptance?
● a declination?

68

Past progressive

You make the past progressive with 'was' / 'were' + -ing form of the verb.
Example: I **was running**.
We **weren't working** last Sunday.

You use the past progressive:
1. to describe two actions that were happening at the same time in combination with 'while'.
   Example: The man **was walking** down the center of the road *while* **carrying** a whisky bottle in one hand.

2. to express a longer action that was in progress when a second (shorter) action began.
   Example: Baba **was taking** Ammu to the hospital *when* the car broke down.

3. to describe the background action of a story.
   Example: It was nearly midnight and he **was lying** on his bed, a torch in one hand and a book in the other …

Have to / Need to / Needn't

You use 'have to' when you must do an action.
Example: You **have to** pay your bills.

You use 'need to' when an action is necessary.
Example: You **need to** eat food to stay alive.

You use 'needn't' when an action is not necessary.
Example: You **needn't** eat chocolate to stay alive.

Filler words / Showing interest

Actually, …	Really!
Anyway, …	Oh!
Well, …	Oh no!
After that …	What happened then?

Inviting and accepting/ declining an invitation

Would you like to come to dinner? –
Yes, I'd love to. / I'm sorry, I can't come because …

Do you fancy watching that new film? –
That would be lovely. / I'm afraid, I can't …

my notes

Cultures

1 Cultural behaviour

a In groups of four find out what things people like about different cultures.

> *Examples:* Which culture do you like? – I like the Spanish culture.
> What do you like about it? – Well, I like the way they eat late, go out late, and dance all night.

b Tell the rest of the class what you've found out.

c Please don't be offended by the following text. It is written by an American travel critic who has a 'humorous' critical style of writing!

Before you read the text, however, can you guess which nationality the writer is describing.

	which nationality?
1. They aren't able to drive.	_____
2. They don't know how to have fun.	_____
3. They find it normal to eat at midnight.	_____
4. They can't use a knife and fork correctly.	_____
5. They aren't able to queue properly.	_____
6. They cannot understand humour.	_____

Now read the text to see if you were right.

> Some things from a particular nation are so clever that we associate them with that country alone – double-decker buses in Britain, windmills in Holland, sidewalk cafés in Paris.
> And yet there are some things that most countries do without difficulty that others cannot do at all. The French for example, can't understand the concept of queuing. The British do not understand how to use a knife and fork. Many of them turn their fork upside down and balance the food on the back (which may result in peas bouncing all over the table). Germans aren't able to understand humour, the Swiss have no concept of fun, the Spanish think there is nothing ridiculous about eating dinner at midnight, and the Italians should never, ever have been let in on the innovation of the motor car …
>
> *(Bill Bryson, 'Neither here nor there')*

Have you had some of the same experiences as the writer, or what different ones have you had? What do you think of these clichés?

d Write down the first association that you have when you think of the following nationalities (it doesn't have to be a negative association!). Make your sentences with 'can' or 'able to', 'can't' or 'aren't able to'.

1. The Australians _____
2. The Brazilians _____
3. The Americans _____
4. The Greeks _____
5. … _____

Now compare your list with the rest of the class.

> When you talk about ability you use **can** or **be able to**. The negative is **can't** (or **cannot**) and **am/is/are not able to**. In everyday conversation 'can' is normally used. In written English both are possible.
>
> *Example:* She **can** play the saxophone. = She**'s able to** play the saxophone.
> He **can't** speak Spanish. = He **isn't able to** speak Spanish.

e In groups can you think of one country (if you can't find a country take a city) for each letter of the alphabet.

Example: **A**ustralia, **B**elgium, …

> **Learning Tip – Vocabulary**
> When you have a large vocabulary field like different countries and nationalities, you can record them in your word bank in alphabetical order. This is one way that can help you to check words again.

2 Cultural symbols quiz

With a partner, test your cultural knowledge of other countries.

a Can you match the cultural symbol with the explanation and the country?

India ✔ • *China* • *Malaysia* • *Jamaica* • *Turkey*

1. Jasmine flowers are not an acceptable wedding gift. ✔
2. People in this country carry an 'eye' ornament to keep away bad spirits.
3. Someone touching the top of your head is not wished for here.
4. People in this country often wear clothes in red, green and gold.
5. Invitations are usually written on red paper.

    a. This symbol watches over you and protects you from evil.
    b. This is regarded as the seat of the soul and is therefore sacred.
    c. Red symbolises blood, green the land and gold the sun.
    d. These flowers are usually sent to funerals in this country. ✔
    e. This colour is the symbol for joy and happiness.

2b **Different cultures**

Tell the rest of the class about any
cultural symbols from your own
country or a country you know well.
How important are these symbols?

3 Special rituals

Each country has special rituals that they may observe at certain times.
What do you know about weddings in Turkey?

a Read the statements below about the rituals leading up to a Turkish wedding
and decide which are true and which are false.

1. The future groom must ask the father of the prospective bride
   if he may marry their daughter.   **True** ☐ ☐ **False**
2. On the first meeting, the future groom's parents give the future
   parent-in-law a gift of a particular brand of expensive chocolates
   and a diamond ring. ☐ ☐
3. Before the wedding the bride-to-be has a party where she invites
   her very close female friends, her female relatives (sisters, aunts,
   cousins) and the female relatives of her future husband. ☐ ☐
4. At the wedding reception the bride receives gifts of money. ☐ ☐

b Now listen to this radio interview with Senay talking about wedding
rituals in her country and see if you answered correctly in **3a**.

Question Tags
In the dialogue the interviewer used question tags to check information. Question
tags are mini-questions you add to the end of the sentence in spoken English.

When the sentence is positive, the tag is negative.
Example: 'Senay' **is** the correct pronunciation, **isn't** it?

When the sentence is negative, the tag is positive.
Example: Your first name **isn't** Senay, **is** it?

When making a question tag, you should keep the same tense in both parts of the
sentence. In the tag you use auxiliary verbs (do, did, have, has, is, was) in the
positive or negative form.
Examples: You **come** from France, **don't** you?
            You **stayed** in Greece last year, **didn't** you?
            You **have** been to Spain, **haven't** you?
            She **is** Spanish, **isn't** she?

c Supply the question tags in these sentences and then listen to the dialogue from **3b** again to correct your answers.

1. It isn't the man who asks the woman's parents for permission to marry her, _____ it?
2. They take gifts on this first meeting, _____ they?
3. So it's quite serious from the beginning, _____ it?
4. The bride-to-be holds a party for her friends, _____ she?
5. It has always been a tradition to give the bride gifts of silver bracelets, _____ it?

Now take it in turns to ask your partner and to give the appropriate answer.
Example: It isn't the man who asks the woman's parents for permission, is it? – No, it isn't. It's the man's parents.

4 The guessing game

a In groups take it in turns for one person to think of a country and for the others to make a guess which country the person has chosen. Ask questions using question tags.

Examples: It's a hot country, isn't it?
Your country has got lots of mountains, hasn't it?
Lots of tourists go there in the summer, don't they?

b As you have just practised in **4a**, when you use question tags to ask real questions, your voice goes up at the end of the tag.
Example: You are allergic to cheese, aren't you?
↗

You can also use question tags when you expect the other person to answer your question with 'yes'. In this case your voice goes down at the end of the tag.
Example: This summer has been great, hasn't it?
↘

Listen to the sentences and decide whether somebody is:
● expecting the listener to say 'yes' (↘)
● asking a real question (↗)

1. You live in the city-centre, don't you? (↗)
2. That film wasn't very good, was it?
3. Frieda changed jobs last month, didn't she?
4. The Olympics hasn't been very interesting, has it?
5. You aren't vegetarian, are you?
6. You went to Greece for your holidays, didn't you?

c Now practise asking the questions in **4b**.

5 Indonesia

a Indonesia has a very different culture to Europe.
Discuss with a partner what you imagine
Indonesia to be like.

Before you read the text in detail, see if you can guess which number fits in the gaps.

2-3 • 30 • 300 • 365 • 13,000

Indonesia consists of lots of small islands; _____ plus. While places like Bali, Lombok and
Torajaland attract many tourists each year, other places remain free of mass tourism.

There are _____ ethnic groups which speak some _____ languages and dialects.
English is the first foreign language, but most Indonesians can only speak _____ phrases.
As education is expensive, few Indonesians actually go to university. As a result of little industry,
lots of Indonesians are farmers. Unfortunately, the average Indonesian farmer doesn't earn much
money. However, you will always find the people welcoming, friendly and willing to share what
few things they have with you.

If you like the sun and enjoy being outside, there are many things to do from sunbathing in Bali
to paddling in rivers, surfing off the coast, and eating over _____ different types of fruit.

Bring as little luggage as possible as you can buy most things in Indonesia. The only problem
with clothes is that as the Indonesians are quite small, there are few large sizes.

(adapted from 'Indonesia – a travel survival kit')

b Listen to the text and read it at the same time
to check if you were right.

c Now compare your ideas about Indonesia in **5a**
with the text. Are you surprised by anything?

You use **many** and **few** with plural countable nouns.
Examples: There are **many** things to do in Indonesia.
There are **few** large sizes of clothes in Indonesia.

You use **much** and **little** with uncountable nouns.
Examples: As a result of **little** industry, lots of Indonesians are farmers.
The average Indonesian farmer doesn't earn **much** money.
(money is a concept, therefore uncountable)

d Look at these sentences and guess where to put 'much', 'many', 'few' or 'little'.
Then compare with the text in **5a**.

1. Places like Bali, Lombok and Torajaland attract _____ tourists each year.
2. The average Indonesian farmer doesn't earn _____ money.
3. Bring as _____ luggage as possible as you can buy most things in Indonesia.
4. The Indonesians are quite small, so there are _____ large sizes.

Now try to put 'much', 'many', 'few' or 'little' in the following sentences.

5. I'd love to go to Indonesia, but the flight costs too _____ money.
6. I've never been to Indonesia, I know very _____ about this interesting country.
7. How _____ travellers cheques are you taking with you on holiday?
8. _____ visitors come to visit in the rainy season.

e Write a 'Culture Profile' of about five to ten sentences of your country or a country
you like. To make your profile interesting, look back at the text in **5a** to see how you
can combine ideas within sentences and how to put individual sentences together.
Give information about the culture, the people, the country, the food, customs etc.
Use 'much', 'many', 'little', 'few' in your sentences.

> **Learning Tip – Writing**
> Try to combine parts of sentences using connecting words like:
> 'as', 'because', 'but', 'which'.
> Try to combine sentences using connecting words like:
> 'While', 'As', 'If you like', 'However'.

6 The Japanese visitor

a A Japanese agent is coming to visit his European partner.
Listen to the dialogue between Sam and Stewart
and make a note of the three tips that Sam gives Stewart.

1. Don't be surprised if _____ .
2. Why don't you take him to a _____ .
3. Don't be nervous if he _____ .

b Sometimes it's necessary to check and clarify what a speaker
has said. Listen to the dialogue again and fill in the missing words
in the phrases below.

Asking for clarification

Sorry, did you say _____?

Can you _____ that, please?

Sorry, I didn't _____ that.

You said _____, didn't you?

6c Find a partner to work with.

Partner A looks at this page.
Partner B looks at **page 121**.

Partner A

You've got an itinerary of the Japanese Agent's visit but some of the points are missing. Phone your partner to check that the facts are correct and to find out the missing information. Go through each point using the expressions from **6b** and any appropriate question tags to help you check the facts.

Example: *Partner A:* Where will Masatoshi Fujisawa arrive?
             Partner B: At …
             Partner A: Sorry, I didn't catch that.

Schedule for Visit
Masatoshi Fujisawa

Arrival Time	18.30 at _____ Airport
Accommodation	Jolly Hotel, Media Park
Length of Stay	14-17 _____
Day 1	company visit – get to know contact partners
	presentation from marketing department
	lunch in _____
	demonstration of key products from sales department
	dinner: Sushi bar (near _____)
Day 2	visit to a sales outlet
	lunch with _____
	visit to _____
	dinner: Lemon Grass Restaurant in Jolly Hotel
Day 3	meeting to discuss sales conditions
	company car to _____
Departure Time	14.15

Question tags

Question tags are a way of making conversation. You can use them to ask real questions.
At the end of these tags your voice goes up.
Example: **You have been** to Mexico City, **haven't you**?

In spoken English you add question tags to the end of the sentences.
When the sentence is positive, the tag is negative.
Example: **He likes** baseball, **doesn't he**?

When the sentence is negative, the tag is positive.
Example: **She didn't** drink beer, **did she**?

You can also use question tags when you expect the other person to answer your question
with 'yes'. In this case your voice goes down at the end of the tag.
Examples: This summer **has been** great, **hasn't it**?

It's a lovely day, **isn't it**?

Ability

When you talk about ability you use **can** or **be able to**.
The negative is **can't** (or **cannot**) and **am/is/are not able to**.
can is normally used in everyday conversation. In written English both are possible.
Examples: She **can play** the saxophone = She**'s able to play** the saxophone.
He **can't speak** Spanish = He **isn't able to speak** Spanish.

Asking for clarification

Sorry, did you say 'eight o'clock'?
Can you repeat that, please?
Sorry, I didn't catch that.
You said 'on Thursday', didn't you?

Much/Many and Little/Few

You use **many** and **few** with plural countable nouns.
Examples: There are **many** people living in Germany.
There are **few** big cities in Bavaria.

You use **much** and **little** with uncountable nouns.
Examples: She has too **much** work to do.
He earns very **little** money. *(money is a concept therefore uncountable)*

In the Mood

3

scent

1 Describing things

a Look at the pictures. Work in pairs and choose words that match the pictures. Some adjectives can go with more than one picture.

*regular • delicious • classical • pleasant • fit • relaxing •
strong • sweet • soft • healthy • tasty • exotic*

4

sport

1

food

2

music

1. _____ 2. _____ 3. _____ 4. _____

_____ _____ _____ _____

_____ _____ _____ _____

Add two or three other adjectives that go with each picture.

> **Remember**
>
> Adjectives tell you something about the noun. You use an adjective before a noun or after the verb 'be'.
> *Example:* The **young** man is my cousin.
> She is **polite**.

(**Learning Tip – Helping your memory**
You can remember words better if you classify them in groups and give them a heading.)

b Odd one out

Circle the word that is different and say why. Look at the above pictures to help you.
Example: frozen — fresh —(new)— grilled

1. strong — junk — spicy — vegetarian   _____
2. dangerous — rough — mild — competitive   _____
3. salty — sweet — foul — powerful   _____
4. guitar — careful — pop — background   _____

(**Remember your word bank.**)

Now match one of the following four 'headings' to each line of adjectives. All the words are word partners.

smell • music • sport • food

c In pairs, make up a set of three similar words and one that doesn't match. Exchange the set with another pair and see if they can find the 'odd one out.'

2 It makes sense

a The five senses are smell, taste, sight, touch and hearing. Listen to three different pieces of music and write down what comes into your head in the columns below.

	sight	smell	hearing	touch	taste
	I see	*I smell*	*I hear*	*I feel*	*I taste*
Music (1)	_____	_____	_____	_____	_____
Music (2)	_____	_____	_____	_____	_____
Music (3)	_____	_____	_____	_____	_____

Work in groups of four. Share your words with the others. Which music did you like best? Why?

b A haiku is a short Japanese poem of three lines. Listen to two poems written by children in a Primary School in England and count the syllables in each line. How many syllables does a haiku have?

A DRESS FLOWING ROUND
THE DANCE FLOOR TO THE MUSIC
SLOWLY, FAST, SLOWLY.
(Emily Suddaby, 10)

Freckles all over,
Ginger hair but very kind
Christopher my friend.
(James Baker, 10)

In your group write a haiku using words from **2a**.
Read your haiku to the others.

c Listen to two riddles. Fill in the adjectives and guess the answer.

It smells _____   It smells _____

It tastes _____   It tastes _____

It feels _____   It feels _____

It looks _____   It looks _____

It's _____   It's _____

> You use adjectives after the verbs 'look', 'feel', 'sound', 'taste' and 'smell'.
> *Example:* She looks **good**.
>   It feels **soft**.

d Now in your group, write a similar riddle. Exchange your riddle and see if the other group can guess what it is.

3 In the mood

a Mood food

> *"Most people know what it feels like*
> *to be in a bad mood.*
> *What they don't realise is*
> *that food can change your mood."*
>
> (Elaine Harrison, a dietician and food consultant)

Do you agree? Tell your partner and give an example.
Example: I agree with that. When I'm tired, I eat a piece of chocolate.

Now listen to David Bates interviewing Elaine Harrison
and complete the table.

	what you should eat	how you will feel
worried?	a bagel,	
stressed?		
tired?		energetic
sleepy?		

Do you find
anything surprising
in the interview?

b Besides food, what else can you do to improve your
mood? Move around the classroom and tell the others.
Example: When I'm in a bad mood, I go for a walk.

Which idea did you like best?

c Now read the following article and find out
why it is called 'Moody Moves'.

Besides food, regular exercise changes moods most powerfully. Exercise increases blood flow to the brain and releases hormones, giving us a feeling of well-being. If you work out regularly, you will feel happy and optimistic.

Make it a point to do something physical every day – walk quickly around the block, take the stairs instead of an elevator, take up dancing. You can dance at home, right in your own living room. Here are some useful tips.

Start slowly and move gently to your favourite music. Warm up your body gradually for at least 5 minutes. Increase the pace and dance freely to fast music for 10 to 20 minutes.

Finish with 5 minutes of slow dancing to bring your heart rate down gently.

Whether it's salsa or swing, the twist or the tango, fox trot or free style, you can dance your way to a good mood.

(adapted from 'The Weekender', Times of Malta)

> **Note**
> BE: lift
> AE: elevator

It is called 'Moody Moves' because _____ .

d Underline all the adjectives and adverbs in the article 'Moody Moves'. Put the underlined words in the correct columns below.

> **Adverbs of manner**
> If you want to describe the way you do something, you use an adverb of manner. Most adverbs are formed by adding **-ly** to the adjective
> *Example:* slow – slow**ly**

> **Learning Tip – Underlining**
> Underlining means highlighting important points in a text. You can use different colours to highlight different types of information (vocabulary or grammar points).

adjectives	adverbs	verb + adverb
regular	*powerfully*	*changes powerfully*

Now look for the verbs which go with these adverbs and write them down in the third column. Put these new word partners (verb + adverb) in your **word bank**.

Is the use of adverbs in English the same as in your own language?

4 Doing it your way

a Answer these questions and then ask your partner.

How do you …?

… do your English homework? (regularly/carefully) – *I do my English homework regularly.*

… speak to your partner? (gently/loudly) – _____

… celebrate your birthday? (noisily/quietly) – _____

… drive? (carefully/fast) – _____

… speak English? (well/badly) – _____

… work? (hard/systematically) – _____

Note
The words 'fast' and 'hard' are both adjectives and adverbs. The word 'well' is the adverb of the adjective 'good'.

4b Now ask your partner another three questions using 'How do you …?' When you answer your partner's questions, don't forget to use an adverb.

Adverbs of manner normally come after the verb or after the object.
Examples: I drive **carefully**.
I listen to the news **regularly**.

c Tell a different partner three things you do …
- regularly.
- well.
- carefully.

Example: I cook well.

5 Smells

a Work in groups of three or four.
Make a list of things that you can smell.

Example: roses, freshly-baked bread, dirty socks

b Now group your words on a mind map.

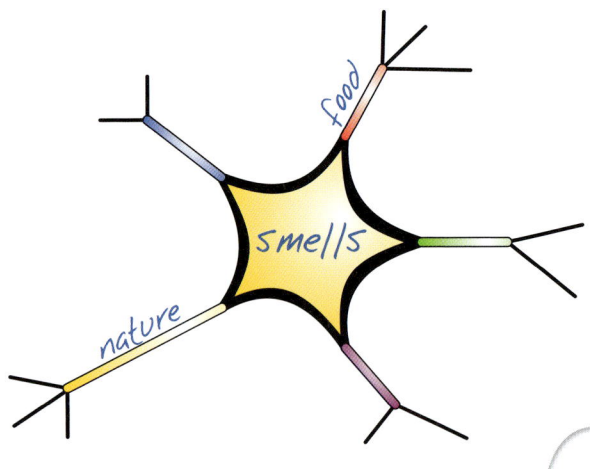

Learning Tip – Mind mapping
A mind map is a diagram in which the key concept is in the centre and is linked to related vocabulary by lines or arrows. A mind map is a visual picture of how ideas or words fit together and therefore makes it easier to remember vocabulary.

c Join another group and compare your mind maps.
Do they have any different words? Agree on three things that you think are most pleasant/unpleasant to smell.
Examples: We like the smell of soap.
We hate the smell of strong cheese.

d The French like the smell of aniseed.
What do you think are the most/least favourite smells in your country? Discuss in groups.

6 Smells and memories

a Work in pairs. You're going to hear a reporter from "Sky News" talking about the discovery researchers have made in England. Before you listen, discuss whether there is a connection between smells and memories.

Look at the notes below. Some information is missing.
Listen to the report and fill in the missing information.

main points	details
psychologists	_____ of Liverpool
smells	more powerful than _____
27 smells	_____ , boot polish, _____
Dr. Simon Chu	a psychology lecturer at _____
smell of an apple	stronger than _____
link	between memory, _____ , words _____

> **Learning Tip – Taking notes**
> Taking notes is an important strategy for increasing your understanding of listening or reading texts. You can write the key points of information in a T-format and this will help you organise what you hear while you are hearing it.

b Discuss in groups of four. Does a particular smell bring back memories?
Share your personal experience with the others in the group.
Select the most interesting experience you hear and tell the class.

7 Writing a summary

a Work with a partner. One of you reads text A below, the other text B on **page 122**. Outline the gist of the article by taking notes.
Use your notes to write a short summary (about 3-4 sentences) of the newspaper article. Finally, think of a headline.

Text A

Artificially created smells of fresh grass and sea air were introduced yesterday in the arrivals lounge of British Airways at Heathrow Airport. The scents came from heated capsules hidden at floor level in the lounge. British Airways said that 70,000 business travellers a year use the arrival lounge and spend at least 20 minutes there. The company spokesperson said that they had the idea of introducing smells to reduce stress and tension. From a choice of about 100 aromas, from leather to chocolate, British Airways chose the scents of the sea and grass because of their stimulating qualities. The use of aromas is an extension of their growing popularity in shops and supermarkets.

Learning Tip – Summarising
Summarising helps you sort out and organise information you read or hear. It is helpful to write the key points first and then to write a summary from your points.

7b Read your summary to your partner. Find out in which way your article is similar/different.

8 Putting more life into speech!

a Underline the adverbs and say the sentences in a lively way.

Joe is absolutely crazy.
You're completely mad.
I had dinner with Ramon. He's incredibly nice.
The whole evening was simply wonderful.
The musical was absolutely great.

b Now listen to the recording and repeat once more.

> **Adverbs of degree**
> Adverbs of degree are used to show the intensity of an action. These adverbs go before adjectives or other adverbs.
> *Examples:* He ran **incredibly** quickly. *(before an adverb)*
> She was **terribly** upset. *(before an adjective)*

9 Problem-solving – Changing moods

You are the human resources manager of a hotel and travel company.
You are having lunch with your colleague who is in charge of customer services.
You want to discuss the problem of low work morale in the head office.
Some employees start work late or leave early, are unfriendly to customers, seem bored or take long coffee breaks.

You make a number of suggestions to improve the working environment in your company:

➜ INTRODUCE TAI CHI IN THE MORNINGS
➜ CHOOSE THE BEST EMPLOYEE OF THE MONTH
➜ INTRODUCE AROMATHERAPY IN THE OFFICE
➜ ORGANISE A COMPANY FOOTBALL TEAM
➜ CONSULT A COLOUR THERAPIST TO CHANGE THE COLOUR OF THE OFFICE ROOMS
➜ ...

Discuss the problem with your colleague and make up a plan of action.

PLAN OF ACTION
● USE FIRST NAMES
● HAVE REGULAR TEA/COFFEE BREAKS
● …
● …
● …

You can use the following expressions to help you.

What do you think?	That's a good idea!
How do you feel about that?	I'm all for it.
Do you agree?	Sure. / I'm afraid I don't agree.
Shall we give a Christmas bonus?	Yeah, why not?

Report your ideas to the others.

Remember your word bank.

Memory Box

Adjectives

Adjectives describe a person or thing.
Example: I bought an **expensive** suit.

Adjectives normally go before a noun or after some verbs like 'be', 'smell', 'look', 'feel', 'taste' and 'sound'.
Examples: She looks **sad**.
 It tastes **good**.

fast/hard/late/early

The words 'fast', 'hard' , 'late' and 'early' are both adjectives and adverbs.
Examples: She takes the **early** train.
 She goes to work **early**.

friendly/lovely/lonely

Not all words ending in **-ly** are adverbs. Some are adjectives.
Example: My teacher is very **friendly**.

Asking for an opinion

What do you think? Do you agree?	That's a good idea. Sure. / I wouldn't agree with that. That's true / right.
What's your opinion? How do you feel about that?	I'm all for it.

Adverbs of manner

Adverbs of manner describe the verb and tell you how you do something. They normally go after the verb, or after the object.
Examples: The man spoke **angrily**.
 She drives the car **carefully**.

Most adverbs are formed by adding -ly to the adjective.
Example: quick – quickly

good/well

'good' is an adjective, 'well' is the adverb.
Example: He is a **good** chef. He cooks **well**.

Adverbs of degree

You use adverbs before adjectives or other adverbs as an intensifier.
Examples: It was **really** cold in Alaska.
 (adverb + adjective)
 She took her work **very** seriously.
 (adverb + adverb)

Suggesting something

Shall we give the staff a Christmas bonus? –
 Yeah, why not?

1 Social skills

a Match the beginnings and the endings of these 'social expressions'.

1. Bless		a. I'm afraid.
2. Black		b. interesting.
3. Would Friday		c. care.
4. Sorry, I didn't		d. at eight then.
5. Say		e. you.
6. I can't,		f. or white?
7. Oh		g. catch that.
8. I'd		h. or without?
9. That's		i. didn't!
10. See you		j. love to.
11. Take		k. did you?
12. You didn't,		l. no!
13. You		m. when.
14. With		n. suit you?

b Can you think of possible reactions, questions etc.
that match these 'social expressions'?

1. Achoo! *(someone sneezes)* – Bless you!
2. Could I have a coffee, please? – Black or white?
3. _____
4. _____
5. _____
6. _____
7. _____
8. _____
9. _____
10. _____
11. _____
12. _____
13. _____
14. _____

c Now listen to possible sentences
to check your answers to **1a & b**.

86

2 The adventures of an English teacher in Cologne – a true story

Put in the appropriate tense (simple present, simple past, past progressive)
in the following sentences.

drink • didn't drink • drank ✔ • was drinking

Example: I _____ (drink) too much whisky last night.

Day 1

Nearly missed my flight from Edinburgh this morning. I _____ (drink) too much
whisky last night and I _____ (not hear) the alarm clock ring this morning.
I _____ (get) to the airport with only 10 minutes before take off.
In Cologne I _____ (buy) the wrong ticket for the express train so I _____
(have to) pay for a new ticket. I _____ (arrive) at my new flat tired but happy.

Day 2

I _____ (survive) my first day of teaching OK. Teaching managers Business
English isn't that much different to teaching small children in the primary school,
_____ (be) it?

Day 3

While I _____ (play) my bagpipes in the kitchen, the bathroom mirror
_____ (fall) off the wall and _____ (smash) into the bath. What will the
flat owner say?

Day 4

As I _____ (travel) to Bonn for a new lesson in a company, I _____ (look)
into my diary – one week too early for the lesson – oh no!

Day 5

You learn a foreign language quicker by reading and listening to it, _____ (do)
you?
So, I _____ (buy) some German books to read – still too difficult for me. While
_____ (watch) the Big Brother soap this evening, I _____ (realise)
I _____ (not understand) one single word – I prefer the British version –
it's funnier.

Day 6

I _____ (take) my flat owner's dog for a walk when she _____ (run) into
the next door's garden. While I was running after her, she _____ (run) after the
little white rabbit. The owner and next door neighbour _____ (scream) at me
but it _____ (be) in German and I couldn't understand. Result: dead rabbit,
happy dog, angry neighbour and furious owner – what a shock!

Day 7

I _____ (stay) in bed today – it's safer …

Time

1 Not a waste of time!

Work in pairs and complete the crossword puzzle.
Student A looks at **page 124** and student B looks at **page 123**.

Take it in turns and ask your partner for the clues of the missing words on your crossword puzzle.

2 Time for yourself

a A big problem nowadays is that many people are pressed for time.
They complain that they are too busy to take proper care of themselves.
Do you have enough time for yourself?

Answer the following questionnaire and find out.
Work with a partner and compare your answers.

	You		Your partner	
	Yes	No	Yes	No
Do you have enough time to …				
go on holiday?	■	■	■	■
socialise with friends?	■	■	■	■
do sports?	■	■	■	■
prepare healthy food?	■	■	■	■
go shopping?	■	■	■	■
read the newspaper?	■	■	■	■
fix things in the house/flat?	■	■	■	■
take up new hobbies?	■	■	■	■
enjoy life?	■	■	■	■

Mostly Yes: You are lucky! You know how to live. You find enough time for the nice things in life.

Mostly No: You need to take better care of yourself. Relax and find time to enjoy life!

b In groups of four discuss the following.
- Do you have enough time for yourself?
- Are you too busy? Do you have too many things to do?
- What don't you have enough time for?

> **'too', 'too many' and 'enough'**
> 'too' goes **before** an adjective. 'enough' goes **after** an adjective.
> *Example:* I didn't buy the shirt. It was **too** expensive.
>   It wasn't cheap **enough**.
>
> 'too many' and 'enough' go before a noun.
> *Example:* I spent **too many** hours watching TV.
>   I didn't have **enough** time for my English homework.

c **Pressed for time!**

Two friends meet on their way to work.
Complete this dialogue with 'too', 'too many' and 'enough'.

Barbara: I'm _____ busy at the moment. I don't have _____ time for myself.

Sheila: You're right. You look very tired. You're working _____ hard.

Barbara: I'm working _____ hours, but I'm saving to buy a new car. I still don't have _____ money.

Sheila: I know you are old _____ to look after yourself, but I worry about you.
You smoke _____ cigarettes and you don't eat _____ vegetables.

Barbara: Don't worry about me! I'm healthy _____ .

3 "If I had my life to live again"

a Work in pairs. Read the poem and fill in the words which describe the pictures.

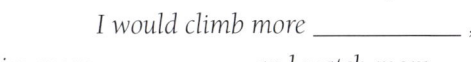

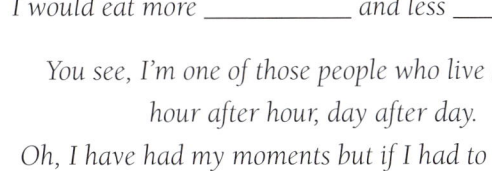

If

I had my life to live again, I'd try to make more mistakes.
I would relax.
I would be sillier than I have been this time.
I would take more chances.
I would take more trips.
I would climb more _____ ,
swim more _____ and watch more _____ .
I would eat more _____ and less _____ .

You see, I'm one of those people who live sensibly,
hour after hour, day after day.
Oh, I have had my moments but if I had to live again,
I'd have nothing else. Just moments, one after another.

I would walk bare-footed in the spring
and stay that way till the _____ .
I would play more with _____ .
I'd pick more _____ .

(adapted from a poem by Jorge Luis Borges)

 Now listen to the poem
and check your answers.

Learning Tip – Helping your memory
Linking words to pictures or creating visual
images of words makes it easier for 'visual'
learners to remember those words.

If-sentence type 2
You use this type of if-sentence to talk about an imaginary and unreal situation or condition.
Example: If I **won** the lottery, I **would travel** around the world.

If-sentences type 2 are made up of two clauses:

if-clause	main/conditional clause
simple past	would(n't) + verb

b The poem contains many main clauses with 'would(n't)'. Read it again and use a highlighter to mark at least six clauses.

Learning Tip – Highlighting
Highlighting is a good strategy for emphasizing certain important parts in a text – through colour, underlining, circling and so on. You can mark **key words** or **key structures**.

c What would you do if you had your life to live again? Complete the following sentences, then find out one or two things from your partner.

I would try ___to take things easier._____ .

I would take _____ .

I would go _____ .

I would eat more (less) _____ .

I would _____ .

4 Imaginary situations

a Imagine what you would do! Answer these questions, then find out what your partner would do in the following situations.

Example: What would you do if you had more time? – I would sleep longer.

What would you do …
… if you were your boss? – I would _____ .
… if you had a million dollars? – _____ .
… if you were the President of your country? – _____ .
… if you were twenty years older/younger? – _____ .
… if you were invisible? – _____ .

Now write two more questions using "What would you do if …?" and ask your partner.

1. _____

2. _____

Note

You don't have to start
the sentence with **if**.
Example: I'd be frightened
              if I got lost in a big city.

b Imagine how you would feel! Finish these sentences
and then find out about your partner.

Example: In what situation would you be very pleased? –
              I'd be very pleased if I passed the English exam next month.

I'd be very pleased if _____

I'd be angry if _____

I'd be shocked if _____

I'd be embarrassed if _____

I'd be disappointed if _____

Remember your word bank.

5 "If I had $1,000,000"

a Work in pairs and tell your partner what you would buy
if you had a million dollars.
Then listen to the song 'If I had a million dollars' and tick
the things the singer would buy if he had a million dollars.

furniture ▢

house ▢

emu ▢

car ▢

Picasso painting ▢

woollen coat ▢

monkey ▢

grey dress ▢

b Tell your partner what you *wouldn't* do if you had a million dollars.

Example: If I had a million dollars, I wouldn't have to go to work.

Now listen to the song once more and complete the sentences.

If I had a million dollars, we wouldn't have to walk …
If I had a million dollars, we wouldn't have to eat …

I.

Once upon a time, God the traveller felt very tired and since it was already dark, he looked for somewhere to sleep. He saw two houses opposite each other – one large and beautiful, the other small and poor. God thought to himself:

"I am sure I can stay in the big house. It obviously belongs to a rich man."

He knocked on the door. The rich man opened a window and asked the man what he wanted.

"I need somewhere to sleep."

The rich man looked at the man's shabby clothes, and since he did not

6 A fairy tale

a Work in pairs. Are there any fairy tales that you can remember?
Name three things that you normally find in fairy tales.

_____

You're going to listen to a fairy tale called "The Rich Man And The Poor Man".
In this fairy tale, both men are granted three wishes.
What do you think their wishes are? Tell your partner.

 Listen to the fairy tale.
Did you guess correctly?

> **wishes + simple past**
> You use the simple past after 'I wish' but you are not talking about past time.
> *Example:* **I wish** I **had** a house in the mountains.

b If you had three wishes, what would they be?
Write them down using the following phrases.
Examples: I wish I was (were) rich.
I wish I had more time.

1. _____ .
2. _____ .
3. _____ .

7 Personal services

The majority of Americans spend too many hours at work. They have no time to cook, to clean, to go shopping, to do the laundry – not even time to go to the post office. The number of personal service professionals is growing rapidly in the United States.

a Work in groups of four. Write a list of personal services that you can think of.
Example: gardener, baby-sitter

Put the services in three lists under the following headings.

necessary	unnecessary	desirable
_____	_____	_____
_____	_____	_____
_____	_____	_____

Show your list to another group. Compare.

b Read the magazine article and in the list below tick the services that Ms Edgell uses.

services available in the US	Ms Edgell	services available where you live
cleaner	▨	▨
gardener	▨	▨
dog-sitter	▨	▨
nanny	▨	▨
window cleaner	▨	▨
laundry service	▨	▨
party service	▨	▨
cook	▨	▨
interior decorator	▨	▨
food shopper	▨	▨
butler	▨	▨
_____	▨	▨
_____	▨	▨
_____	▨	▨

Running out of time

Most Americans haven't got enough time for themselves. They are buying themselves a little time. Take Angie Edgell, for example. She has no time for the daily chores. She doesn't do anything herself, she hires a firm to clean the outside of her house and another firm to plant flowers in her garden. One man cuts the lawn, another comes to the house to wash the family's cars. A woman comes to wash the dog. A company organises her parties, wraps and sends her presents to friends. When she leaves town, she pays for a 'dog-sitter' and at Christmas she hires someone to decorate the house and the Christmas tree.

Harvard University economist Juliet Schor calls it 'time poverty'. Families in which both partners not only work full-time but have a second job have become the norm in the United States. Americans are spending more and more of their income on themselves and on services that make them feel good.

(adapted from Spotlight magazine)

c Now look at the list again and add some personal services that were mentioned in the text 'Running out of time'. Then tick the services that you can find in the place where you live.

d Work in pairs. What personal services would you recommend to your partner, who has no time?
Example: If I were you, I'd hire a window cleaner.

> You also use an if-sentence type 2 when giving someone advice.
> *Example:* If I **were** (was) you, I'd **work** only part-time.
>
> You often say 'were' and not 'was' in the if-sentence.

7e Find different examples of reflexive pronouns from the text in **7b**. Then complete the following sentences using a reflexive pronoun (myself, yourself etc.) and one of the following verbs.

Example: Jerry always talks about **himself**.

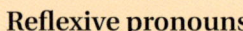

take care • have • think • talk • tell

1. He's such an egoist. He only _____ of _____ .
2. Maria is old enough to _____ of _____ .
3. My parents are very busy. They _____ no time for _____ .
4. _____ me about _____ . I haven't seen you for over a year now.
5. Sometimes I _____ to _____ .

> **Reflexive pronouns**
> You use a reflexive pronoun (myself, yourself, herself etc.) when the subject and the object are the same.
> *Example:* I bought **myself** a diamond ring.
>
> You also use a reflexive pronoun as the object of a preposition.
> *Examples:* I have no time for **myself**.
> She can take care of **herself**.

8 Business situations

Imagine yourself in the following business situations. What would you do? What would you say? Discuss in groups of four and choose what you think is the best response
- in your country.
- in a foreign country.

1. You go for a meal with a business partner. You would like to order. What would you do/say to the waiter?
   a. "Hey, waiter."
   b. Snap your fingers.
   c. Try to catch the waiter's eye.

2. You have just been introduced to a new colleague. What would you do/say?
   a. Shake her hand.
   b. Kiss her on the cheek.
   c. You bow.
   d. "Pleased to meet you."

3. You have been invited by a business partner to his house for a meal. What would you do/say?
   a. Take a small present (a bottle of wine or chocolates).
   b. Take nothing.
   c. "Shall I bring something?"

4. You don't like the food at your colleague's house. What would you do/say?
   a. "Thank you – I can't eat it."
   b. "Would you mind if I only take a little?"
   c. Eat it and say nothing.
   d. "Thank you but I'm not hungry."

Learning Tip – Understanding different cultures
Knowledge of a new culture helps you to understand better what you read or hear in the new language.

9 Sentence stress

In English the key words in a sentence are stressed.
Listen to this poem about "Time" and write down the words
that are stressed.

_____   _____   _____   _____

_____   _____   _____   _____

Now, on a separate piece of paper,
write out the poem. Use the stressed
words to help you.

Memory Box

Expressions of quantity – 'too', 'too many', 'enough'

'too' goes before, 'enough' goes after an adjective.
Examples: The sun is **too** hot today.
It is hot **enough** to go for a swim.

'too many' and 'enough' go before a noun.
Examples: There are **too many** rainy days in Norway.
There isn't **enough** sun.

If-sentence type 2

You use an if-sentence type 2 to talk about an
imaginary situation or unlikely condition.
Example: If you **stopped** smoking, you
would feel better.

If-sentences type 2 are made up of two
clauses:

if-clause	main/conditional clause
simple past	would (n't) + verb

The if-clause can come at the beginning or at
the end of the sentence. If it is at the end, you
don't separate the sentences with a comma.
Example: You would feel better **if** you
stopped smoking.

You don't normally use 'would' in the if-
clause. Instead of 'would', you can also use
'could' or 'might'.
Example: If you **stopped** smoking, you **could
(might) feel** better.

Asking for and giving advice

What would you do? – If I were you,
I would eat less.

'were' is often used instead of 'was' in the
if-clause.

Expressing wishes

To express a wish you can use 'wish +
verb in the simple past'.
Examples: **I wish** I **were** on holiday.
I wish I **had** five cats.

Reflexive pronouns

You can use a reflexive pronoun (myself,
yourself etc.) when the subject and the
object are the same.
Example: She bought **herself** a new car.

You can use a reflexive pronoun after a
preposition.
Example: The children are old enough to
look after **themselves**.

Shapes

1 All shapes and sizes

a   Look at the photographs. Work in pairs and choose a door each.
Describe it to your partner. Use the following sentences to help you.
Can your partner guess which one you are describing?

1. It's made of _____ .   (e.g. wood, glass, steel, aluminium, wrought iron)
2. It's about _____ .   (e.g. 2 metres by 1 metre)
3. It's _____ .   (e.g. brown, black, white, grey)
4. It's _____ .   (e.g. modern, plain, old, rustic, traditional)

> **Learning Tip – Labelling**
> Putting a label on a group of
> words can help you remember
> them later on.

Put the four sentences above
under these headings.

colour   ☐
description   ☐
material   ☐
size   ☐

b   Now take it in turns and describe a door that was important to you in your life.
Your partner then draws it in her/his notebook. She/he may ask questions.
Examples: What's it made of?
What shape is it?
How big is it?
What colour is it?

Show your drawings to each other.

c   Work in groups of four. Look at the photographs again
and talk about the following.
In which countries can you find these doors?
Who do you think lives behind these doors? (Age? Family? Job?)
Which house would you choose to live in? Why?

2 First impressions

a You are going to read about front doors and personalities.
Do you think front doors tell you something about the people who live behind them?

Read the newspaper article and guess which of the adjectives fit the gaps.

bright • fashionable • neutral • natural • attractive • aggressive • coloured

The front door is the gateway to the home. It is not only a thing that you open or close to go in or out of a house. It tells you about the people who live behind it.

The most popular doors are the polished wooden doors. Wood is _____ , but it needs to be treated to prevent peeling and cracking. So you need to invest time and money if you choose a wooden door. Personalising your front door with a fresh coat of paint will add interest and charm to your home. However, choose the colour with care!

"Doors that are painted black are _____ , smart and elegant," says Helen Green of Lifestyle Interiors. "Although pale colours are _____ , they can get very dirty, particularly in towns. Very dark blue and dark green is _____ and sophisticated and red is considered _____ ." Traditionally, doors have been painted black or white. However, a door painted in _____ colours makes the house look cheerful and welcoming.

Generally the British protect their privacy. The doors of British houses are always closed. They are meant to keep the weather and other people out. There are always blinds or curtains in the windows and, if there is glass in the door, it is normally _____ or frosted, so that people cannot look in.

(adapted from 'The Daily Telegraph')

Now check your answers with a partner.

b Read the article again and find three words that you don't know.
Go round the class and ask for their meaning.
Examples: What's the meaning of 'paint'?
What does 'sophisticated' mean?

If the other students don't know the meaning of the words,
you can use a dictionary or ask your teacher.

> **Learning Tip – Vocabulary**
> Learn only the words that are important to you. Decide which words are useful for you to learn. Don't try to learn every word you come across in English.

c What do you think? In groups of four talk about the following:
Is privacy important in your country?
Do you always have curtains in the windows?
Are the front doors in your country always closed/locked?

> **Remember**
> **Linking words**
> 'But', 'however' and 'although' are used to link two different or contrasting ideas.
> 'However' begins a new sentence.

d Look at the text again and find the words 'but', 'however' and 'although'.
Do they have the same meaning?

2e Write at least four general sentences about your front door.

Example: My front door is made of wood.
              It is painted white.

Now work on your own and link your sentences to make a short paragraph. Put your sentences in any order you want. You can use other linking words, for example, 'and', 'because' and 'so'.

> **Learning Tip – Writing**
> When you write you usually need to make some connection with some other thing that you have just written. A common way of making a connection is by using linking words (e.g. 'however', 'because', 'although').

3 Shapes

a What shape is it?
Label these diagrams with one of these words.

oval • oblong • square • round

b Work in pairs. Tell your partner the name of an object. Your partner will tell you the shape.
Example: Partner A: water melon
              Partner B: A water melon is round.

Tell your partner which shape you like best. Why?

4 What's it called in English?

a Listen to these people describing some things they don't know the English word for. Do you know the name of the object?

1. _____
2. _____
3. _____
4. _____
5. _____

b Now listen again and number the expressions as you hear them.

☐ It's stuff to …
☐ It's a kind of …
☐ It's a machine …
☐ It's a thing you need …
☐ It's something like …

> **Learning Tip – Speaking**
> The above expressions (e.g. It's stuff to … / It's a thing you need …) are useful to know when you don't know the exact English word and need to describe it.

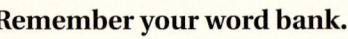
Remember your word bank.

c Work in pairs and complete the crossword puzzle.
Student A looks at this page.
Student B turns to **page 125**.
Use the expressions from **4b** to explain your words. All these words are objects you can find in the house. Take it in turns. Look at the example first.

Example: *Student B:* What is '1 across'?
Student A: '1 across' is a kind of machine for weighing things.

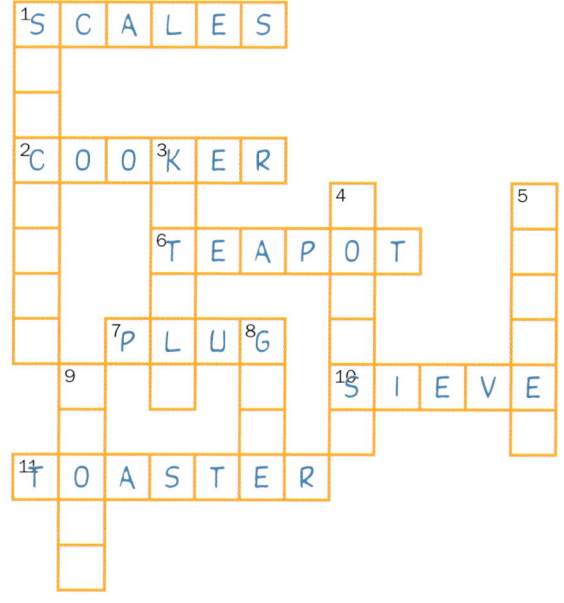

d What's that stuff for?

'Stuff' can mean a number of things in English. Work in pairs.
Read the poem and guess what the word 'stuff' is referring to.

Lovers lie around in it.
Broken glass is found in it.
_____ .
I like that stuff.

Eskimos and tramps chew it.
Madame Tussaud gave status to it.
_____ .
I like that stuff.

Tuna fish get trapped in it.
Legs come wrapped in it.
_____ .
I like that stuff.

Cigarettes are lit by it.
Pensioners get happy when they sit by it.
_____ .
I like that stuff.

Well, I like that stuff.
Yes, I like that stuff.
The earth
Is made of earth.
And I like that stuff.

(*adapted from 'Stuff' by Adrian Mitchell*)

Then listen to the recording and check your answers.

Now in groups of four, think of a 'stuff' and write a similar poem.
Read it out to the other groups. Can they guess what your 'stuff' is?

5 The sky's the limit!

a There are many kinds of outdoor activities.
Work in pairs. Write down as many names
of outdoor activities as you can think of in sixty seconds.
Example: parachuting

_____

_____

_____

Now listen to Steve describing an outdoor activity that he enjoys.
Do you know what it is? Have you ever tried it?

Write down some key words which helped you find out.
Examples: light frame, take off

_____

_____

b In the recording, there are many examples of multi-word
verbs – verbs that consist of more than one word.
Examples: consist of, find out

Listen to Steve again and complete the multi-word verbs.

find *out*	pull _____
take _____	bring _____
falls _____	bring _____
give _____	blow _____
meet _____	

> **Multi-word verbs (1)**
> A multi-word verb is a combination of a verb plus
> another short word called a particle (e.g. off,
> down, on, with, after).
> *Examples:* He **sat down**.
> She **turned off** the radio.

6 Multi-word verbs

a How many multi-word verbs can you make from the following words?
Tick the combination you think is possible.

	on	off	away	out	in	down	back
take	☐	✔	☐	☐	☐	☐	☐
give	☐	☐	☐	☐	☐	☐	☐
put	☐	☐	☐	☐	☐	☐	☐
switch	☐	☐	☐	☐	☐	☐	☐

Now check with a partner.

b Complete these sentences.

1. Hello, you're early. Come _____ and sit _____ .
2. I told Jan to come _____ at 10.00.
3. I'm feeling hot. I'll take _____ my coat.
4. Write _____ the name in my notebook. I forget names quickly.
5. You have to sign here and fill _____ your date of birth.
6. Darcy had to put _____ the suitcase. It was too heavy for him.

Remember your word bank.

c Complete the following mind map with the words from below.

radio • job • TV • page • cooker • the lights

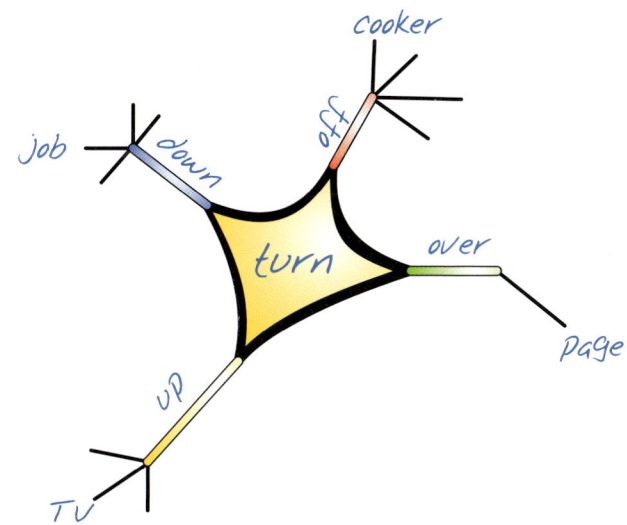

The different combinations have different meanings. Do you know all the different meanings of these multi-word verbs?

Learning Tip – Mind Map
A mind map is a creative way of learning vocabulary. The main word is linked with other related words by means of lines or arrows.

Multi-word verbs (2)
You can sometimes put the object of a multi-word verb in front of or after the particle (e.g. down, off, over, up etc.).
Example: I **turned up** the radio. / I **turned** the radio **up**.

If the object is a pronoun, it always goes between the verb and the particle.
Example: I **turned** it **up**.

6d Write two examples with the multi-word verb
'turn down' and 'turn up' to demonstrate
the three different combinations.
Examples: I **turned off** the cooker.
I **turned** the cooker **off**.
I **turned** it **off**.

_____

_____

_____

_____

7 Describing a product

a Ms Kline is visiting Kay, her business partner in England.
She, Kay, is showing her their latest products.
Listen to their conversation and complete the notes that Ms Kline has taken.

	Product 1	Product 2
Name	Harmony	_____
Weight	_____	260 g
Material	recycled paper	_____
Description	_____	striped, with dots or stars
Shape	rectangular	_____
Dimensions	_____	30 cm in diameter, 12 cm high
Price	60 p	_____
Delivery	_____	_____

What are the two products?

_____

Check your answers with your partner.

b Ask your partner about the dimensions of
her/his office or of a room in the house.
Example: How large is your office? –
It's _____ long/wide/high.

Identifying and describing simple objects – shape, size, colour, material

What shape is it?	It's oblong.
What size is it?	It's about 2 metres long, 2 metres wide and 2.5 metres high.
What's it made of?	It's made of glass.
What colour is it?	It's dark grey.

Expressing that you don't know a word

What's the meaning of …?
What's the English for …?

Expressing that you don't know what something is called in English

I don't know what it's called in English.
What's that in English?
What do you call …?

Compensation strategies

It's something like …
It's a thing you need …
It's stuff to …
It's a kind of …

Talking about weights and measurements

How long/wide/high is it?
How much does it weigh? / How heavy is it?

Multi-word verbs

A multi-word verb is a combination of a verb plus another short word called a particle (e.g. off, down, on, with, after).
Example: He **sat down**.

The object of a multi-word verb can sometimes go before or after the particle.
Example: I **took off** my jacket. / I **took** my jacket **off**.

If the object consists of many words, it goes after the particle so that the two parts of the verb are not separated too widely.
Example: I **took off** my mother's old green jacket.

If the object is a pronoun, it always goes before the particle.
Example: I **took** it **off**.

With some multi-word verbs (verb + preposition) you cannot separate the preposition from the verb. In this case, the object is always after the particle.
Example: She **looks after** her grandmother.

Memory Box

A Global Language

1 Map of the world

Work in pairs and look at the map of the world. On the map, circle five countries where English is spoken as a mother tongue and five countries where English is spoken as a second language.

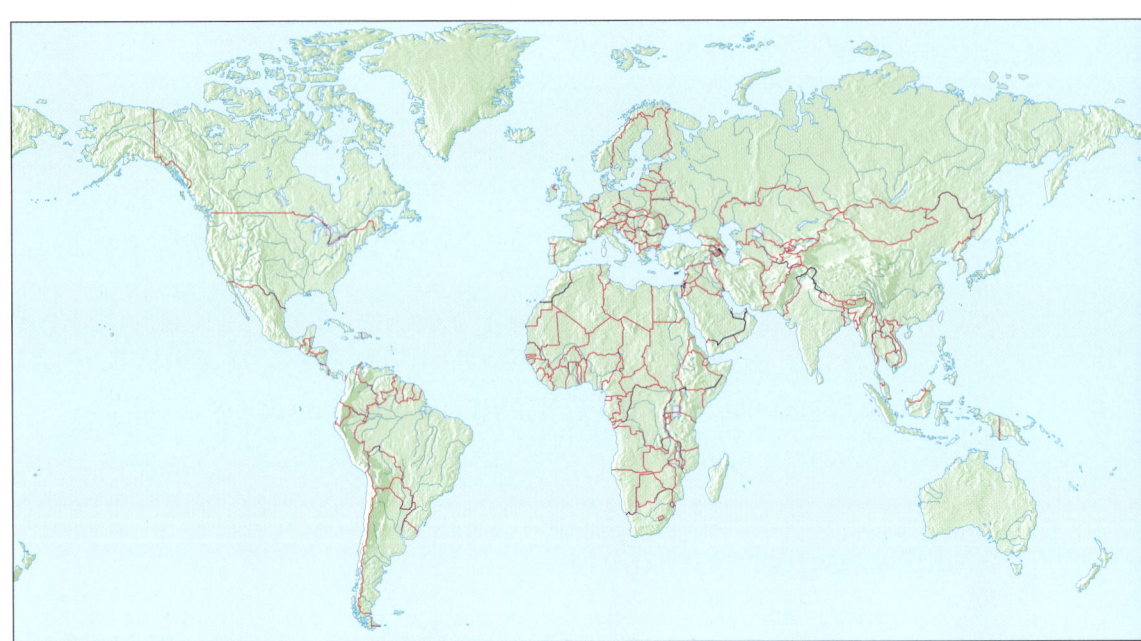

2 The English language

a Write down one or two things you know about the English language.
Example: In Austria, children learn English at an early age.
English is spoken in many countries.

_____

Work in groups of three or four. Talk about your sentences.

b Read this short extract about the English language.
Try and fill in the missing numbers in the text.

400 million • 70 • 1.5 billion • 1/4 • 1996 • 100

English is a global language. You hear it on television, spoken by politicians from all over the world. Wherever you travel, you see English signs and advertisements. Around _____ people, a _____ of the world's population, are already fluent in English. In the USA, Canada, Great Britain, Ireland, Australia, New Zealand and South Africa, English is spoken as the mother tongue by _____ native speakers. English is also the official or second language in over _____ countries, such as India, Singapore, Gibraltar, Malta and Nigeria. In these countries, it is used as the language of the government, the media, education and commerce. Furthermore, English is also the language most widely taught as a foreign language – in over _____ countries, such as China, Russia, Germany, Brazil and Egypt. This number is constantly increasing. In _____ French was replaced by English as the main foreign language in schools in Algeria, a former French colony. No other language is used by so many people - not even Chinese, which is spoken by 1.1 billion people. *(adapted from 'English as a Global Language' by David Crystal)*

Compare your answers with a partner. What is the most interesting piece of information in the text? Tell your partner.

c Look at the sentences below. Rewrite these sentences using the passive form. You can check your answers in the text in **2b**.

Examples:

active form	passive form
People in New Zealand **speak** English.	English **is spoken** in New Zealand.
Politicians from all over the world **speak** English.	English **is spoken** by politicians from all over the world.

1. 400 million native speakers speak English.

   English is spoken _____ .

2. The Indian government uses English as an official language.

   English is used _____ .

3. Teachers teach English as a foreign language in over 100 countries.

   English _____ .

4. The schools in Algeria replaced French by English.

   French _____ .

Which do you think sounds better – the active or the passive form?

In **passive** sentences you use the verb 'to be' (is, are, was, were, has been) plus the past participle of the verb (e.g. spoken, used).
If you are more interested in the subject, you use a verb in the **active form**.
Example: Marie **teaches** French at a primary school in Germany.

If you are more interested in 'what is done' than 'who does the action', you use the **passive form**.
Example: French **is taught** in some primary schools in Germany.

If you want to say 'who' or 'what' does the action in the **passive** form, you use **by**.
Example: English is spoken **by** 400 million native speakers.

d Read the text again and sort out the information about the English-speaking countries, using the following word wheels.

> **Learning Tip – Sorting out information**
> Sorting out information helps you remember it. Word wheels are one way of organising your work.

The English Language

USA

countries using English as a first language

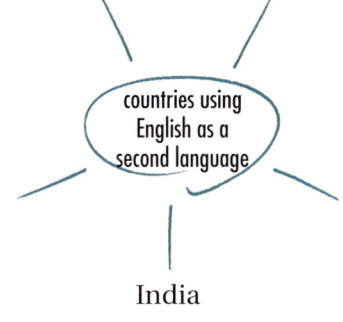

countries using English as a second language

India

countries using English as a foreign language

China

3 How numbers are spoken

a Working with numbers. Say these numbers aloud.
Now listen and repeat.

70p	17	$108
555	£9,999	€ 155,417
¹/₄	5,987,379	³/₄

Note

In **BE** you can say:
five hundred *and* fifty-five (555)
In **AE** you often say:
five hundred fifty-five

b Listen and write the numbers you hear.

_____   _____   _____

_____   _____   _____

4 Esperanto quiz

a What do you know about Esperanto ? Have a look at this quiz
and tick the correct answers. Work with a partner.

Note

In **British and American English** a **comma** is used to separate the digits in numbers greater than 999 (1,000 or 6,698,234).
A **point**, not a comma, is used in writing decimals (4.75).

1. What is Esperanto?
   (a) an artificial language   **(b)** an English dialect
   (c) a language spoken in Poland

2. When was it invented?
   (a) 1854   **(b)** 1887
   (c) 1910

3. How many people speak it?
   (a) 80,000   **(b)** 995,000
   (c) 2,000,000

4. Where does Esperanto's vocabulary come from?
   (a) French   **(b)** German and English
   (c) several European languages

5. Can you read Shakespeare in Esperanto?
   (a) Yes   **(b)** No

6. What is the role of Esperanto today?
   (a) it brings about peace   **(b)** it slows down the growth of English
   (c) it will become the official language of the EU

b ABC Radio Station interviews Mr. Kepp Enderby during the
84th annual "Universala Kongreso de Esperanto" in Berlin.

Listen to the interview and check
your answers in the quiz.
You score one point for each
correct answer.

Who has the most points?

Learning Tip – Listening
Don't worry if you don't understand everything!
You can still get the main ideas if you listen to the
key words first and disregard the rest.

c Now listen once more and notice the passive constructions. Complete the following sentences. Compare your answers with a partner.

1. Esperanto was _____ by Ludwig Zamenhof.
2. Esperanto _____ published in 1887.
3. A world-wide census _____ never been _____ .
4. Esperanto _____ by about two million speakers.
5. Every word is pronounced exactly as it _____ .
6. The congress has _____ every year since 1905.

d Write the passive verb forms from **4c** in the columns below.

present simple passive	past simple passive	present perfect passive
_____	_____	_____
_____	_____	_____

Note

Both in the passive and in the active form you use the same rules for the tenses.

5 What do you think?

a Talk about the following questions in groups of four.

1. Is it useful to learn Esperanto?
2. Do you think children should learn it at school in addition to English?
3. Does Esperanto have a role to play in the third millennium?
4. Would you like to learn Esperanto?

b Now listen to these young people talking about different aspects of Esperanto. Tick the table according to which aspect they are talking about.

aspects:	communication	travel	culture	easy to learn
Speaker 1	✔			
Speaker 2				
Speaker 3				
Speaker 4				
Speaker 5				
Speaker 6				
Speaker 7				

6 English signs

a When you travel, you see many English signs and advertisements. Here are some typical English signs. Where would you see these signs? Choose from the following places.

bar • department store • street • Bed & Breakfast • hotel • restaurant • hospital • airport

 Dear Smoker, you are entering a non-smoking passenger terminal. Smoking is not allowed.

Breakfast is served between 6.30 and 9.30 a.m.

Credit cards are accepted.

English is spoken here.

Under-18s will not be served beer.

Visitors are asked to leave before 7.00 p.m.

<u>Our guests are kindly asked not to smoke in bed.</u>

 **Cars will be towed away**

b Work in pairs. Look at the signs again and underline all the passive forms. Talk to a partner and rephrase the sentences using 'can', 'can't', 'must' or 'mustn't'. Take it in turns.
Examples: You can have breakfast between 6.30 and 9.30 a.m.
You can't (mustn't) smoke here.

Remember

The passive is often used in the written form. In the spoken form you use **can** plus infinitive (or can't + infinitive) to talk about what you are allowed (or not allowed) to do.
Examples: You **can** pay by credit card.
You **can't** park your car here.

You use **mustn't** to say strongly that something is not permitted.
Example: You **mustn't** smoke in the office.

Warning signs are normally written in the imperative form.
Example: **Reduce** speed now!

You often use the negative form by putting 'Do not' or 'Don't' in front of the verb.
Example: **Don't drink** and drive!

c Look at 1.-7. and decide where these 'warnings' can be seen.

1. Don't feed the animals! _____
2. Keep off the grass! _____
3. Mind the gap! _____
4. Don't lean out of the window! _____
5. Beware of the dog! _____
6. Keep Malta tidy! _____
7. Private. Don't enter! _____

d Signs have to be short. In the spoken form, you can use 'should' and 'shouldn't'. Can you change 1.-7. below using 'should' or 'shouldn't'?
Example: Don't feed the monkeys! – You shouldn't feed the monkeys.

1. Bikes are not allowed.
2. No left turn!
3. Don't drink and drive!
4. Use the other side of the road.
5. Reduce speed now!
6. Keep to the path!
7. Pay cash at exit.

7 Mixing socially – mysterious expressions!

a Here are some expressions commonly used in social situations in Britain and in the USA. What do you think they mean? Discuss in groups of four.

Learning Tip – Word Bank
It is important to notice how native speakers express things when they speak or write. Put these short expressions in your **Word Bank** so that you can use them later on as part of your own English.

b What do you say?

Do you use such expressions in your own country?
Do you use any other polite expressions, for example,
do you say anything in your country before you start a meal?

8 The press conference

a Mr. Jordan, the managing director of Chrisler, is giving a press conference about his company. Listen to his speech and look at his notes below.

- 1985/COMPANY STARTED
- IN JANUARY / NEW FACTORY OPENED
- 60 WORKERS HIRED
- CARS SOLD IN 50 COUNTRIES
- GOOD WORKING CONDITIONS, HIGH WAGES, CHILDCARE
- TWO YEARS AGO / LANGUAGE CLASSES STARTED
- IN DECEMBER / $10,000 TO UNICEF

Now use the notes to write an e-mail to a friend who is interested in getting a job at Chrisler's.

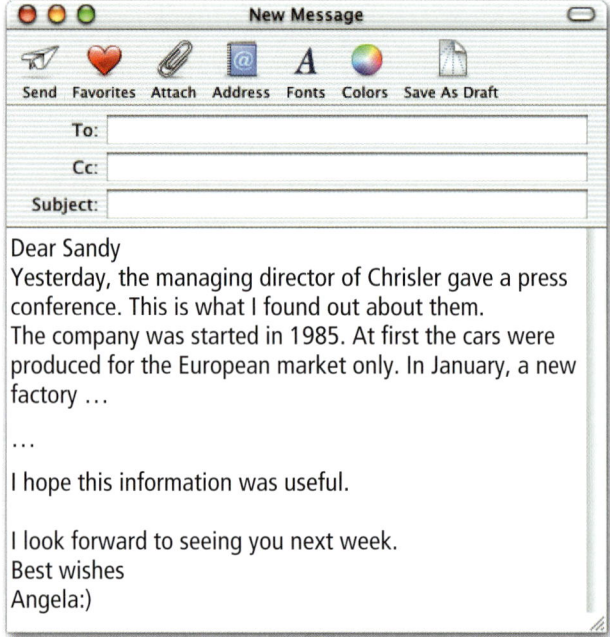

New Message

Send Favorites Attach Address Fonts Colors Save As Draft

To:

Cc:

Subject:

Dear Sandy
Yesterday, the managing director of Chrisler gave a press conference. This is what I found out about them.
The company was started in 1985. At first the cars were produced for the European market only. In January, a new factory …

…

I hope this information was useful.

I look forward to seeing you next week.
Best wishes
Angela:)

Note

You use the passive form both in speaking and in writing but it is more common in writing.

b   Verbs and nouns

Listen to Mr. Jordan again. Which nouns go with these verbs?
Example: start a company

produce _____

open _____

hire _____

sell _____

Adjectives and nouns
Some adjectives and nouns often go together.
Example: a successful company

Look at the word wheels. Which adjective does not go with the noun in the middle.

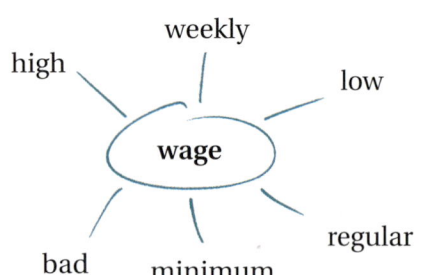

high   weekly   low

wage

bad   minimum   regular

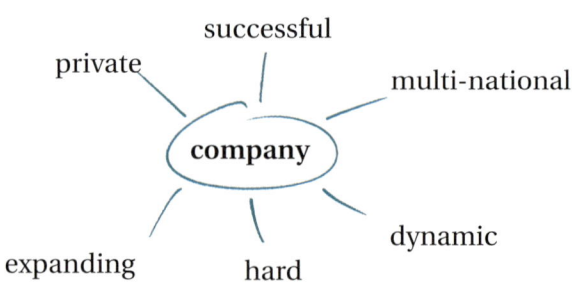

private   successful   multi-national

company

expanding   hard   dynamic

Remember your word bank.

Learning Tip – Word partners
Dictionaries show you which words go together.
wage *A weekly wage of $200* – 'weekly' is an adjective that goes together with 'wage'.

Passive

You use the passive when it is not so important to say 'who' or 'what' did the action. In passive sentences you use a form of 'be' (is, are, was, were, has been) plus the past participle of the verb (e.g. written, opened).

Present passive:	Coca-Cola **is sold** all over the world.
Past passive:	Romeo and Juliet **was written** by Shakespeare.
Present perfect passive:	A new factory **has been opened**.
will-future:	Dinner **will be served** at 6 p.m.

You use an **active verb** to say what the subject does.
Example: My father **built** this house.

You use a **passive verb** when 'who' or 'what' does the action is not important or is unknown.
Example: English **is spoken** all over the world.

If you want to say 'who' or 'what' does the action in the passive form, you use **by**.
Example: He was arrested **by** the police.

Talking about what you are allowed (not allowed) to do

You use 'can' + infinitive for permission. You talk about what you are allowed to do.
Example: You **can** pay by cheque.

You use 'can't' + infinitive for prohibition. You talk about what you aren't allowed to do.
Example: You **can't park** your car here.

You use 'mustn't' to say strongly that something is not allowed.
Example: You **mustn't** smoke in the office.

Talking about numbers

679	six hundred and seventy-nine
2,455	two thousand four hundred and fifty-five
54,734	fifty-four thousand seven hundred and thirty-four
999,456	nine hundred and ninety-nine thousand four hundred and fifty-six
1,000,000	one million
1,000,000,000	one billion

In **British English** you can say: five hundred *and* fifty-five (555)
In **American English** you leave out 'and', so you often say: five hundred fifty-five (555)

Warning someone

You should be careful.
You shouldn't drive so fast.

Imperative

You use the **imperative** in signs to give warnings. The imperative is the same as the infinitive form of the verb without a subject.
Example: **Mind** the step!

Don't or **Do not** are used in strong warnings.
Example: **Don't** drink and drive!

Final Game

Rules

1. Put your markers on START and throw the dice.
2. Move your marker along the board according to the number on the dice.
3. Complete the task on the square you land on.
4. Make up a sentence with your word.
5. If you are correct, you can stay on the square until your next turn. If your answer is not correct, you must go back two squares.
6. The other players decide whether your answer is correct or not. If they are not sure, they can turn to **page 208** for the answers.
7. The first player to reach FINISH is the winner.

Congratulations!

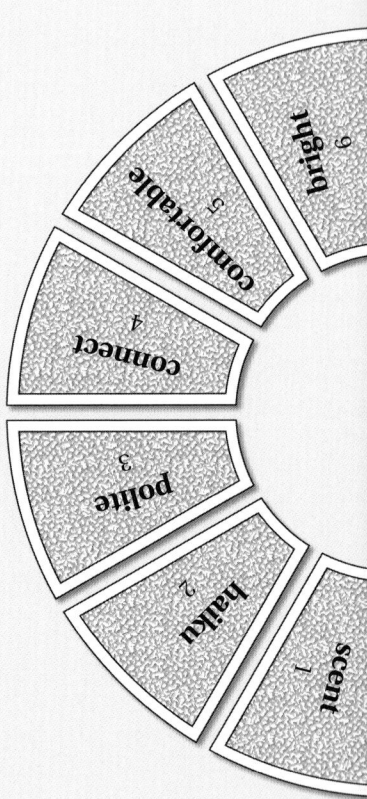

1 Find a synonym

wages
company
scent
employee
commuter

2 Explain the meaning

managing director
fairy tale
haiku
aromatherapy
global language

3 Find the opposite

lazy
necessary
polite
light
tired

4 Add a suffix to change the verb into a noun

inform
describe
connect
explain
govern

5 Find the stressed syllable in the word

advertisement
hotel
comfortable
thirteen
education

6 Find the silent letter(s) in the word

foreigner
vegetable
bright
climb
psychologist

7 Make-up two multi-word verbs

take
put
give
turn
switch

START

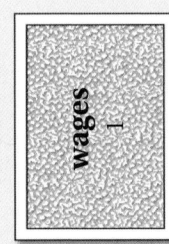

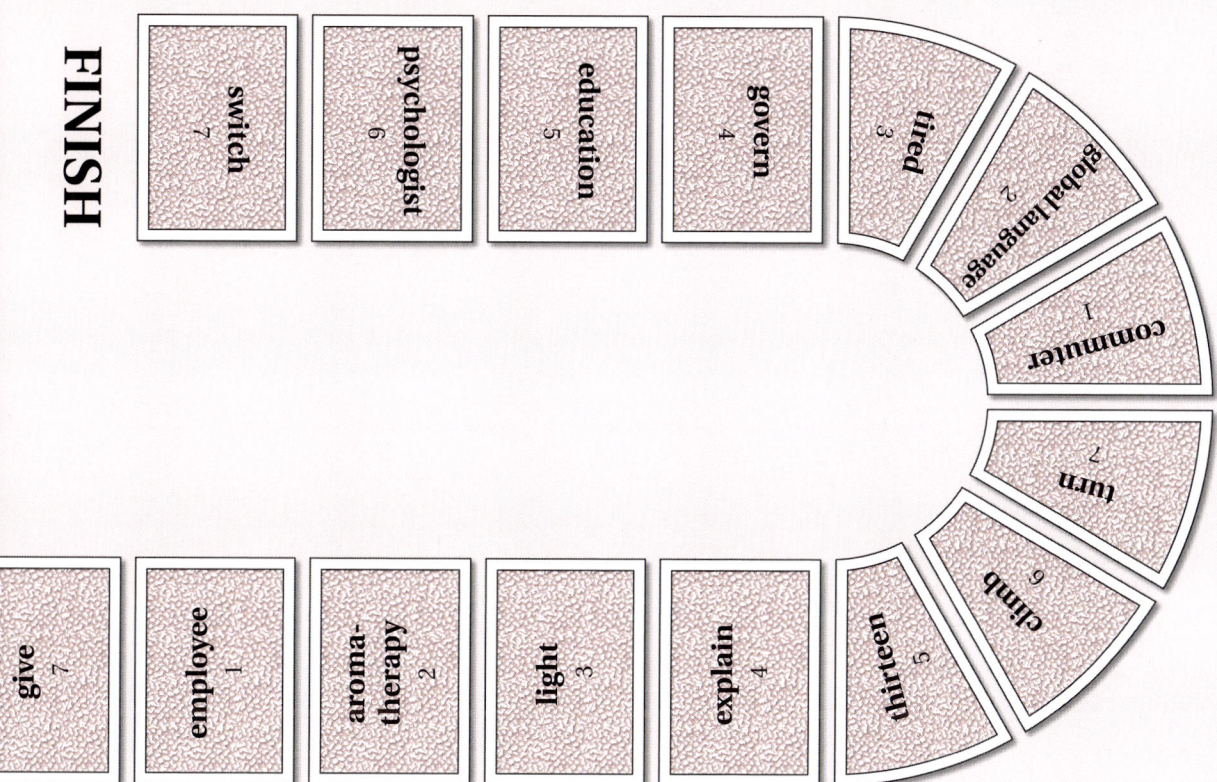
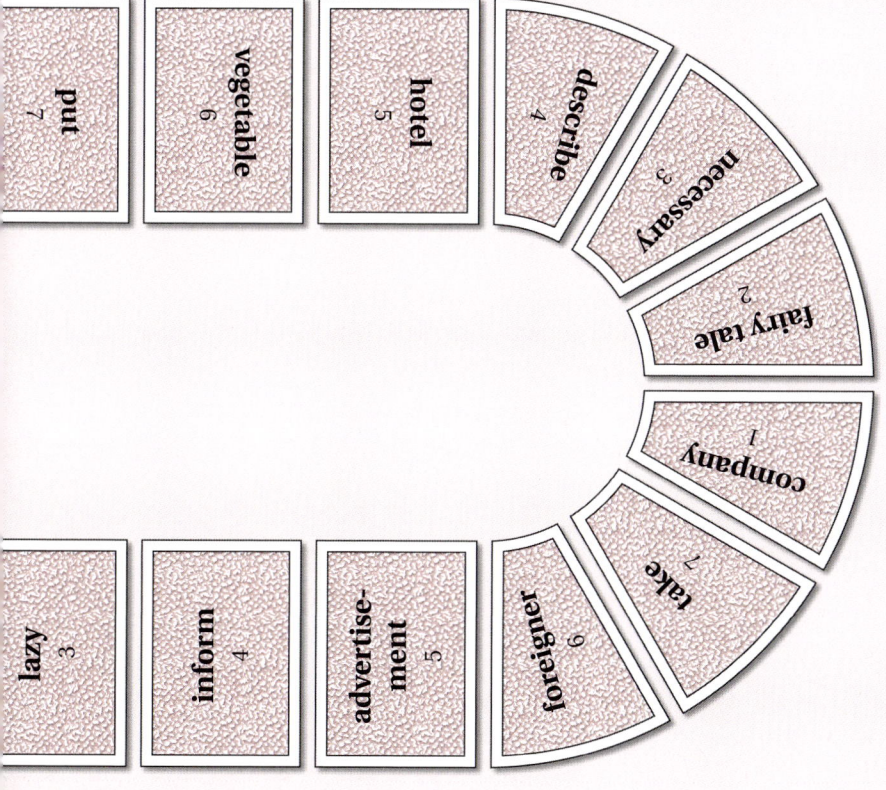

switch 7

psychologist 6

education 5

govern 4

tired 3

global language 2

commuter 1

turn 7

climb 6

thirteen 5

explain 4

light 3

aroma-therapy 2

employee 1

give 7

Final Game

put 7

vegetable 6

hotel 5

describe 4

necessary 3

fairy tale 2

company 1

take 7

foreigner 6

advertisement 5

inform 4

lazy 3

4 A week in the life of Hal Heckam

b Role Card 9
You are Hal's yoga teacher. He's having a session with you on Thursday evening at
7.00 p.m. He likes to see you after his psychiatrist as it helps him to calm down.

3 How fit are you?

b Partner B
Ask partner A the following questions
starting with 'Have you ever …?'

Have you ever …?
1. watch TV all day
2. drive to the shop round the corner
3. eat chocolate in the evening
4. spend a lazy weekend
5. take the lift up one floor only

Results for partner A
Less than 3 'yes' answers:
  *You are right on track! Little rewards are an
  essential part of your fitness programme!*

More than 3 'yes' answers:
  *You've lost the track completely!
  Stop thinking about the rewards and
  concentrate on getting fit.*

8 Telephone expressions

b Sit back to back with your partner.
Practise phone conversations using the expressions
on **page 24** and the situations below.

Partner B
1. You work for MacQueen Balloons.
   Find out your partner's name and address.

   Name: _____

   Address: _____

2. You want to go trekking in Nepal and
   want to book a flight soon. You know that
   your colleague has downloaded some
   information from the internet about this.
   Phone her/him and ask to send you the
   information via e-mail. Your e-mail
   address is lewes@aol.com.

9 Making suggestions   Partner A

Work in groups of three. Choose a situation and explain it to your group. Your group then makes suggestions and you reply. You can use the expressions on **page 25**.

Situation 1
You have become a couch potato. Every evening you sit in the living room, eat crisps and chocolate and just watch TV. You know you should break this habit, but how?

Situation 2
You are a workaholic. You spend all your week and weekends working. You can only talk and think about your work. Perhaps it's time to find a way to relax …

Situation 3
Help! You have made a bet with your friends to lose 5 kilos in one month. You have eaten a lot less but it hasn't made a difference …

File Section • Revision 1

2 Information exchange

Work in pairs. Ask your partner questions in the simple past to find the missing information in the text below.

Example: 'In the early 1970s Tony Wheeler and his wife, Maureen, travelled from _____' –
Where did the Wheelers travel to in the 1970's?

Partner B

In the early 1970s Tony Wheeler and his wife, Maureen, travelled from _____ across _____ , the Middle East and Asia to _____ . They left England in a £_____ mini-van and drove across Europe, Turkey and Iran into Afghanistan. They made a £3 profit on the van and went on by _____ and _____ through Pakistan and India. They trekked in _____ , hitchhiked through Malaysia and took boats to Java and then on to Sydney. 'People asked us our _____ and where we stayed. We decided to put what we knew into a small book.' Maureen brought her typewriter home from work at weekends to write up the book and Tony drew all _____ and _____. They spent all their savings on printing 'Asia on the Cheap'.

8 Asking for permission   Partner A

c Using the situations ask someone in your group for permission. Another person in the group should give permission or refuse, giving a reason why.

Situation 1
You want to borrow a car to take your mother-in-law out on a day trip and your car has broken down.

Situation 2
You have two tickets to a concert. You need someone to baby-sit for your five children and dog.

Situation 3
Your friend has just got a fantastic job in Spain. Ask if it's OK for you to apply for a job at the same company as you would love to live and work in Spain, too.

File Section • Unit 4

1 The hurry sickness quiz

Results
More than 4 'yes' answers
Oh dear! You seem to have difficulty keeping up with yourself. You could be suffering from hurry sickness.

Less than 3 'yes' answers
Well done! You seem to have no problems managing your time.

4 Company regulations

a In pairs exchange information to complete the memo on **page 38**.

Partner B
Use the prompts below to make up the company regulations using 'must', 'don't have to' and 'mustn't' in your answer. Then answer your partner's questions.

Example: What are the regulations for meetings? –
You must attend weekly meetings.

1. **Must**
   meetings – You must attend weekly meetings.
   travel expenses – …
2. **Don't have to**
   holiday entitlement – …
   flexitime – …
3. **Mustn't**
   overtime – …
   private phone calls – …

8 Secret eating habits

b Work in pairs. Find out your partner's secret eating habits at work / at home. In your answers use one of the words from the scale on **page 42**.

Example: Do you like eating cheese and jam sandwiches? – No, I can't stand them! / Yes, I love them!

Partner B
1. putting lemon in your early-morning peppermint tea
2. munching a whole bag of liquorice when writing a report
3. eating pizza with your fingers during your working lunch
4. eating a chocolate croissant when photocopying
5. …
6. …

4 A week in the life of Hal Heckam

b Role Card 8
You are Hal's psychiatrist and he has an appointment at your clinic on Thursday afternoon at 3.05 p.m. You keep trying to tell him he's just a normal person but he won't believe you …

H4 Habits quiz

Results

Mostly A
You like your habits. You always do the same things every day.
You should try to change your routines. Remember: variety is the spice of life!

Mostly B
You sometimes like to be adventurous, but you feel safe with your routine.
Make sure that you keep that little bit of spice in your life!

Mostly C
You are 'Mr/Ms Spontaneity'! You don't like routines. You always do different things at different times. However, don't fall into complete chaos!

9 Making suggestions   Partner C

Work in groups of three. Choose a situation and explain it to your group. Your group then makes suggestions and you reply. You can use the expressions on **page 25**.

Situation 1
You are always tired. You could fall asleep day or night any time anywhere. You know you need to find some energy, but how?

Situation 2
You want to do something adventurous – to go on a bike holiday in Spain with a group for two weeks. You want to train before you go but there are no hills where you live …

Situation 3
Your favourite hobby is cooking and eating good food (and drinking good wine). You don't want to give up this hobby but you now need a larger size of trousers …

4 A week in the life of Hal Heckam

b   Role Card 7
You are Hal's Public Relations Officer and have a date with him on Tuesday at 2.45 p.m. at his city flat. You want to show him your plans for a 'Hal Web Page' on the Internet …

8 Asking for permission   Partner B

c   Using the situations ask someone in your group for permission. Another person in the group should give permission or refuse, giving a reason why.

Situation 1
You are a member of a book club and you will get one free book every month if you send the name of someone who would like to become a member. Ask someone if it's OK to write their name.

Situation 2
You want to do a fast for two weeks and don't want to see other people eating – ask your boss if you can work from home for the two weeks.

Situation 3
Your sister is coming to visit and she has a very expensive car. Ask your neighbour if you can use his/her garage (he/she doesn't have a car) as your sister won't leave her car on the street.

8 Asking for permission   Partner C

c Using the situations ask someone in your group for permission. Another person in the group should give permission or refuse, giving a reason why.

Situation 1
Ask someone if you can use their computer in the evenings to practise surfing the internet until you have one of your own – you have ordered one but you have to wait six weeks.

Situation 2
You want to have a barbecue party but you don't have a garden. Ask your neighbour if you can use their garden – you know they are going on holiday this weekend.

Situation 3
You are trying to stop smoking but need to have five a day at work. Your new colleague is an anti-smoker. Ask your colleague if you may smoke just five a day in the office.

9 Making suggestions   Partner B

Work in groups of three. Choose a situation and explain it to your group. Your group then makes suggestions and you reply. You can use the expressions on **page 25**.

Situation 1
You have never been interested in sports but you think now is the time to start. The question is what sports and how?

Situation 2
You have become a computer freak. You spend all your time in dark rooms in front of the computer. You love computer games and can play for hours. You really must spend some time outside …

Situation 3
You are a book worm. Your favourite way to spend the weekend is with a pot of tea, lots of toast and a good book. Sometimes you think you should find time to give your eyes a rest and exercise the rest of your body …

4 A week in the life of Hal Heckam

b Role Card 3
You are Hal's hairdresser. Hal has an appointment at your hair salon on Friday afternoon at 3 o'clock. He wants his hair dyed blonde again.

6 Invitations   Partner B

d Your partner wants to invite you. Accept or decline your partner's invitations. If you decline an invitation don't forget to give a reason why. You can use the expressions in **6b** on **page 67**.

Now it's your turn to invite you partner to the following events.
1. a modern art exhibition
2. rock-climbing
3. a parachute jump
4. a day trip to the mountains
5. a talk about the local wildlife

4 A week in the life of Hal Heckam

b Role Card 5
You are Hal's fiancé. As you are a singer and a model you don't have much time to see each other. This Saturday you are giving a concert in London and then are going to a celebrity party with Hal at 11.00 p.m. You must phone Hal to tell him what to wear!

6 The Japanese visitor

c Partner B

You have got an itinerary of the Japanese Agent's visit but some of the points are missing. Phone your partner to check that the facts are correct and to find out the missing information. Go through each point using the expressions from **6b** and any appropriate question tags to help you check the facts.

Example: *Partner B:* What time will Masatoshi Fujisawa arrive?
Partner A: At …
Partner B: Sorry, I didn't catch that.

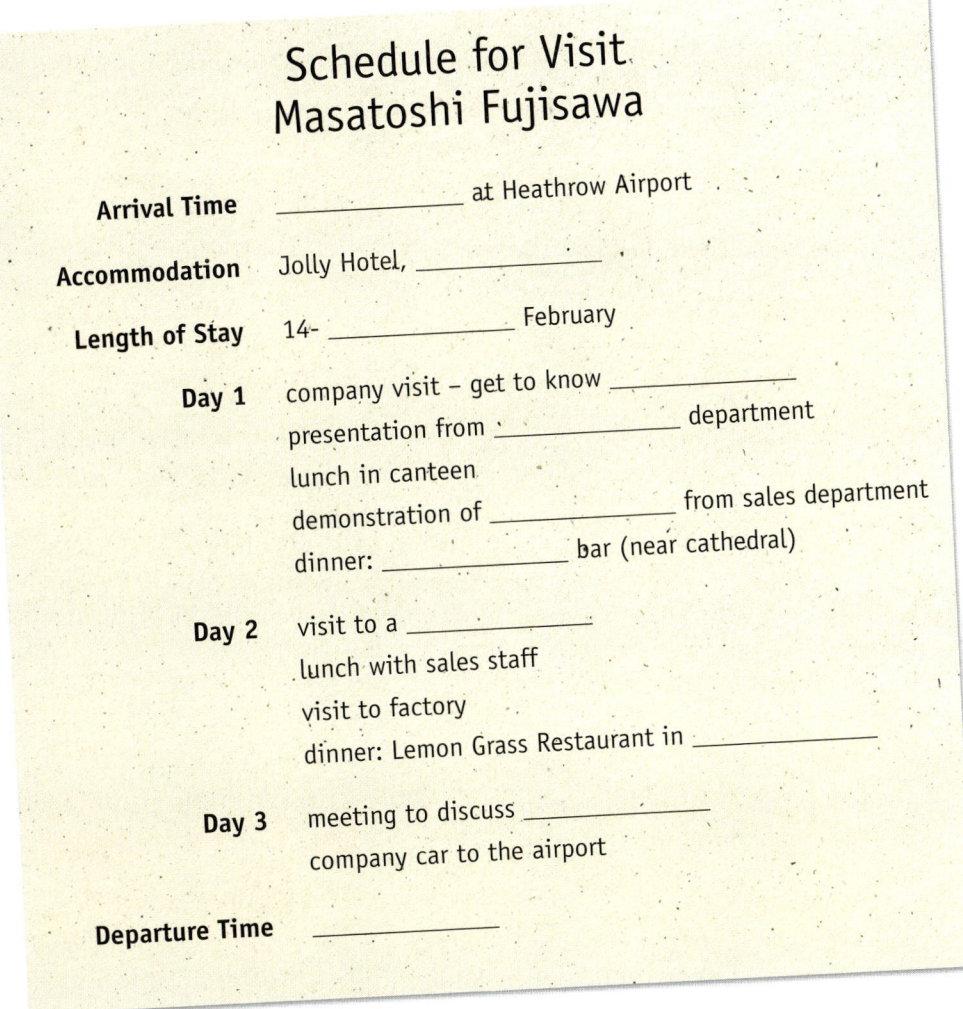

Schedule for Visit
Masatoshi Fujisawa

Arrival Time _____ at Heathrow Airport

Accommodation Jolly Hotel, _____

Length of Stay 14- _____ February

Day 1 company visit – get to know _____
presentation from _____ department
lunch in canteen
demonstration of _____ from sales department
dinner: _____ bar (near cathedral)

Day 2 visit to a _____
lunch with sales staff
visit to factory
dinner: Lemon Grass Restaurant in _____

Day 3 meeting to discuss _____
company car to the airport

Departure Time _____

4 A week in the life of Hal Heckam

b Role Card 1

You are Hal's masseur. You are meeting Hal every weekday next week at 11.00 a.m. for his massage and facial. He likes his face to be as fit as his body is!

7 Writing a summary

a Work with a partner. One of you reads text B below, the other text A on **page 83**. Outline the gist of the article by taking notes. Use your notes to write a short summary (about 3-4 sentences) of the newspaper article. Finally, think of a headline.

Text B

Scientists say they know how to cut down the rush-hour aggression. Scents of the seaside can be introduced in the Underground to reduce the stress of the travellers. The most effective smells are seaside salt since they remind the commuters of sunny relaxing holidays on the beach. They claim that scents could also calm down football hooligans in stadiums. The theory behind the research is based on aromatherapy – the use of oils for healing purposes.

> **Learning Tip – Summarising**
> Summarising helps you sort out and organise information you read or hear. It is helpful to write the key points first and then to write a summary from your points.

b Read your summary to your partner. Find out in which way your article is similar/different.

4 A week in the life of Hal Heckam

b Role Card 10
You are Hal's oldest friend. You are meeting Hal at a fruit juice bar on Sunday evening at 7.25 p.m. for two hours (Hal likes to be in bed for 10.00 p.m.). You remember the days when he would go down the pub and drink 'men's drinks' but now it's only fruit juice …

4 A week in the life of Hal Heckam

b **Role Card 4**
You are Hal's financial advisor. You are having a working lunch with Hal on Monday at
1.15 p.m. You want to report to him how well his shares are doing, where he should
invest his money now, and how much money he can spend this week.

1 Not a waste of time!

Student B
Student A writes the clues for the words across.
Student B writes the clues for the words down.

Now take it in turns and ask your partner for the clues of the missing words
on your crossword puzzle.
Example: *Student A:* What is '3 down'?
　　　　　Student B: '3 down' is a period of 24 hours.

Clues down

1. _____

3. a period of 24 hours

4. _____

5. _____

8. _____

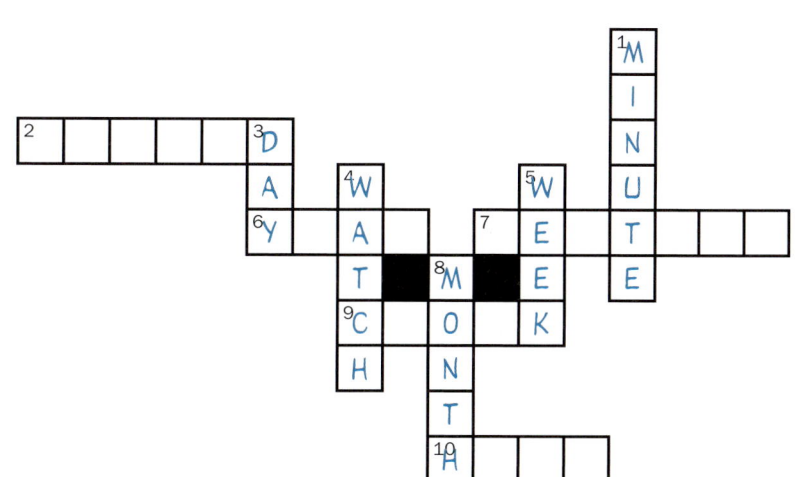

4 A week in the life of Hal Heckam

b Role Card 6
You are Hal's image designer. On Wednesday at 2.20 p.m. you are meeting Hal at the designer Clothes Complex in Covent Garden as it's time to choose Hal's spring collection. You can't decide if he should wear yellow or orange this spring …

File Section • Unit 10

1 Not a waste of time!

Student A
Student A writes the clues for the words across.
Student B writes the clues for the words down.

Now take it in turns and ask your partner for the clues of the missing words on your crossword puzzle.
Example: *Student B:* What is '2 across'?
              Student A: '2 across' is one of 60 parts which make a minute.

Clues across

2. one of 60 parts which make a minute

6. _____

7. _____

9. _____

10. _____

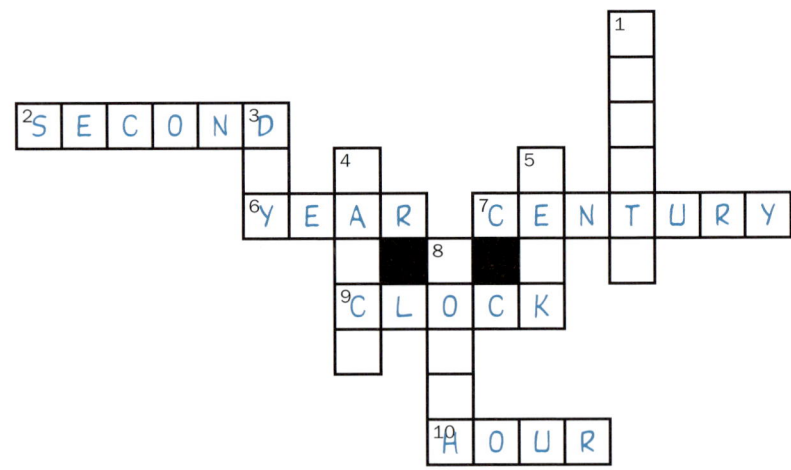

4 A week in the life of Hal Heckam

b Role Card 2
You are Hal's trainer. Hal is attending your training session on Monday, Wednesday and Friday from 9.00 a.m. to 11.00 a.m. You like to keep your star player in good form!

4 What's it called in English?

c Student B
Work in pairs and complete the crossword puzzle. Use the expressions from **4b** on **page 98** to explain your words. All these words are objects you can find in the house. Take it in turns. Look at the example first.

Example: Student A: What is '1 down'?
Student B: '1 down' is a kind of round pot used for cooking things.

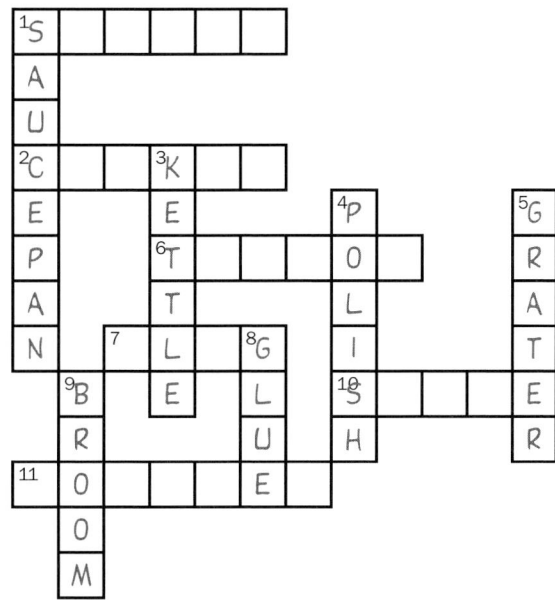

H1 Questions

It is not always easy to form correct questions so practice is important.
Can you find the correct questions for the following answers?

1. I'm Spanish.   _____?
2. He's a cook.   _____?
3. We like climbing.   _____?
4. They've got two cats and a dog.   _____?
5. Sylvia can speak English and German.   _____?

H2 The clothing puzzle

Can you find ten words to do with clothing? Read the clues and then fill in the missing words.
The ten letters in the middle boxes make up two more words to do with clothing.

What are they? _____

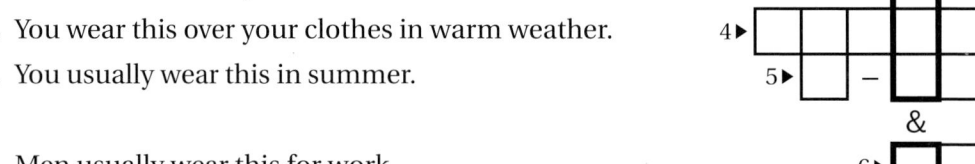

1. You wear this on your legs.
2. You need these to walk in snow.
3. You wear this over your clothes in cold weather.
4. You wear this over your clothes in warm weather.
5. You usually wear this in summer.

6. Men usually wear this for work.
7. This is like number 5 but has long sleeves.
8. This is like number 7 but women usually wear this.
9. This is made of wool and you wear it in winter.
10. Women often wear this.

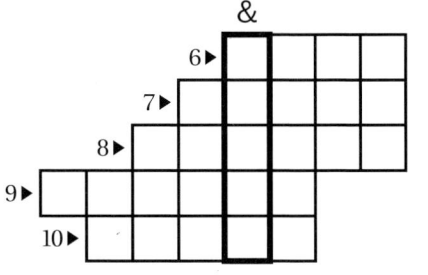

H3 Habits

a Listen to the recording to find out how often the speakers do the following.

How often?

1. have a cup of tea in bed   _____
2. have a cold shower in the morning   _____
3. have only fruit for lunch   _____
4. have dinner with friends   _____
5. have a hot bath in the evening   _____

b Can you now put the words you found in **H3a** on to the scale below.

100% ————————————————————————— 0%

C The habits in **H3a** are all used in combination with the verb 'have'.
Below are four more words which are used in combination with 'have'.
Can you unjumble them?

have … / have (a) …

1. cknas   _____
2. tfskraeba   _____
3. ffeoec   _____
4. nnride   _____

H4 Habits quiz

Are you a creature of habit or the spontaneous type?
Try our fun quiz to see what type of person you are.

1. When do you get up?
   a. You always get up at the same time every day. ☐
   b. You normally get up earlier in summer than in winter? ☐
   c. You usually get up as soon as you wake up? ☐

2. Are you
   a. trying lots of different new evening courses at the moment? ☐
   b. doing one new course? ☐
   c. doing the same procedure as every year? ☐

3. When do you learn English?
   a. You learn your English vocabulary every week on the same day. ☐
   b. You usually learn English when you feel like it. ☐
   c. Are you learning your vocabulary at this very minute? ☐

4. When do you do the household chores*?
   a. Every Saturday? ☐
   b. Normally when you have time? ☐
   c. Never. You have a cleaner because you're always doing different things and don't have time. ☐

5. What are your typical eating habits?
   a. Do you never eat in-between meals? ☐
   b. Do you sometimes have snacks between meals? ☐
   c. Are you eating now? ☐

* household chores = Hausarbeiten

Add up mostly A's, mostly B's or mostly C's and look at **page 117** in the **File Section** to find out if you are a creature of habit or the spontaneous type.

H5 Simple present or present progressive?

Put the correct form of the verb in the sentences below.

1. I _____ (learn) English at the moment.
2. Every Sunday he _____ (play) tennis with his friends.
3. We _____ (work) for a large international company.
4. Sylvia usually _____ (get up) at 8.00 am.
5. I _____ (no eat) meat or fish.
6. He _____ (have) got a new job.
7. Sylvia _____ (have) a holiday in Portugal this week.
8. They _____ (watch) the football match now.
9. This month we _____ (do) an English course.
10. Boris never _____ (work) on Sundays.

H6 An application form

You would like to do a course at a language school.
Complete the application form with your own details.

APPLICATION FORM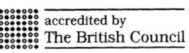

accredited by
The British Council

PERSONAL DETAILS

Family name ....   Home address ....
First name(s) ....
Nationality ....
Date of birth .... Age .... Tel No. ....
Passport No ....   Tel No. ....
Male ☐   Female ☐

TYPES OF COURSE YOU WOULD LIKE TO STUDY

General English - Programme 1	☐	Tailor-made English Programme	☐
General English - Programme 2	☐	Teacher Development Programme	☐
Part-time English:		English and Activities:	
Business English	☐	Art	☐
TOEFL	☐	Indoor climbing	☐
Cambridge Proficiency	☐	Outdoor Climbing	☐
Cambridge Advanced	☐	Horse Riding	☐
First Certificate	☐	Golf	☐
Academic English	☐	Walking	☐
Spring Junior Vacation Course	☐	English for Bankers	☐
Summer Junior Vacation Course (residential)	☐		
Summer Junior Vacation Course (home-stay)	☐		
Summer Adult Vacation Course - Option 1	☐		
Option 2	☐		

Course start date .... Course end date .... Length of course ....

LOCATION OF STUDY

Sheffield ☐   Colchester ☐

H7 Letters

Do you remember different ways to start and finish a letter?

Start	Finish
1. _____	1. _____
2. _____	2. _____

H8 Mix and match

Match the following statements/questions to the correct answers.

1. Nice to see you again.
2. What about learning ten new words a day?
3. What do you do?
4. This is Katja.
5. After you.
6. Sorry, what was your name?

a. I'm a journalist.
b. It's Jennifer.
c. Thank you.
d. Yeah, why not.
e. Nice to meet you.
f. Good to see you, too.

H9 Sounds: The weak form

Many words in English have strong forms when they are stressed and weak forms when they are spoken normally.
If you want to sound natural, don't stress every word.

Example: Nice **to** meet you.
strong form [tu] – weak form [tə]

Listen to the following sentences and underline the words which are said using the weak form.

1. I'm an engineer for Dupont.
2. I'm from Sweden.
3. I can speak a little Spanish.
4. Good to see you again.
5. Where do you work?

Pinboard

The most common words which are normally not stressed are the following:
a, an, the, some
to, from, for, at, as, of
are, have, has, was, can, do

You can compare the [ə] sound with the sound at the end of the German word 'bitte'.

H1 Healthy body & mind

Match the correct word partners.

1.	to run	mind & body
2.	to ride	a couch potato
3.	to relieve	squash
4.	to harmonise	a bike
5.	to play	a gym
6.	to become	stress
7.	to join	fit
8.	to get	a race

Which one is not a healthy 'activity'? – _____

H2 The Fast Track Gym

a Can you unjumble these words?
They all have to do with sports.

1. iracseob   _____
2. ggionjg   _____
3. nbsailegi _____
4. wmgisinm   _____
5. iktrknge   _____
6. xesercei   _____
7. gayo   _____
8. nngurin   _____

b Can you now put them to the correct word wheels?

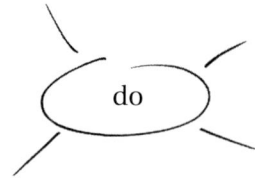

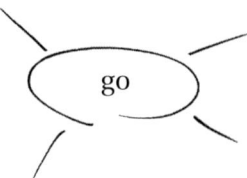

H3 Comic Relief – Red Nose Day

Find out more about Red Nose Day. Read the short text
and match the titles to the paragraphs below.

Where is the money spent?

Who gets involved?

What sort of things do people do?

What is Red Nose Day?

What is special about Red Nose Day?

When is Red Nose Day?

1. _____

Red Nose Day is a national fund-raising event organised by the charity 'Comic Relief'.

2. _____

Red Nose Day is once every two years. It's usually on a Friday in March.

3. _____

On Red Nose Day everyone in the country is encouraged to forget their inhibitions*,
put on a red nose and do something wild to raise money for charity.

4. _____

On Red Nose Day people in the UK go a little bit crazy. In schools the children don't wear
their school uniforms but fancy costumes instead. In offices secretaries are bosses for the
day. Everyone also watches the 6 hours of fantastic Red Nose television in the evening.

5. _____

Sporting heroes, leading business people, film stars and, of course, comedians are all
happy to get involved.

6. _____

Two thirds of the money raised by the public Red Nose Day goes to secure long term
development projects in Africa. One third of the money goes to projects in the UK.

inhibitions – Hemmungen

H4 Present perfect or simple past?

Put the verb in the correct form.
Examples: I**'ve** never **tried** ballooning. / I **went ballooning** last week.

1. I _____ (be) to Indonesia.
2. I _____ (go) mountain climbing last weekend.
3. _____ you ever _____ (ride) a camel?
4. He _____ (run) in three marathons.
5. It _____ (take) him 10 hours to drive home yesterday.
6. Ten years ago we _____ (live) in Brazil.
7. We _____ (not/swim) _____ in the Mediterranean.
8. Last year I _____ (collect) £150 for charity.
9. _____ they _____ (spend) all their money?
10. They _____ never _____ (think) about going on a balloon trip.

H5 Telephone dialogue

Can you fill in the missing words to complete the dialogue?

Caller   **Receiver**

1. Fast Track Fitness Centre. Can I _____ you?

2. _____ is George Jones speaking. I'd like _____ information about your courses, please.

3. Would you _____ me to send you a brochure?

4. Yes, that would be _____ .

5. OK. Could you _____ me your address, please?

6. It's 12 HumbledonView, Surrey SRX 4T8.

7. Right, I'll send it to you right _____ .

8. Thank you very _____ .

9. You're _____ . Bye

10. Bye.

 Now listen to see if you are correct.

H6 A Hen Night

The week before a couple gets married in Britain the man goes out with his male friends on a 'Stag Night' and the woman goes out with her female friends on a 'Hen Night'. What do you think each group would do on this evening or day?

a Before you read the text to find out what Di and her female friends did on her 'Hen Night', can you match these words from the text with the correct definition.

1. to coincide		a.	to feel sad / to have a negative feeling about a situation
2. to hop		b.	to collect money together for an organisation / person
3. to be disappointed		c.	when two things happen at the same time
4. to raise money		d.	to walk on only one leg

'It was the most unusual Hen Night I've ever been to,' says Di, 29. 'I enjoy running and in fact I ran in many marathons in the past. I even came eighty-third in the woman's category in the 1996 London marathon! We decided on the date for my hen weekend but then I found out that it coincided with the *Richmond Race for Life Run*.

I was really disappointed that I would miss the race, but then my friends suggested we all do the run together. "Yeah, well, oh, OK" was my reaction as I thought that my non-running friends would not enjoy it. But I was wrong.

They all finished the race, and they raised several hundreds of pounds for the *Imperial Cancer Research Fund*. This fund spends over £7 million each year on research into cancers that specially affect women.

If you would like to help raise money for this research, why not take part in one of this year's 'Race for Life' events? Remember you can walk, jog, skip or hop the 5 km course!

b Can you complete the questions below to ask about an unusual story?

1. When? – _____
2. Where? – _____
3. What? – _____
4. Why? – _____
5. How many friends? – _____
6. What first? – _____
7. After that? – _____
8. Finally? – _____
9. How ... home? – _____
10. How much ? – _____

c Using the question prompts above can you now write / make up an unusual story.

H7 Making suggestions

Look at the following situations and make suggestions. How many different constructions can you use?

1. I've got a headache.
   Why _____?
2. I can't find the time to do sports.
   Have _____?
3. I can never get up in the mornings.
   Have _____?
4. I do too much sport.
   _____?
5. I'm too lazy.
   _____?

H1 'Some' and 'any'

You are planning a trekking holiday with a friend. Check this list and write out some sentences/ questions using 'some' and 'any'.

Trekking in the Himalayas — check list

suntan lotion ✔
Plasters ✗
water bottles ?
insect repellent ✗
accommodation ✔
guide books ?

1. We've got some suntan lotion.
2. _____
3. _____ ?
4. _____
5. _____
6. _____ ?

* insect repellent = Insektenspray

H2 Fire and water

How many things in self-catering accommodation can you remember that are associated with 'heat' or with 'water'?

heat	water
1. f __ __ __ p __ __ __ __	1. b __ __ h
2. m __ __ r __ __ __ v __	2. d __ __ __ w __ __ h __ __
3. s __ __ v __	3. f __ __ d __ __
4. o __ __ n	4. s __ __ __ e __

Can you think of one thing you use in the kitchen which is associated with both 'heat' and 'water'?

c __ __ __ __ e   m __ __ h __ __ __

H3 Different lives

Everyday life can be different in different countries in Europe. More and more people notice this when they move on from one job in one country to another one in another country.

Listen to the dialogue and write in the table below the differences the speaker has noticed between life in Germany and life in the UK.

	UK	Germany
people	_____	more efficient
lifestyle	_____	_____
cars	_____	_____
homes	_____	_____
holidays	shorter	_____

H4 Irregular verbs

a Can you make seven more irregular verbs in the simple past out of this letter box?
Some letters are used more than once (sometimes also in the same word).

Example: D-R-E-W

D	K	M	R
A	B	O	W
U	V	N	G
E	T	H	S

b Can you now put the infinitive
next to the verbs in the simple past?

	simple past	infinitive
1.	*drew*	*draw*
2.		
3.		
4.		
5.		
6.		
7.		
8.		

H5 'Since' and 'for'

a Put 'since' or 'for' in front of these time phrases.

1. _____ last week
2. _____ 2 weeks
3. _____ a long time
4. _____ 1st January
5. _____ this morning
6. _____ a decade
7. _____ the spring
8. _____ 10 years

b Now write five sentences about yourself using the time phrases
above with the present perfect.

Example: I've worked in this company since last week.

1. _____
2. _____
3. _____
4. _____
5. _____

H6 A short biography

a Put the verbs in brackets in the correct tense – simple past or present perfect or simple present.

> Margaret Atwood _____ (be) born in Ottawa in 1939. She _____ (spend) most of her early life in northern Ontario and Quebec. She _____ (be) Canada's most famous novelist and poet. Up till today she _____ (publish) nine novels, five collections of short fiction and fourteen volumes of poetry.
> 'The Circle Game' (1966) _____ (win) her the Governor-General Award.
> Since then she _____ (go) on to win many more awards. In 1989 and 1996 she _____ (be) shortlisted for the Booker Prize with 'Cat's Eye' and 'Alias Grace'.
> Margaret Atwood _____ (live) in Toronto with the writer Graeme Gibson and their daughter.

b Now write a short biography about yourself to read out to the rest of the class next lesson.

H7 Books

Complete the word wheel with different types of 'books'.

1. This gives you information about a foreign country.
2. Another word for number 1.
3. This gives you short sentences in a foreign language.
4. This tells you the history of religion.
5. This gives you information about products or services to buy or rent.

H8 Booking a hotel room

a Can you find the word partners in these two lists?

1. double		of payment
2. room		reservation
3. written		bath
4. advance		confirmation
5. receipt		rates
6. private		room

b Look at the two advertisements and write a fax to one to make a booking for you and your family or friends. In your fax include:

1. dates you want to stay
2. number of rooms required
3. number of people in the party
4. method of payment
5. request confirmation of booking

Fax

To:
Subject:

H9 Intonation

a Can you mark the stressed syllable in the following words?

Examples: de**po**sit, **lin**en

furniture	balance	accommodation	Asia
countryside	Turkey	mountain	cabins
confirmation	result	fascinated	Nepal
independent	facilities	equipped	exclusive

b Now listen to check.

H1 You and your job

a Put the following words under the three headings below.

sales • overtime ✔ *• office • service • working hours • personnel •*
reception • canteen • flexitime • marketing • break • meeting room

time	departments	places
1. overtime		
2.		
3.		
4.		

b Can you add some words to the lists in **H1a**?

H2 Prepositions and the telephone

What are the missing prepositions in this dialogue?

CC: Cornerstone Company. Can I help you?

Mike: Hello, this is Mike Shaw _____ Johnstone & Johnstone.
Could I speak _____ Colin Fleet, please?

CC: Just one moment and I'll put you _____ .

Mike: Thanks.

CC: Oh, I'm afraid he's talking _____ the other line at the moment.
Would you like to hold _____?

Mike: Yes, that's OK.

CC: Hello, I'm sorry, it's still engaged. Would you like _____ leave
a message?

Mike: Could you ask him to phone me _____? He's got my number.

CC: Right, I'll ask him to call you _____ . Thanks _____
your call. Bye.

Mike: Bye.

 Now listen to the recording to check your answers.

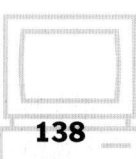

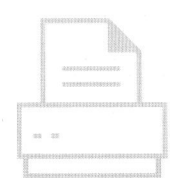

H3 Body & soul

a Read this extract from Ruth Elm's book about her company the 'Body Beautiful Store'.
What facial gesture do you think is most important when talking to customers? – _____

Ruth Elm's 20 second crash-course in Customer Care
- Never treat* customers as enemies*, approach them as potential friends.
- Think of customers as guests, make them laugh.
- Acknowledge their presence within 30 seconds: smile, make eye contact, say hello.
- Talk to them within the first 3 minutes.
- Offer product advice where appropriate.
- Smile! Always thank customers and invite them back ...
- Treat customers as you'd like to be treated!

* treat – behandeln, enemies – Feinde

b Can you complete these sentences from the extract using 'mustn't', 'don't have to' and 'must'?

1. You _____ treat customers as enemies.
2. You _____ to talk to customers within 30 seconds.
3. You _____ smile at the customers!
4. You _____ give product advice if it's not appropriate.
5. You _____ treat customers as you'd like to be treated!

c Can you now write three sentences of you own to add to the list in **H3b** using 'mustn't', 'don't have to' and 'must'?

6. _____

7. _____

8. _____

H4 American English versus British English

a How many American English words do you remember?
First fill in the missing vowels (a, e, i, o, u,) in the words below.

American	British
1. d __ wnt __ wn	a. *city centre*
2. c __ ll __ l __ r	b. _____
3. c __ – w __ rk __ r	c. _____
4. r __ str __ __ ms	d. _____
5. l __ n __	e. _____
6. s __ bw __ y	f. _____
7. ch __ ck	g. _____

b Now write the British equivalent next to the American words in **H4a**.

H5 The working puzzle

Use the clues to fill in this 'working puzzle'. What's the 'missing' word?

1. The place where you keep your pens and pencils.
2. The person you work for.
3. When you work extra hours.
4. When you stop working for a short while.
5. The system that allows you to start work between 8 and 10 in the morning.
6. The place where you can eat in a company.
7. An electronic device that tells you somebody is trying to reach you.

8. The American word for the people you work with.
9. The British word for the people you work with.
10. The area where you enter a company.
11. The machine that takes you from the first floor to the second.
12. The area where you work is your …

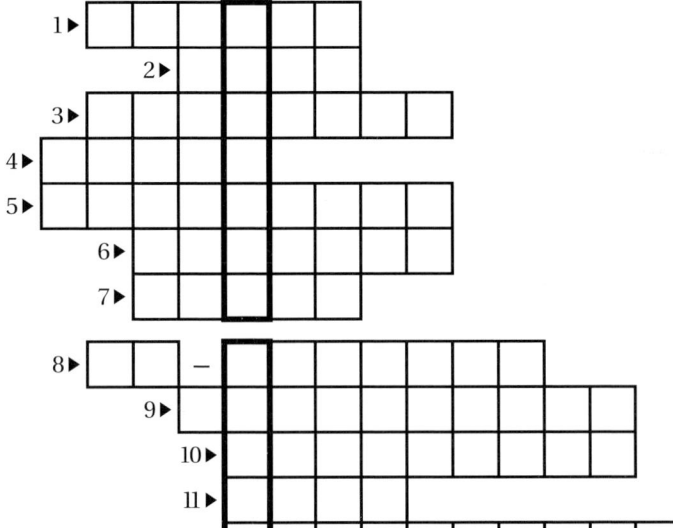

H6 Love/hate relationship

a Listen to the speakers talking about their jobs and decide which jobs the people do.

Speaker 1: _____ 2: _____ 3: _____

b Listen again and fill in the table below.

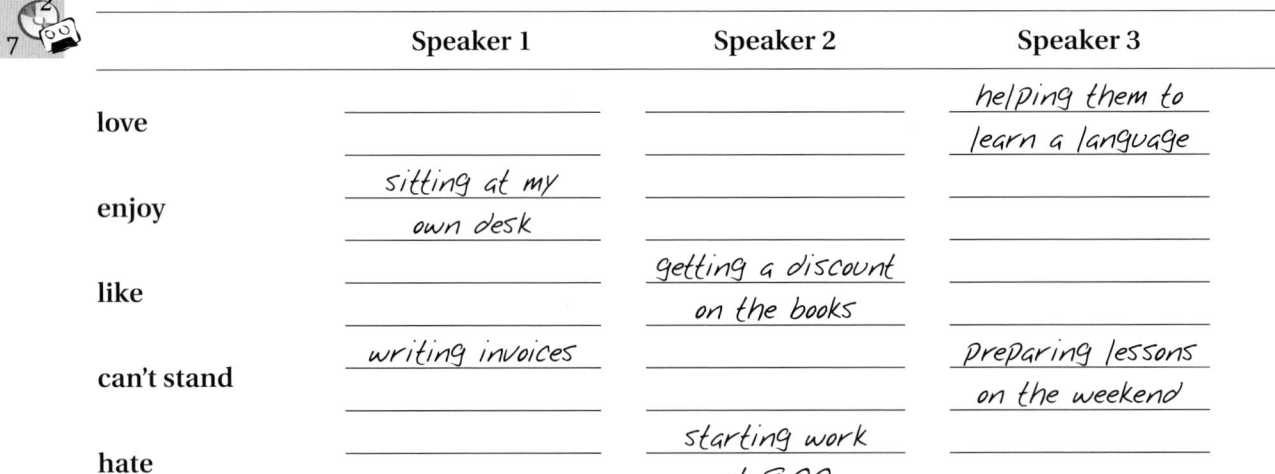

	Speaker 1	Speaker 2	Speaker 3
love			helping them to learn a language
enjoy	sitting at my own desk		
like		getting a discount on the books	
can't stand	writing invoices		preparing lessons on the weekend
hate		starting work at 8.00	

c Now write five sentences about a job you have/had using the words (e.g. love, hate) from **H6b**.

1. _____
2. _____
3. _____
4. _____
5. _____

H1 How 'computer fit' are you?

Answer these questions and then check the answers to see your score.

1. A smaller more practical version of a computer
   is a _____ . (2 possible answers)
2. If you work at home for your company and send your work to the
   company via a computer, you are a _____ .
3. To look for information using your computer you can
   _____ the internet.
4. Instead of putting a letter into an envelope you can send it by
   _____ or by _____ .
5. The abbreviation 'www' means _____ .
6. When your computer doesn't work any more it has _____ .
7. An 'umbrella word' for computer, modem, printer etc. is electronic
   _____ .
8. To go to a computer course regularly is to _____
   a course.
9. Another word for the technological business world is
   e-_____ .
10. The (.) in a web address is a _____ .

Score

Three out of ten:
You are not really interested in sitting in a dark room and spending hours on watching a screen BUT be careful that the electronic age doesn't leave you behind!
Three to six:
You are quite interested in computers and know enough to survive BUT you may need to know more in the future!
Seven to ten:
You are a 'computer freak'! You feel quite comfortable with the electronic age!

H2 If and will

Can you put the correct form of the verb into the following sentences?

1. If he catches the 8.20 train, **he'll** be in Hamburg at 12.30 pm.
2. If you _____ (send) me an e-mail with the details, I _____ (order) it for you.
3. They _____ (miss) the concert if they _____ (arrive) at 9.00 pm.
4. If she _____ (not come) tonight, I _____ (not see) her until after my holiday.
5. If the company _____ (ask) you to have a home office, _____
   you _____ (take) it?
6. I _____ (cancel) the barbecue party if it _____ (rain) tomorrow.

Remember

'If' and 'will' are never in the same part of the sentence.
In if-sentences type 1 'if' is followed by the simple present.
Example: What **will** you do **if** your company **moves** to Berlin?

H3 Permission

Think of what you could say in the following situations to ask for permission.
Use as many different possibilities as you know.

1. You're sitting in the doctor's waiting room. You're nervous and it is hot in the room.
   _May I open the window_____?

2. You're in a pub. You want to smoke a cigarette but you have forgotten your lighter.
   _____?

3. You have forgotten to reserve a seat on the train. The only seat free has a rucksack on it.
   _____?

4. Your car has broken down but you have promised to collect your parents from the airport.
   Your partner has his/her own car.
   _____?

5. You're friend has a kickboard. You've always wanted to try it.
   He won't be using it in the next few weeks because he's broken his leg.
   _____?

H4 AIBO

a Do you think AIBO is …
  1. … a Japanese meal?
  2. … a Japanese flower?
  3. … a Japanese robot?

Read the press release below to find out.

b Read the text again and complete the spaces with the correct form of the verbs in brackets.

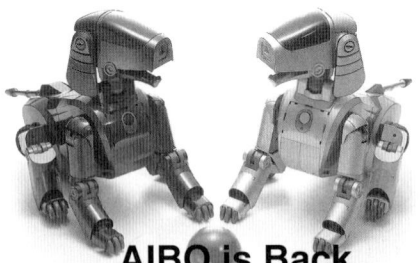

> ### Remember
> Future plan = going to = **I'm going to** read a book.
> Definite future date = present progressive = **I'm visiting** my friend in Munich next week.

AIBO is Back

An adorable pet, sensitive as a child, autonomous as any individual, quick to learn and as lively as any playful animal, AIBO is back! On the 25th of January, the Sony Corporation press relations officer stated 'We _____ (make) as many AIBO's as the customers in Japan, the United States and Europe want.'

The Heads of Marketing _____ (meet) in Tokyo next week to analyse how many additional orders for AIBO, the entertainment robot model, are expected. The Head of the European Company _____ (stay) in Tokyo for one week, too.

From the 15th of February to the 1st of March, customers in Europe can place orders by the internet or by the telephone. From the beginning of April, the factories in Tokyo _____ (ship) the goods to Europe.

The Sony press relations officer added that 'Sony _____ (create) more different robots in the future.'

c Can you now write three sentences about your own future plans and three sentences about definite future dates?

1. _____
2. _____
3. _____
4. _____
5. _____
6. _____

H5 Letters

Can you fill in the spaces in this letter?

Dear Sir / _____

With _____ to your advertisement in the weekly edition of 'The Electronic',
I would like to have more _____ about your range of products. _____
you please send me your latest product _____ and current _____ list?
I look _____ to _____ from you in the near future.

Best _____
Jennifer Hendrix

H6 The body and the car

a Can you think of words for parts of the body and parts of the car that fit the following descriptions?

	car	body
1. This part helps you to move.	wheels	_____
2. Without these you can't see in the dark.	_____	_____
3. You need this to store luggage / knowledge.	_____	_____
4. This is the place for energy / 'food'.	_____	_____
5. You use this to get attention.	_____	_____

b Can you add five more 'parts' to each list?
(They don't have to be corresponding.)

6.	doors	hands
7.	_____	_____
8.	_____	_____
9.	_____	_____
10.	_____	_____

H1 Infinitive or -ing form?

Can you put the correct form of the verb in brackets into these sentences?
Example: 'to meet' or 'meeting'

1. I'm afraid I have to postpone **meeting** you until next week.
2. He decided _____ (go) to Greece for his holidays.
3. Can you finish _____ (play) that game because the dinner is ready.
4. She offered _____ (look) after our dog when we go on holiday.
5. I have to continue _____ (attend) the course so that I can improve.
6. I plan _____ (jog) every morning next week.
7. Could you stop _____ (watch) TV and come and help me?
8. Can you imagine _____ (live) in a hot country with sunshine the whole year?
9. I hope _____ (spend) one year studying in the US.
10. Keep _____ (smile)!

H2 Furniture

a Can you write down ten things that you have in a living room?

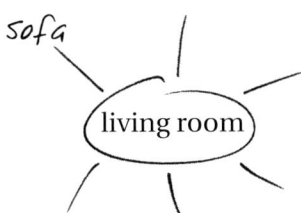

sofa

living room

b Can you now fill in the vowels (a, e, i, o, u) to complete the furniture for other rooms?

bedroom	kitchen	bathroom	study
b __ d	fr __ dg __	b __ th	d __ sk
l __ mp	__ v __ n	sh __ w __ r	c __ mp __ t __ r
w __ rdr __ b __	ch __ __ r	b __ s __ n	pr __ nt __ r
c __ pb __ __ rd	s __ nk	m __ rr __ r	ph __ n __
c __ rt __ __ ns	d __ shw __ sh __ r	t __ __ l __ t	sh __ lv __ s

H3 Stress

a What advice would you give to the following people?
Use 'ought to' or 'should' in your answer.
Example: You **ought to** get some fresh air.

1. I feel dizzy. – You _should get some fresh air_ .
2. I've got backache. – You _____ .
3. I can't switch off. – You _____ .
4. I feel exhausted. – You _____ .
5. I've got stomach-ache. – You _____ .
6. I can't relax. – You _____ .

b Now listen to the following three people and write down what problem they have with time.

	problems
1. the single mum	_____
2. the manager	_____
3. the schoolboy	_____

c Write down what advice you would give to the three speakers.

1. _____

2. _____

3. _____

H4 Relaxation

Can you put these phrases together?

1. to cope with	calm
2. to be	the mind
3. to let off	the muscles
4. to relax	steam
5. to focus	stress

H5 Simple present or present progressive?

a Which future tense do you use in the following sentences?
Examples: The train **leaves** at 20.30. *(simple present for timetables)*
We**'re having** a party next Friday. *(present progressive for fixed plans)*

1. The train _____ (arrives) at 3 p.m.

2. What _____ you _____ (do) tonight?

3. My sister _____ (come) to visit next Friday.

4. The flight _____ (arrive) in Düsseldorf at 13.15.

5. The conference _____ (start) at 9.30 a.m. with an opening talk by Professor Hill.

6. Phil and Charlie _____ (sail) in the Netherlands this weekend.

7. I _____ (have) a party next Friday.

8. _____ the ferry _____ (depart) at 11.20 tomorrow?

9. We _____ (not visit) friends this weekend after all because our car has broken down.

10. Don't forget that the meeting _____ (begin) at 2.30 this afternoon!

H5b Now look at your diary for next week and write down
one definite arrangement that you have for each day of the week.

1. On Monday I'm meeting my boss at 9.00 a.m.
2. On Tuesday …
3. On Wednesday …
4. On Thursday …
5. On Friday …
6. On Saturday …
7. On Sunday …

H6 Energy medicine

Can you put the words into the correct place in the text?

diet • *medicine* • *imbalanced* • *energy* • *emotional* • *colour* • *conventional* •
harmonise • *healthy* ✔

It seems that doctors are waking up to a view held by alternative therapists – that we all have an invisible energy system that fights disease and keeps us _____*healthy*_____ . For thousands of years, ancient systems, such as traditional Chinese _____ and the Indian Ayurvedic system have been working with body _____ in a successful way.

Poor _____, stress, _____ problems, even weather cause the energy to become blocked, stagnant or _____ – and that's how we become ill.

Therapies such as acupuncture and herbs, even light, sound and _____, all have their own energy patterns which are believed to _____ our energy and restore health. Until recently, most _____ doctors would have considered this to be mumbo jumbo. However, many experts believe that, in time, these 'alternative' techniques will be integrated into conventional medicine …

H7 The curious [k] words

a Look at the phonetic script below.
Can you try and say the words out loud
and then write them down?

1. [kɑ:m]   *calm*
2. [kɔ:z]   _____
3. [kəʊp]   _____
4. [kʌpl]   _____
5. [ki:p]   _____
6. [kɔ:s]   _____
7. [saɪkl]   _____
8. [kɒnflɪkt] _____
9. [kəntɪnju:] _____

b Now listen to the recording
to check your answers.

H1 What were you doing?

The police are trying to solve a crime – a lot of paintings have gone missing from the city art gallery.

a Listen to the interview with a suspect and complete the suspect's answers in the table below.

Where? – _____

When? – _____

Why? – _____

Who with? – _____

b Listen again to check if the following sentences are true or false.

1. He flew from Berlin to Pafos.   **True** ☐ ☐ **False**
2. He landed at 3:40.   ☐ ☐
3. At 4:00 he was sitting in the sun drinking a beer.   ☐ ☐
4. He was only walking in the hills.   ☐ ☐
5. While he was walking in the hills he met a lot of tourists.   ☐ ☐
6. Cyprus has over 14 different kinds of orchids.   ☐ ☐

c Now write a few sentences about what you were doing in the first three weeks in May / last year on holiday. Try to include sentences / situations in the past progressive.

H2 Simple past or past progressive

a Put the verb in the correct tense in the following sentences.

1. While the detectives _____ (talk) to the reporter, the police team _____ (look) for the criminal.
2. When the elephant _____ (arrive) all the other animals _____ (talk).
3. The peace talks _____ (break) down last night.
4. Batman _____ (speak) to Robin in a quiet voice when the Joker appeared.
5. Every film star I _____ (meet) in Hollywood _____ (have) a guru.
6. Mozart _____ (die) at the age of 35 in 1791.

b Which types of writing (books / papers) are the extracts in **H2a** from?

1. _____
2. _____
3. _____
4. _____
5. _____
6. _____

c Can you add three more types of books / papers to the list in **H2b**?

7. _____
8. _____
9. _____

H3　Programmes

How many different types of TV programmes can you remember under the three headings below?

factual programme	fictional programme	mixture of both
1. c_____t	1. c_____y	1. c_____'s
2. q_____z	2. s_____p	2. c_____l
3. n_____s	3. f_____m	
4. w_____r		
5. d_____y		

H4　Emigration?

Put 'have to', 'need' or 'needn't' into the spaces in this text.

If you are thinking of emigrating to Australia or New Zealand you should think about the following points. You _____ have a work permit otherwise you can't work in these countries. You also _____ to possess a residence permit. You _____ to speak a good level of English so that you can understand and of course make yourself understood! You _____ have visited either country before, but we think it is better to experience a holiday there first, so that you have a realistic picture of what life is like. You _____ have family or friends already living there, but it is useful to have a few contacts. However, we believe you _____ to be very flexible and open to change as your life will be completely different to what you left behind.

H5　Invitations

Decline three of the following invitations giving reasons why, and accept two.

1. Do you want to book a 'health & fitness weekend' with me?

   _____

2. Would you like to do a bungy-jump with me next month?

   _____

3. Do you want to watch a Spanish film with us tonight?

   _____

4. Would you like to go roller-blading on Saturday?

   _____

5. Would you like to come on holiday with me this summer?

   _____

H6 Mix & match

Which words fit together?

1. house		a. work
2. mid		b. confidence
3. home		c. shop
4. news		d. warming
5. work		e. paper
6. self		f. night

H7 A business letter

Can you fill in the spaces in this letter?

_____ Roberto

I am writing to _____ our appointment on the morning of June 29th.
I _____ by train at 6.00 in the evening. I'm _____ at the
Sitges Hotel and would be _____ to accept your dinner _____
that evening.

Could you let me know when and where we should _____ for dinner?
I'm looking _____ to seeing you next week.

_____

Lucia

H8 Nouns and verbs

Can you write in the missing noun or verb?

noun	verb
1. application	1. to apply
2. _____	2. to invite
3. cancellation	3. _____
4. _____	4. to inform
5. a walk	5. _____
6. _____	6. to eclipse
7. sleep	7. _____
8. _____	8. to act

H1 The wedding quiz

a How many words belonging to the vocabulary field of 'family' do you remember from the unit? Use the clues to help you.

1. A special 'wedding word' for the future wife.   _____
2. A special 'wedding word' for the future husband.   _____
3. The couples 'second' parents are their …   _____
4. Your mother's / father's sister is your …   _____
5. Your sister's / brother's daughter is your …   _____

b Unjumble the following words to find more members of the family.

1. The husband of 4 in **H1a**.   lcune   u_____
2. Your mother's mother.   drgathremon   g_____
3. Your 'boy' is your …   nso   s_____
4. Sisters and …   thorbres   b_____
5. Nieces and …   epwhnes   n_____

H2 Question tags

a Can you complete the following sentences with the appropriate question tag?

1. You don't know a good street café, _____?
2. August is a rainy season in Australia, _____?
3. You didn't hear my music last night, _____?
4. He has a northern dialect, _____?
5. You went to a sushi bar last week, _____?
6. You have flown on a long-distance flight, _____?
7. He looks like a film star, _____?
8. They haven't been here before, _____?

b Now make up five statements that you believe to be true about a member of your class.

1. You _____
2. _____
3. _____
4. _____
5. _____

In the next lesson ask questions to find out about your statements.
Don't forget to use question tags.

H3 Mix and match

a Can you match the correct phrases together?

1. to stand	a. off the coast
2. to sunbathe	b. on the beach
3. to be	c. in rivers
4. to surf	d. in a queue
5. to paddle	e. on holiday
6. to visit	f. in a hotel
7. to stay	g. in the dry season

b Write a postcard to a friend about a holiday trip including as many of the phrases from **H3a** as possible.

Dear …

PORTUGAL

H4 'many'/'few' and 'much'/'little'

Put either 'many'/'few' or 'much'/'little' in the text below.

Portugal

'Get away from it all' type holidays are no real problem in Portugal as, apart from the big resorts on the coast, very _____ of the country has _____ tourism. Only a _____ tour operators deal with areas outside of the main centres, so there are _____ possibilities to get away from the crowds. Throughout the interior there are _____ small villages or towns which you can use as a base. Here there are _____ signs of modern life as the villages are very traditional. You can see _____ farmers working with ox and carts.

As there is _____ noise, you can enjoy the peace and quiet of holiday away from busy everyday life …

H5 Business noun-endings with '- ion' or '-ing'?

Can you make nouns from the following verbs?
Be careful with the spelling of the nouns.

verb	noun
1. to present	1. presentation
2. to meet	2. _____
3. to discuss	3. _____
4. to market	4. _____
5. to produce	5. _____
6. to begin	6. _____

H6 The bad line

a Look at this phone conversation and fill in the missing words.

Roger: Hello?

Kate: Hi, Roger. Kate here. How _____?

Roger: _____ , thanks, Kate. And _____?

Kate: Not so bad, thanks. Listen, shall we meet for dinner tonight?

Roger: Great _____! _____ shall we go?

Kate: Well, what about Café Fleur?

Roger: Sorry, can you _____ that?

Kate: Café Fleur.

Roger: Oh dear. It's a bad line. Can you _____ that, please?

Kate: It's Café F-L-E-U-R.

Roger: Got you, like 'flower' in English?

Kate: That's right. About 8.00?

Roger: Sorry, didn't _____ that.

Kate: About 8.00?

Roger: That's fine. See you at 8.00.

Kate: See you. Bye.

Roger: Bye.

b Now listen to check your answers

H7 What's in a number?

a Listen to the short text and write down why the following numbers are important for the speaker.

1. 108 – _____
2. 7 – _____
3. one – _____
4. three – _____
5. five – _____
6. 91 – _____

b Can you now write a few sentences about numbers that are important in your life and say why they are important.

H1 Alternatives

The little word 'nice' is nice but can you find a better adjective
to express 'nice' in the following sentences.

1. Last Sunday the weather was nice. – _____

2. She is such a nice person. – _____

3. The pizza was nice. – _____

4. Last night, the Hitchcock film on TV was very nice. – _____

5. Have a nice time! – _____

6. The bride looked nice. – _____

7. I bought a nice armchair. – _____

8. Spain was nice. – _____

H2 Talk about people!

Use these adverbs and make sentences about yourself or other people.
Example: fluently – I speak French fluently.

1. carefully _____

2. noisily _____

3. badly _____

4. easily _____

5. gently _____

6. quickly _____

7. well _____

H3 Adjectives or adverbs?

a Choose an adjective or an adverb to complete the sentences.

1. Yesterday I listened to the news very _____ (careful).

2. My sister is not only a _____ (good) violinist, but she sings
   _____ too (good).

3. I got up _____ (early) to go to the office, but there was such
   a _____ (bad) traffic accident that I arrived twenty minutes
   _____ (late).

4. Our English teacher speaks five languages _____ (fluent).

5. The coffee tastes a bit _____ (strange).

H3b   Are the underlined words adverbs or adjectives?

1. You look <u>lovely</u>.   adjective 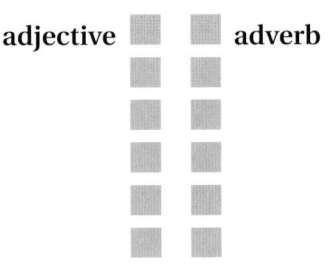 adverb
2. Michael Schumacher is a <u>fast</u> driver.
3. The train is travelling <u>fast</u>.
4. Karen is such a <u>friendly</u> person.
5. She works very <u>hard</u>.
6. My husband plays the piano <u>well</u>.

H4   Jumbled sentences

a   Put the words of these sentences in the correct order.

1. THE / SPENT / OFFICE / A / MORNING / IN / MARY / QUIET

   _____

2. SPOKE / HIS / PHILIP / BOSS / QUIETLY / TO

   _____

3. SEEMED / THE / VERY / COUPLE / HAPPY / YOUNG

   _____

4. GARDEN / THE / HAPPILY / PLAYED / IN / CHILDREN / THE

   _____

5. ANGRY / FATHER / ME / AN / LOOK / MY / GAVE

   _____

6. HE / AMAZED / FIRST / SHOUTING / THEN / HE / ANGRILY / LOOKED / STARTED

   _____

b   Use two different colours to highlight
the adjectives and the adverbs.

H5   Suffixes

a   A suffix is a letter or a group or letters at the end of a word to make another word.
It can tell you if the word is an adjective or an adverb.

Examples: quick – quick**ly**,   suffix -ly: adverb
care – care**ful**,   suffix -ful: adjective
care – care**less**,   suffix -less: adjective

Add the suffix **-ful** or **-less** to these nouns. Four words can take both **-ful** and **-less**.

beauty • use • taste • peace • end • help • care

_____   _____

_____   _____

_____   _____

_____

b Now match the adjectives with these nouns.

beautiful		day
useless		dinner
tasteless		actress
peaceful		secretary
endless		book
helpful		driver
careless		fun

H6 Aromatherapy

a Look at the title of the passage. What do you know about it?

Aromatherapy is the <u>ancient</u> <u>art</u> of using the <u>healing</u> <u>power</u> of <u>essential oils</u>. The oils are <u>distilled</u> from plants, flowers, leaves or <u>the bark of trees</u>. They are highly concentrated and contain natural <u>fragrances</u>. Aromatherapy helps you to keep the balance of mind, body and soul.

b Match the underlined words from the text with their meaning.

words from the text		meaning
ancient		natural oil
art		the outer part of a tree
healing		very, very old
power		a sweet smell
essential oil		making healthy
distilled		energy
bark of tree		heated to make pure
fragrance		the way of doing something

Read the passage again and decide which words are important to be able to understand the meaning of the text.

c Now listen to the report and complete the notes.

main points	details
Egyptians	*massaged*
Greeks	*wrote*
Romans	*imported*
scientists in Europe	*began*
a French chemist	*published*

H7 Homophones

a Homophones are words with the same pronunciation
but with a different spelling and meaning.
Example: meet / meat

 Listen to this story and underline the homophones. Something went terribly wrong
with some of the words in the text.

> An unfinished story
>
> Joe took Monica to Paris on there honeymoon. He new that she
> had never bean their. She was very excited. At the airport
> they had to weight four ours. There plain was delayed.
> Monica went to by too postcards. She walked threw the
> weighting lounge, went up some stares till she found the
> write shop.
>   On hair way back, she followed the signs for British
> Heirways. She was shore that she would find Joe in the same
> plaice - next to the cheque-in counter. Joe was knot their.
> Won minute passed, too minutes passed. She looked at hair
> watch. The plain was leaving at ate minutes past for. She
> asked a man if he had scene hair husband. She was getting
> nervous. Halve an our later, she saw Joe walking between too
> policemen. What had happened?

b Can you now correct the underlined homophones?

H8 Word partners

a Some adverbs and adjectives are word partners.
Match the adverbs with the adjectives.

adverbs	adjectives
highly	pretty
extremely	easy
bitterly	qualified
elegantly	ill
seriously	cold
surprisingly	dressed

> **Learning tip – Word partners**
> When you learn an adjective, it is
> a good idea to learn the word
> you can use with it.

b Now complete the sentences with one of the above expressions.

1. The company employed a _____ person.
2. Madonna is _____.
3. It is _____ in Alaska.
4. Sophia Loren is always _____.
5. Unfortunately the President is in hospital. He is _____ .
6. The driving test was _____.

H1 'too short' or 'not long enough'?

Change these sentences using 'enough'.
Example: It's too short. – You're right! It isn't long enough.

1. She's too young. – _____

2. The water is too cold. – _____

3. The tea is weak. – _____

4. The T-shirt is too small. – _____

5. The sea is too dirty. – _____

H2 Match

Match these sentences and join them with 'if'.
Example: If I lived in Japan, I'd speak Japanese.

1.	She ate less.	You could pass the exam.
2.	I might save some money.	They would come to visit us.
3.	He would feel better.	She would lose weight.
4.	They had more time.	I had an extra job.
5.	You studied harder.	He stopped smoking.

> ### Remember
> Instead of 'would', you can also say 'could' or 'might'. You don't use 'would' in the 'if-clause'.

H3 If-sentence type 1 or 2?

a Complete the following sentences with the correct tense of the verb. Decide whether to use the first or the second conditional.

1. It will be better if you _____ (go) outside and get some fresh air.

2. Mr. Dunmore would take a year off if he _____ (win) the lottery.

3. You will be late if you not _____ (hurry).

4. Malta _____ (be) the ideal holiday place if it wasn't so hot.

5. If I _____ (be) you, I would study harder.

6. If I go to France this summer, I _____ (visit) the Louvre.

b Explain the differences in meaning between the following pairs of sentences.

● She'll come to see me if she has time.
▲ She'd come to see me if she had time.

● If I have enough money, I'll buy a new bicycle.
▲ If I had enough money, I'd buy a new bicycle.

H4 Word partners – verb + noun

Cross out the verb that does not go with the noun.

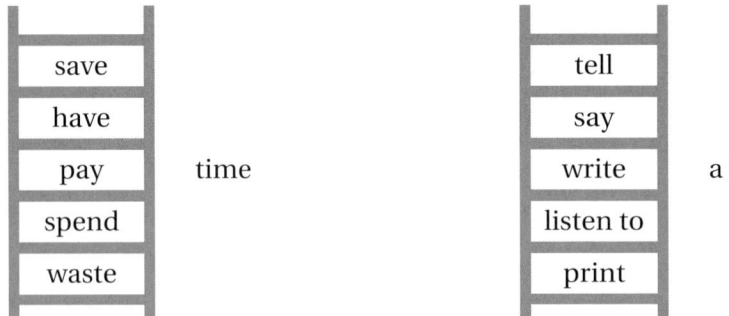

save	
have	
pay	time
spend	
waste	

tell	
say	
write	a fairy tale
listen to	
print	

H5 Fairy tale

a Do you remember the fairy tale 'The Rich Man And The Poor Man'?
(If not, you can listen to the fairy tale again.)

Which adjectives went with these nouns?
Write them down in these word wheels.

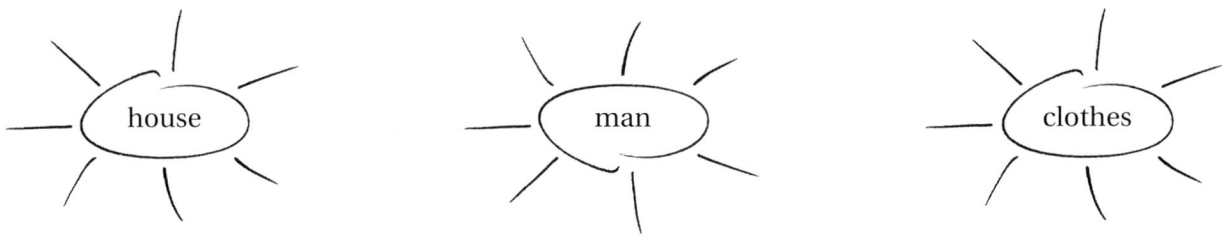

b Now also add the adjectives below to the word wheels above.
You can put some under two headings.

second-hand • comfortable • happy • dream • spacious • cosy • proud •
warm • brave • busy • hard-working • trendy • elegant • fashionable

> Remember your word bank.

> **Learning Tip – Adjectives and nouns**
> When you learn a new noun,
> try to learn an adjective
> that goes with it.

c Here are some of the words and
expressions from the fairy tale.
Write the fairy tale using these
expressions as a framework.

once upon a time
a traveller
felt tired
knocked on the rich man's door
granted the poor man three wishes
health
something to eat every day
a wish came true
lived happily ever after

H6 Not enough time!

The biggest problem to our health today is lack of time.
You are going to hear Dr. Singh from the Centre for Stress Management talking about stress and how to reduce it.

What do you expect to hear? – _____

Listen to Dr. Singh and check if you were right. Complete the notes below.

length of time	tips
1 minute	*drink a glass of water*
5 minutes	
10 minutes	
20 minutes	

> **Learning Tip – Listening**
> Don't look at the tapescript before you listen. In real life you don't read something before you hear it.

H7 Question and answer

Read the letter to the magazine 'Health and Living', asking for some advice.

Dear Doctor,
My wife is a bank manager. She works too many hours, drinks too much alcohol and is always in a bad mood. She smokes 20 cigarettes a day and is very nervous. How can I help her?

Answer the letter for the magazine using the following phrases.
Remember to keep it short.
– She should …
– She could …
– She (you) might …
– If I were you, I'd …

Bring your letter to class and exchange it with another student.
Who gave the best (the funniest) piece of advice?

H8 Rhythm

a English sentences normally have a regular rhythm. We emphasise only the important words in a sentence. Read the following limericks and highlight the stressed words.

* uncommonly – ungewöhnlich
stout – korpulent, untersetzt

There was an Old Man of Berlin
Whose form was uncommonly* thin;
Till he once, by mistake,
Was mixed up in a cake,
So they baked that Old Man of Berlin.

There was an Old Man, who when little
Fell casually into a kettle;
But, growing too stout*,
He could never get out,
So he passed all his life in that kettle.
(from Limericks, Edward Lear, Reclam)

b Then listen and repeat.

H9 Talking about 'Time'

When would you say the following expressions?

Time to go. – _____

Time is up. – _____

Time flies! – _____

Time is money. – _____

Dead on time! – _____

Behind the times. – _____

H10 Mixed-up nouns

a Match the words from column 1 with words from column 2 to form compound nouns.

1	2
French	bag
baked	fries
mineral	gum
chewing	beans
tea	water

1	2
youth	centre
police	office
health	property
post	hostel
lost	station

1	2
film	driver
baby	manager
pen	star
bank	sitter
bus	friend

Find a heading for each group of words.

> ### Note
>
> The word **'fairy tale'** is a **compound noun** – a fixed expression which is made up of more than one word.
> *Example:* We bought a new **washing machine** yesterday.
>
> You can put a hyphen between the two words, but this is not usually necessary.
> *Example:* washing-machine
>
> You can sometimes write the two nouns as one word
> *Example:* headache, toothpaste

b Can you fill in the missing parts of these compound nouns?

swimming _____

_____ tennis

junk _____

zebra _____

T-_____

_____ room

make- _____

science _____

_____ conditioner

H1 English sayings

a In English, there are a number of sayings with the word 'door'.
Can you guess what the missing words are?

1. As one door _____ , another one _____ .
2. The meeting was held behind _____ doors.
3. She _____ the door in her face.

b Listen to three short texts and check your answers.
Are there any similar sayings in your language?

H2 What's it made of?

Fill in the missing letters.

It's made of ... p ⬜⬜⬜ t i c.
s t ⬜⬜⬜ .
a l ⬜ m ⬜⬜⬜⬜ m.
⬜ o o ⬜ .
g ⬜⬜⬜ s.
⬜ r ⬜ n.

H3 Linking words

a Complete these sentences with 'however' or 'although'.

1. I drink wine. _____ , I don't drink beer.
2. _____ the weather was terrible, we went for a long walk.
3. She went to the supermarket. _____ , she forgot to buy milk.
4. She cannot speak German , _____ she lived in Austria for 10 years.
5. He bought a new car, _____ he couldn't afford it.
6. I thought Mary was older than George. _____ , I was wrong.

b Complete the following sentences.

1. Although I was very hungry, _____
2. His English is not very good, although _____
3. She didn't feel well. However, _____
4. Jane said that the musical was very good. However, _____
5. Although it was raining, _____

H4 Multi-word verbs

Complete the sentences by putting in multi-word verbs.
Decide where you are going to put the object.
Sometimes more than one answer is possible.

1. Mr. Lipsey phoned while you were out. OK, I'll (ring up) _____ him.
2. She (threw away) _____ all his letters into the waste paper bin.
3. They had to (pay back) _____ the money.
4. The radio is too loud. I'll (switch off) _____ it.
5. My husband (cut down) _____ the old cherry tree in the corner of the garden.
6. It's so dark. Please (turn on) _____ the lights.

> *Note*
> Multi-word verbs are never written as a single word.

H5 Verbs with the same meaning

Rewrite this paragraph, changing the verbs in *italics* with multi-word verbs.
Choose the verbs from the following list. Be careful with the tenses.

make up • *come back* • *go away* • *fix up* • *find out* • *turn up*

Susanne *discovered* that her brother was in Vienna. She asked him *to return*.
Her parents wanted to see him. She *arranged* a meeting at a motorway
restaurant. He *arrived* two hours late, *invented* a story of losing his passport
and said that he had to *disappear* for some time. Susanne's parents broke
down. I think they will never stop looking for him.

H6 Word order

Rewrite these sentences using a pronoun.
Remember that you cannot separate the preposition from the verb.
Example: I listened to the radio last night. I listened to **it** last night.

1. She looked at the children in amazement.

   _____

2. He waited for his girlfriend all evening.

   _____

3. The dog belongs to our neighbours.

   _____

4. He always agrees with the conservative politicians.

   _____

5. She paid for her father.

   _____

H7 Not just a toy

a We usually think of the kite as a toy. But history tells us that the kite is more than that. Read the article and find out more.

IN 1847, THE CITY OF NIAGARA FALLS decided that they should build a bridge across the valley gorge. They had the technology to build the bridge, but they did not know how to get the first line across. The cliffs were steep, the waterfalls rapid and the winds strong.

They finally came up with an idea – to fly a kite across the gorge. The 10-year-old Homan Walsh crossed the water by ferry, walked back to the narrowest part of the gorge and set his kite free. The kite went high up above the cliffs. Homan just had to wait till sunset when the winds dropped for his kite to come down. Sunset came but the kite didn't drop. During the night, the kite line fell into the gorge. There was a heavy ice storm all night and he could not cross the river to get his kite back. He had to stay on the other side of the valley for 8 days. After some necessary repair to his kite, he tried a second time. It was a complete success. The engineers used the kite line and pulled a heavy cable across. The bridge was constructed.

Homan Walsh was given a prize of 10 dollars and in 1847 that was a lot of money.

A fact that is less known is that hundreds of years before, Leonardo da Vinci had also planned the use of kites in bridge construction.

(adapted from member.forterie.com/xeno/history.htm)

* valley gorge = Talschlucht

b The summary of the text below has a number of mistakes.
Rewrite the sentences correctly.

1. The city of Niagara Falls wanted to build a bridge across the valley in 1874.

   _____

2. They did not have the technology to build the bridge.

   _____

3. Homan Walsh, a 12-year-old boy, swam across the river.

   _____

4. His kite flew high over the cliffs and came down at night, when the winds dropped.

   _____

5. There was a snow storm and Homan could not cross back to get his kite.

   _____

6. After 10 days, the weather was better and he returned home.

   _____

7. He was successful the third time.

   _____

8. Homan was only given ten dollars.

   _____

9. Leonardo da Vinci had also used kites to build bridges.

   _____

H8 Describing a product

Write the questions for these answers. Then listen and check.

1. _____?

   It's very light – around 200g.

2. _____?

   Cardboard.

3. _____?

   It's mostly used for cornflakes.

4. _____?

   It's 30 cm high and 10 cm wide.

5. _____?

   If you order more than a thousand packets, it costs 10 pence per packet.

H9 Word-building

a If you add a prefix to the beginning of a word, you change the meaning of that word.
The prefixes **im-**, **in-**, **un-** + adjective mean NOT.

Examples: polite – **im**polite
correct – **in**correct
friendly – **un**friendly

Find the negative forms of these adjectives by adding the prefixes **im-**, **in-** and **un-**
and write them down in three columns.

patient • *dependent* • *formal* • *happy* • *possible* • *usual* • *able* •
lucky • *tolerant* • *practical*

im+	in+	un+
_____	_____	_____
_____	_____	_____
_____	_____	_____
		_____

> **Learning Tip –**
> **Word-building**
> A prefix can help you guess
> the meaning of a new word.

b In English we do not stress the prefixes as in German.
Example: **un**bequem / un**com**fortable

Read these words aloud, then listen to the recording and repeat.

immoral	imbalance	improbable	impersonal
inexpensive	inaccurate	inefficient	incorrect
unpleasant	unhealthy	unknown	uncertain

c Listen again
and underline the
 stressed syllable in
the words above.

H1 The world of languages

a Write down the languages spoken in these countries.

England   _____
Portugal   _____
China   _____
France   _____
Poland   _____
Hungary   _____
Norway   _____
Greece   _____
Turkey   _____
Japan   _____
Italy   _____
Holland   _____

b Now divide these languages according to their endings.

-ish   **-ese**

_____   _____
_____   _____
_____   _____

-ian   **other**

_____   _____
_____   _____
_____   _____

c Read the words in **H1b** aloud. Then underline the stressed syllable. Now listen and check your answers.

H2 Newspaper articles

a Look at these two newspaper headlines.
Which headline do you think has a story that interests you?

1. **New Language Law Introduced – EU Protests**

2. **Mother Tongue Protected From Anglicisms**

> **Learning Tip – Headlines**
> When you read a newspaper, you do not normally start from the first page and read to the end. You first look at the headlines and then read the article that looks interesting.

H2b Now read the articles quickly and match them with the headline. Find three words in each article that you don't know, check them in your dictionary and write them down in your word bank.

a. The word 'Coca-Cola' has been changed in Russian. Now Coca-Cola directors are protesting. They say: "The name is a trade mark and must remain the same." Julia Safanova, a member of the Russian Language Institute, disagrees. "In the accusative, it is written as Coca-Colu and in the genitive as Coca-Coli. Russian must be spoken correctly."

The Institute opened a hot line giving advice to callers on how to speak and write Russian correctly. New words are the biggest problem. Computer, fashion and pop language is taken from the English language. However, Ms Safanova insists that Russia should not try, like the French, to stop the use of foreign words. "That would be a hopeless task."

(adapted from The Times)

b. A new law has been passed in Poland to protect the Polish language from the influence of English on the Polish vocabulary. As in most places in the world, more and more English is being used in Poland. This has to do with the economic opening to the West and the popularity of American culture. Protests are coming from the European Union and the business world. The language law requires that all import documents are translated into Polish. In this way, imports from EU countries will be kept down.

(adapted from Frankfurter Allgemeine – English Edition)

c Headlines are normally short. The verb before the past participle is often left out. Expand the headlines to proper sentences.

1. A new language law _____ introduced.
2. The mother tongue _____ protected from Anglicisms.

Now read the texts more carefully and underline two examples of passive constructions from each article.

What are the articles about?

> **Note**
> The passive is used very often in newspaper reports.

H3 Advertisements

Look at the following advertisements and write passive sentences using the verbs below.

DUCHESS 020 7494 5075
cc 020 7420 0000 (bkg fee)
The Royal National Theatre production of
MICHAEL FRAYN'S
MULTI AWARD WINNING PLAY
inc. **TONY AWARDS BEST PLAY**
AND BEST DIRECTOR
MICHAEL BLAKEMORE
COPENHAGEN
"Best play of the year" *Independent*
Mon-Sat 7.30, Mats Thu & Sat 2.30

09061 992 012

write   The play 'Copenhagen' is written by Michael Frayn.

produce _____

direct _____

publish _____

design by _____

design in _____

sell _____

make in _____

make of _____

H4 "Die neue lingua per all Europa"

a Can you speak the new European language?

Read the following newspaper article. Put the verbs in brackets in the correct tense – active or passive.

Diego Marani, an Italian translator in Brussels (a.) _____ (invent) his own
language. It (b.) _____ (call) Europanto – a mix of German, Italian and Spanish
with an English foundation. Mr. Marani's weekly column (c.) _____ (publish) in
Belgian and Swiss newspapers. Esperanto speakers, however, don't see the joke.
Mr. Marani, who speaks 5 languages fluently, (d.) _____ (start) Europanto to
amuse his friends. Now he (e.) _____ (receive) letters from readers from all over
Europe, asking him whether he (f.) _____ (write) a dictionary, or where they can
go on a training course. Next year a series of books in Europanto will be published in France.
Europanto (g.) _____ (speak) by a few enthusiasts already. 'Parlez-vous die neue
lingua per all Europa?' *(adapted from 'The Guardian')*

b Which is an active and which is a passive construction?

active verbs	passive verbs
_____	_____
_____	_____
_____	_____
_____	

H5 Telling the time and the date

Say these numbers aloud –
then listen and check your answers.

10.20

31/1/99

9.30

11.15

3.50

5/9/2000

8.45

1996

> **Note**
>
> In **British English** you say 'twenty past ten' (10.20 a.m.).
> In **American English** you say 'twenty after ten'.

H6 Sign language

Write signs from these sentences using 'don't'.
Example: You shouldn't turn right. – Don't turn right.

1. You shouldn't drive so fast. – _____

2. You shouldn't smoke. – _____

3. You shouldn't walk on the grass. – _____

4. You shouldn't litter. – _____

5. You shouldn't talk to the driver. – _____

> **Remember**
>
> **Don't** or **Do not** are used
> in strong warnings.

H7 Dialogues

Listen to these dialogues and decide where you would hear them.

1. _____

2. _____

3. _____

4. _____

5. _____

6. _____

7. _____

H8 Laughter is the best medicine!

What is wrong with these signs? Can you rewrite the messages on these signs?

From a Hotel in Athens:

Visitors are expected to complain at the office between nine and eleven daily.

_____

_____

From a Norwegian cocktail bar:

Ladies are requested not to have children in the bar.

_____

_____

In a Bangkok temple:

IT IS FORBIDDEN TO ENTER
A WOMAN EVEN A FOREIGNER
IF DRESSED AS A MAN.

_____

_____

Remember

You can use **can** to talk about things that are allowed (or not allowed).
You can use **mustn't** to say that something is not permitted.

Functional Language

Meeting people

Hello. My name's …
Nice to meet you.
Nice to meet you, too.

Greeting people

Hello, Carlos. How are you?
Hi, Jason. I'm fine, thanks.
Nice to see you. / Good to see you.
Nice to see you, too. / Good to see you, too.

Asking for information

What's your name?
Where are you from?
What are your hobbies?
Where do you work?
Have you got any children? /
   Do you have any children?
Why are you learning English?

Paying compliments

That's a nice car you've got!
What a lovely flat!
That hair style really suits you!
You look great!

Giving advice

You should do more sports.
You shouldn't smoke so much.
You ought to get some sleep.
If I were you, I would eat less.

Talking about rules and regulations

When you do overtime you must leave the office before 8 p.m.
You don't have to wear a suit.
You can't open the window.
You mustn't smoke in the meeting rooms.

Warning someone

Mind the step!
Don't drink and drive!
You should be careful.
You shouldn't drive so fast.

Expressing wishes

I wish I were on holiday.
I wish you were here.
I wish I had five cats.

Expressing preferences

I love eating chocolate.
We enjoy watching films.
They like living in Spain.
She dislikes eating sauerkraut.
I can't stand getting up early in the morning.
He hates drinking beer.

Functional Language

Making suggestions ...

Why don't you train more often?
Have you thought about dancing classes?
Have you tried yoga?
Shall we give the workers a bonus?

... and replying

That's a good idea
That sounds interesting.
Maybe I'll try that. / Well, I don't know.
Yeah, why not.

Asking for permission ...

May I use your car?
Can I park here?
Could I smoke here?

... and responding

I'm sorry, I can't help you.
That's fine by me. / Yes, of course.
I'm afraid that's not possible.

Inviting

Would you like to come to dinner?
Do you want to visit us on Friday?

Accepting

I'd love to.
That would be lovely.

Declining

I'm sorry, I can't.
I'm afraid, I can't.

Asking for an opinion

What do you think?
How do you feel about it?
Do you agree?

Giving an opinion

I think 5 weeks holiday is enough.
In my opinion petrol is too expensive.
I would like more information on that.

Agreeing

That could be true.
I agree with you.
I would, too.
That's a good idea.
I'm all for it.
Sure.

Disagreeing

I'm not so sure.
Sorry, but I think that's wrong. / I disagree.
I don't agree.
Well, I don't really agree with you on that.
I wouldn't agree with that.

Filler words

Actually, I work there.
Anyway, I accepted the offer.
Well, I missed the flight.
After that, I decided to leave.

Showing interest

Really!
What happened then?
Oh no!
Oh!

Functional Language

Linking words

Although it was raining, she went for a walk.
Would you like tea **or** coffee?
It's an interesting job **but** it's hard work.
She liked the city. **However**, she didn't like her job.

Asking for clarification

Sorry, when are you coming?
Can you repeat that, please?
Sorry, I didn't catch that.
Could you spell that, please?
You said Friday, didn't you?

Checking information

He likes baseball, doesn't he?
You have been to Mexico City, haven't you?
She is Spanish, isn't she?

Expressing that you don't know a word

What's the meaning of …?
What's the English for …?

Expressing that you don't know what something is called in English

I don't know what it's called in English.
What's that in English?
What do you call …?

Compensation strategies

It's something like …
It's stuff to …
It's a thing you need …
It's a kind of …

Identifying and describing simple objects

What shape is it? – It's oblong.
What size is it? – It's about 2 metres long, 2 metres wide and 2.5 metres high.
What's it made of? – It's made of glass.
What colour is it? – It's dark grey.

Writing a letter

Dear Sir / Madam
Dear Mr Tweed / Ms Davis
I would like to …
I'm interested in …
Could you please send me …
I'm happy to send you our brochure.
Thank you in advance. / Thank you for your interest.
If you have any questions, please contact me.
I look forward to hearing from you.
Hope to hear from you soon. / See you soon.
Best wishes / Best regards

Talking on the phone

This is … from …
Could I speak to …, please?
Just one moment, please.
I'll put you through.
How can I help you?
Would you like me to …?
I'm afraid he's talking on the other line.
Would you like to hold?
It's still engaged.
Would you like to leave a message?
Could you ask him to phone me back?
Thank you for your help.
Thanks for calling.

British and American expressions

British English	American English
colleague	co-worker
company	enterprise
curriculum vitae	résumé
bonnet	hood
boot	trunk
café	diner
cartoons	funnies
film	movie
to pull (up)	to hitch (up)
journey	commute
lift	elevator
managing director	president
mobile	cellular
personnel department	human resources
petrol	gas
tights	stockings
to watch a video	to do a video

Different spelling

to practise	to practice
centre	center

Contents

Pronouns

G1 Reflexive pronouns

Usage

You use reflexive pronouns when the object and the subject of the verb are the same.
Example: She bought **herself** a diamond ring.

You also use a reflexive pronoun after a preposition.
Example: They can look after **themselves**.

Form

Reflexive pronouns are:
singular   myself, yourself, herself, himself, itself
plural   ourselves, yourselves, themselves

Determiners

G2 'Some' and 'any' and their compounds

You can use 'some' to say that there is a quantity of something but you don't give exact details or numbers. 'Some' is used in positive sentences and in questions where you expect the answer to be 'yes'.
Examples: He has **some** days holiday next week.
Would you like **some** coffee?

'Any' is used before plural nouns and uncountable nouns. You can use 'any' in questions and in negative sentences.
Examples: Have you got **any** questions?
I'm sorry, I haven't got **any** milk.

When you want to talk about people or things but you don't know who they are or the exact details, you can use 'something / anything', 'somebody / anybody' or 'somewhere / anywhere'.

You use 'something', 'somebody', 'somewhere' in positive sentences.
Examples: I've got **something** to tell you.
There is **somebody** at the door.
Let's go **somewhere** warm this year.

You use 'anything', 'anybody', 'anywhere' in negative sentences and general questions.
Examples: I didn't bring **anything** with me.
Do you know **anybody** who could help us?
I don't know **anywhere** in that town where we could stay.

G3 'little'/'much' and 'few'/'many'

I. 'Little' and 'much' are used with uncountable nouns.
You use 'little' ('not much') to say that there is only a small amount of something.
Examples: He has **little** time.
As a result of **little** industry, many people are farmers.

You use 'much' to emphasize a large amount.
Examples: She has too **much** work to do.
The Indonesian farmer doesn't earn **much** money.

II. 'Few' and 'many' are used with countable nouns.
'Many' refers to a large number of things but you are not very precise.
Example: There are **many** tourists each year.

You can use 'many' in positive sentences but 'lots of' is more usual in spoken English.
Examples: There are **lots of** islands to visit.

You also use 'many' in negative sentences and questions.
Examples: There aren't **many** people who can speak English.
How **many** day holiday do you have?

You usually use 'few' ('not many') with plural countable nouns when you want to talk about a small number of things of a particular kind.
Examples: She has **few** days holiday.
There are **few** large sizes of clothes.

Adjectives

Adjectives are 'describing' words. They give you more information about a noun.
You can put an adjective in front of a noun.
Example: She bought an **expensive** dress.

You can also put an adjective after the verbs 'be', 'look', 'feel', 'seem', 'smell', 'taste'.
Example: The coffee tastes **good**.

G4 'Too' and 'enough'

You use 'too' when you want to indicate that the quality/quantity of something is more than is wanted or needed. You put 'too' *in front of an adjective.*
Example: He is **too** young.

You can also indicate that you think something is sufficient by using 'enough' *after an adjective.*
Example: The coffee is not hot **enough**.

Note: 'too many', 'too much' and 'enough' go *before a noun.*
Examples: I don't have **enough** money.
He has **too many** problems.
They spend **too much** time in the disco.

G5 Comparison of adjectives

The comparative form of most short adjectives is -er.
Example: Joe has become **richer**.

Short adjectives ending in -y, drop the -y and add -ier.
Example: This week was **busier** than last week.

For most two-syllable and longer adjectives you add more + adjective.
Example: Driving has become **more dangerous**.

G6 Superlative of adjectives

The superlative form of many short adjectives is -est.
Example: This is the **slowest** train I've ever taken.

Short adjectives ending in -y, drop the -y and add -iest.
Example: It was the **funniest** show he'd ever seen.

Long adjectives normally use most + adjective.
Example: What was the **most interesting** job you've ever had?

'Best' / 'worst' are irregular superlatives:
good – better – best
bad – worse – worst

Adverbs

G7 Adverbs

Form

You can form an adverb by adding -ly to the adjective.
Examples: nice – **nicely**
quick – **quickly**

Sometimes the spelling changes:
after -y: easy – **easily**
after -le: terrible – **terribly**
after -ic: automatic – **automically**

Not all words that end in -ly are adverbs.
Some are adjectives (e.g. friendly, lively, lovely, lonely).
Example: She has a lovely voice.

Hard, fast, early, late

These words can be used both as adjectives and as adverbs.
Examples: I love **fast** cars.
The driver drove **fast**.

Good and well

Good is an adjective. Well is an adverb.
Examples: My mother is a **good** cook.
She cooks **well**.

Adverbs of manner

An adverb of manner tells you how something happens.
It normally goes at the end of the sentence.
Example: He listened **carefully**.

Adverbs of degree

An adverb of degree makes the meaning of the word stronger or weaker.
Examples: He is **completely** mad.
It is **slightly** colder today.

Adverbs of degree can be combined with an adjective or another adverb.
Examples: The film was **absolutely** fantastic. (adverb plus adjective)
He drove **very** carefully. (adverb plus adverb)

Grammar Reference Section

Multi-word verbs

G8 Multi-word verbs

A multi-word verb is a combination of a verb and an adverb or a preposition, called particle (e.g. down, in, after, off, up).

Some multi-word verbs are easy to understand because they extend the usual meaning of the verb.
Examples: Please, **come in**!
I **went back** to school.

Some multi-word verbs change the meaning of the verb.
Example: He **put off** the meeting.

Types of multi-word verbs

I. Some multi-word verbs don't take an object.
Examples: I **got up** early.
Slow down, please!

II. Some multi-word verbs have a direct object which cannot go between the verb and the particle.
Example: I **looked after** my grandmother.

In this case, you cannot separate 'look' from 'after'.

III. Some multi-word verbs have a direct object which can go between the verb and the particle, or after the particle.
Examples: I **threw** the letter **away**.
I **threw away** the letter.

However, if the object is a pronoun, you have to put it between the verb and the particle.
Example: I **threw** it **away**.

Verbs

G9 Simple present

I. You use the simple present to talk about facts and habits.
The verb form is the same except for 'he/she/it' where you add an -s.
Examples: I **live** in Bristol.
He **works** in an international company.

II. 'Do/does' are used to form questions and 'don't/doesn't' to form negative sentences.
Examples: **Do** you **drive** to work?
Does she **like** detective novels?
He **doesn't play** a musical instrument.
They **don't have** a garage.

III. Adverbs of frequency describe how often something happens. These adverbs – 'always', 'usually', 'often', 'sometimes', 'never', 'normally' – come before the main verb.
Examples: They **often** go to the cinema.
She **usually** cycles to work.

IV. Time phrases like 'every day', 'once a week', 'twice a month', 'three times a year' etc. can come at the beginning of the sentence or at the very end.
Examples: **Every Monday** she plays squash.
They visit their parents **twice a month**.

G10 Imperatives

The imperative is used to give warnings and advice.
Examples: **Keep** Malta clean!
Don't drink and drive!

The imperative does not have a subject and has the same form as the infinitive without 'to'.

G11 Question tags

Question tags are mini-questions you put at the end of a sentence in spoken English. They are formed by using a 'helping verb' in negative or positive form.
When the verb in the sentence is positive the 'helping verb' in the tag is negative, and when the sentence is negative the tag is positive. You use the same tense in the tag as in the sentence

	+	–
Examples:	Your name is Senay, *simple present*	isn't it? *helping verb simple present*
	–	+
	You haven't seen that film, *present perfect*	have you? *helping verb present perfect*
	+	–
	You lived in France, *simple past*	didn't you? *helping verb simple past*

I. When you use them to make real questions your voice goes up at the end of the tag.
Examples: You are vegetarian, **aren't you**? – Yes, I am. / No, I'm not.
He hasn't been here before, **has he**? – Yes, he has. / No, he hasn't.

II. When you expect the listener to agree with you, your voice goes down at the end of the tag.
Examples: It's a beautiful day, **isn't it**? – Yes it is.
He didn't go the concert, **did he**? – No, he didn't.
The film wasn't very good, **was it**? – No, it wasn't.

G12 Modal verbs I

When you talk about ability you can use 'can' or 'be able to'. You use 'can' in every day conversation and you use both in written English.
Examples: **Can** you play the piano?
He **can't** drive.
They **are able to** speak three different languages.

G13 Modal verbs II

I. 'Have to', 'must' and 'need to' are used when you talk about something that is necessary. You use 'have to' for facts, not for your personal feelings.
Examples: He **has to** work at the weekend.
I **have to** attend lots of meetings.

You use 'must' and 'need to' when you talk about your personal feelings.
Examples: I **must** be on time.
I **need to** do more exercise.

II. You use 'needn't' and 'don't have to' to talk about something which is not necessary.
Examples: You **needn't** stay to the end if you are tired.
You **don't have to** come, but it would be nice if you did.

III. You use 'mustn't' when an action is not allowed.
Example: You **mustn't** smoke in here.

G14 The -ing form and the infinitive of verbs

After the following verbs you normally use the -ing form:
continue, finish, keep, imagine, postpone.
Examples: She **finished** clean**ing**.
Imagine liv**ing** in Italy.

After the following verbs you normally use the infinitive form:
decide, hope, offer, plan.
Examples: She **offered to help**.
They **planned to arrive** on Saturday.

G15 Present progressive (continuous)

Usage

You can use the present progressive to talk about things that are true for a certain time.
Examples: He**'s learning** French.
They **are looking** for a new flat.

You can also use the present progressive to talk about things which are happening at the moment of speaking.
Examples: I**'m waiting** for the results at the moment.
I**'m sitting** in a café now and I'm waiting for my friends.
(situation: somebody talking on the phone)

Form

The present progressive contains two parts: am/is/are + -ing form of the verb.

I	am + -ing form
He She It	is + -ing form
We You They	are + -ing form

G16 Present perfect

Usage

I. You use the present perfect to talk about the past with no definite time signals.
Examples: I**'ve done** a computer course.
He**'s been** to Canada.

II. You often use the present perfect in combination with 'ever' and 'never'.
Examples: **Have** you **ever run** in a race?
They**'ve never played** squash.

III. You can also use the present perfect to say how long something has happened – as a link between the past and the present.
Example: How long **have** you **lived** here? – I**'ve lived** here for five years.
(I still live here.)

You use 'since' when you say the beginning of the period.
Examples: I've lived here **since** 2000.
last week.
May.
1st July.

You use 'for' when you say the period of time.
Examples: He's had a dog **for** ten years.
three months.
a year.
a long time.

Form

The present perfect contains two parts: have /has + past participle.

I You We They	have / haven't + past participle
He She It	has / hasn't + past participle

G17 Simple past

The simple past is used to talk about something that happened in the past and which is over. You use time signals like 'yesterday', 'last week', 'last month', 'one year ago', and 'in 1999'.

I. You make regular verbs in the simple past by adding -ed to the verb. It is the same form for all persons.
Examples: Last year I visit**ed** my cousin in Australia.
Yesterday they work**ed** very hard.

II. Irregular verbs have a special form in the simple past but it is the same form for all persons.
Examples: Last summer he **went** to Greece on holiday.
Two days ago I **bought** a new TV.

III. Questions and negative sentences
Except for the verb 'to be' you form questions with 'did' and negatives with 'didn't'. It is the same form for all persons.
Examples: **Did** you **swim** in the new pool last night?
They **didn't (did not) work** in Scotland in 1999.

IV. The verb 'be'
You use was for the past of 'am' and 'is' and were for the past of 'are'.
Examples: **Were** you at the new pool last night?
He **wasn't** at home last night.

G18 wish + simple past

'Wish' plus a verb in the simple past expresses a wish for things to be different.
Example: I **wish** I **had** more money.

G19 Past progressive (continuous)

Usage

I. You use the past progressive to describe actions in the past. This can be two actions that were happening at the same time and are connected with 'while'.
Example: They **were having** a party *while* we **were trying** to sleep.

II. You use the past progressive to express a longer action that was in progress when a second, shorter action began and are connected with 'when'.
Example: She **was having** a bath *when* the phone rang.

III. You can also use the past progressive to describe the background of a story.
Example: It was midday and Dora **was lying** on the beach dreaming …

Form

You make the past progressive with 'was' or 'were' + -ing form of the verb.

You We They	were / weren't singing.
I He She It	was / wasn't watching TV.

G20 List of irregular verbs

infinitive	simple past	past participle
be	was / were	been
become	became	become
break	broke	broken
buy	bought	bought
catch	caught	caught
choose	chose	chosen
do	did	done
draw	drew	drawn
drive	drove	driven
fly	flew	flown
get	got	got
give	gave	given
go	went	gone
grow	grew	grown
have	had	had
keep	kept	kept
know	knew	known
leave	left	left
lie	lay	lain
make	made	made
meet	met	met
ride	rode	ridden
run	ran	run
sell	sold	sold
speak	spoke	spoken
spend	spent	spent
swim	swam	swum
take	took	taken
tell	told	told
think	thought	thought
wear	wore	worn
write	wrote	written

G21 'going to' as a future tense

You use 'going to' when you talk about a plan in the future, but you haven't made final arrangements yet.
Examples: I**'m going to** relax at the weekend.
He**'s going to** learn Spanish.

G22 will-future

You can use the will-future to predict what you think will happen in the future.
Examples: Everyone **will have** a mobile phone in ten years' time.
The letter **won't arrive** tomorrow.

G23 Simple present as a future tense

You use the simple present when you talk about something in the future based on a timetable.
Examples: The flight **leaves** at 13.15.
At 9.30 you **have** a meeting with Mr. Mars.

G24 Present progressive as a future tense

You use the present progressive when you talk about definite arrangements in the future.
Examples: I'm flying to Corsica on Saturday. *(I have already bought the tickets.)*
He's having a party on Friday night. *(He has already invited friends.)*
We're going on holiday next week. *(We have already arranged accommodation.)*

G25 'Zero' conditional

You use this type of 'if-sentence' to talk about situations that are generally true.
Example: **If** I **don't go** to bed early, I**'m tired** in the morning.

If-sentences of this type are made up of two parts:

if-clause	main clause
If + simple present	simple present
If you forget your passport,	you can't fly on holiday.

The 'if-clause' can come before or after the main clause.
Example: If sales increase, the profit grows.
The profit grows if sales increase.

G26 If-sentence type 1

You use this type of 'if-sentence' to talk about situations in the future which can happen. You use it to refer to possible situations and their results.
Example: **If** you work too long at the computer, you**'ll get** a headache.

If-sentences type 1 are made up of two parts:

if-clause	main clause
If + simple present	will-future
If I get up early tomorrow,	I'll be on time for work.

The 'if-clause' can come before or after the main clause.
Example: If it rains tomorrow, I won't cycle to work.

If it is at the end, you don't separate the clauses with a comma.
Example: I won't cycle to work **if** it rains tomorrow.

G27 If-sentence type 2

You use this type of 'if-sentence' to talk about an imaginary or unreal situation. You use it to refer to or to speculate about something that doesn't seem to be possible.
Example: **If** I **had** more time, I**'d help** you.

If-sentences type 2 are made up of two parts:

If-clause	main clause
If + simple past	would
If you went to bed earlier,	you wouldn't be so tired.

The 'if-clause' can come before or after the main clause.
Examples: If I had the money, I'd buy a new car.
I'd buy a new car if I had the money.

You can also use this type of 'if-sentence' when giving advice.
Example: If I were you, I'd go to see the doctor.

You can use 'were' instead of 'was' in the if-clause.

G28 The passive

Usage

The passive form of the verb is used when you don't know or when it is not important to say who performs the action.
Example: English **is spoken** all over the world.

If you want to say who or what did the action, you use 'by'.
Example: English is spoken **by politicians** from all over the world.

Form

A passive verb is a form of the verb 'to be' (is, are, was, were, have been) plus a past participle (e.g. spoken, written).

	active	passive
simple present:	Marie **teaches** French in Germany.	French **is taught** in Germany.
present perfect:	The writer **has sold** a million books.	A million books **have been sold**.
simple past:	They **translated** the text yesterday.	The text **was translated** yesterday.
will-future:	The landlady **will serve** breakfast at 7.00.	Breakfast **will be served** at 7.00.

Usage

You use the passive in both speaking and writing, but it is more common in writing, especially in news reports, in books, in describing processes in industry and in warnings and signs.
Examples: The bank robbers **were caught**.
Water **is heated** to the boiling point.
English **is spoken** here.

G29 Relative clauses

Relative clauses are used to give more information about people and things. You can use the relative pronoun 'who' to define people and 'which' to define things.
Examples: He is the type of person **who** works very hard.
Yoga is a sport **which** helps you to relax.

Tapescripts

Unit 1

4b

Interviewer:
Hello, I'm from the Max Frank Institute and I'm – um – doing a survey about why people are learning English. Can I ask you all why are you attending English courses at the moment?

Student 1:
Well, I'm a student. I need English in my studies every day – you see. This extra course really helps me with my studies.

Student 2:
Oh, I want to visit my sister and her family in Australia, you see, and her children can only speak English.

Student 3:
Well, as you can see I'm over 60 and – well – I just want to train my brain!

Student 4:
Um, as I work for an international company I have to speak English with our business partners. So I just want to speak and speak …

4e

Tom's Diner
(by Suzanne Vega)

I am sitting
In the morning
At the diner
On the corner
I am waiting
At the counter
For the man
To pour the coffee

And he fills it
Only halfway
And before
I even argue

He is looking
Out the window
At somebody
Coming in

"It is always
Nice to see you"
Says the man
Behind the counter

To the woman
Who has come in
She is shaking
Her umbrella

And I look
The other way
As they are kissing
Their hellos

And I'm pretending
Not to see them
Instead
And I pour the milk

I open
Up the paper

There's a story
Of an actor

Who had died
While he was drinking
It was no one
I had heard of

And I'm turning
To the horoscope
And looking
For the funnies

When I'm feeling
Someone watching me
And so
I raise my head

There's a woman
On the outside
Looking inside
Does she see me?

No she does not
Really see me
Cause she sees
Her own reflection

And I'm trying
Not to notice
That she's hitching
Up her skirt

And while she's
Straightening her stockings
Her hair
Has gotten wet

Oh, this rain
It will continue
Through the morning
As I'm listening

To the bells
Of the cathedral
I am thinking
Of your voice...

And of the midnight picnic
Once upon a time
Before the rain began...

And I finish up my coffee
And it's time to catch the train

6b

(P = The Park Language Centre,
S = Student)
P: The Park Language Centre. How can I help you?
S: Hello, um, this is Paul speaking. I got your brochure last week and – well – I'd like to do a two-week intensive course at your school.
P: Right, are you thinking about any particular course?
S: Yes, I would like to know something about your English and Activity Programme.
P: Well, this course gives you the perfect chance to improve your English through controlled study in the classroom and realistic, free practice outside of the classroom, too. So, the 'inside' classroom study offers you the chance to increase your English knowledge with the help of the teacher. The 'outside' activities will additionally increase your confidence to speak and your skill to understand a lot of people.
S: Great! That's just what I need! Which activities can I – er – choose from?
P: OK, well, we usually offer six different activities; painting, golf, walking, horse-riding, climbing and – um – tennis.
S: Right, and how do I spend each day?
P: Well, in the morning you do the General English programme here at the school. As you know from our brochure, that is 15 lessons per week. Then, after lunch you can do an activity session. You can do the same activity each day or a mix of different activities.
S: So, I could do horse-riding one day and then tennis the next?
P: Yes, that's right.
S: Um, do I need any previous experience of the activities?
P: No, none at all. You can be a total beginner or advanced. The trainers will give you the training which is right for your level.
S: So, what do I need to bring with me?
P: Well, for painting you need an old shirt, – um – for golf all the equipment is provided, and – um – for walking – well – your walking boots or a good pair of shoes. Let's see, for both horse-riding and climbing you should – um– bring some comfortable trousers and flat shoes. Additionally, for tennis you need white clothing and soft shoes. OK?

8a

1. Well, every morning on my way to work I look at the adverts for English words.
2. Er – when I arrive at work, I always write down a list of what I want to do in English.
3. Hm, let me think … I talk in English on the phone to a class member once a week.
4. I – um – usually send short e-mails in English to a colleague.
5. Oh, I know, I play my favourite English CD in the evening.
6. Well, I often have an English conversation in a café with a friend.
7. Oh, I never forget to take my English word bank with me.
8. Every night I choose one word in English that I – er – want to remember before I go to sleep.

H3a

Speaker 1
Well, I always get up at 6.30 in the morning, make a cup of tea, go back to bed and just enjoy my cup of tea in bed …

Speaker 2
I – er – find it so difficult to wake up in the morning, so I – um – normally have a freezing cold shower – I'm always awake after that …

Speaker 3
As you can imagine, I'm so busy at work that I just don't find time to have a lunch break – so, I – well – usually eat lots of fruit in my office.

Speaker 4
Well, I love cooking and, you know, trying out new recipes – so I often have dinner with friends.

Speaker 5
When I'm tired in the evening I – um –sometimes have a nice hot bath before I go to bed. It helps me to relax – you see …

H9
(weak forms)
1. I'm **an** engineer **for** Dupont.
2. I'm **from** Sweden.
3. I **can** speak **a** little Spanish.
4. Good **to** see you again.
5. Where **do** you work?

Unit 2

1a
Dialogue 1
- Hi, Mandy, how are you?
- Fine thanks, Robert. That's a nice jacket you're wearing!
- Oh, thank you. I bought it yesterday.

Dialogue 2
- Hello, Sven. Come on in. Let me take your coat.
- Thanks. Oh! What a great flat you've got! It's really big.
- Thanks, we're really happy with it.

Dialogue 3
- Hey, Jo, that haircut really suits you!
- Oh, thanks. I've just had it cut.

Dialogue 4
- Sandra, it's great to see you again. Wow, you look really fit!
- Well, thank you. It must be all the sports I'm doing …

3a
(F = Fast Track Gym, M = Mark)
F: Right, Mark, before I show you around the Fast Track Gym, I'd like to ask you some questions about your level of fitness. OK?
M: Er, OK.
F: Have you ever been to a gym before?
M: Well, actually no, never. I can honestly say I've never been before.
F: OK. Have you ever done any sports before?
M: Well, I've played football before.
F: Right – and –um – have you ever smoked?
M: Yes, I have, but I've just given up.

F: Well, that's a good start! Come on, let me show you around the gym …

4a
First Speaker/Anthony
During the whole of December I went to all my friends and colleagues and collected sponsors to raise money for the Samaritans. On the day after Christmas Day I met all the people at the hotel in front of the beach. It was very cold and windy, but at least it wasn't raining! There were a grand total of 1,000 'swimmers'. We put on our swimming costumes and at 11.00 a.m. we all left together. There was a crowd of about 3,000 people to cheer us as we ran across the sand to the sea. The water was very cold, but I stayed in for five minutes. I even swam when I saw that my daughter was videoing me! I raised £80 for charity and both my daughters want to swim with me next year!

Second Speaker/Gill
Last year I walked up lots of mountains in Scotland, but this was the first time I would climb down one. It was a fantastic summer's day and I was happy I wouldn't get wet. Lots of people came to watch including all my friends. Was I crazy? I had agreed to abseil down a mountain for the charity 'Capability Scotland'. It took me only 10 minutes to abseil down – a lot quicker than walking up! It wasn't as difficult as I thought. In fact, I quite enjoyed it!

Third Speaker/Jenny
March the 12th … This was the special day! Before I left my home for work I put the red round piece of plastic on my nose and looked in the mirror. I looked really terrible, but I knew I had to wear it the whole day. I felt better in the underground as many people in the train also had a big red nose like me. When I got to work my colleagues just smiled at me. They all had big red plastic noses, too. At the end of the day we went to a pub to celebrate that our team had collected £150 for charity.

5

[ɪd]	[d]	[t]
collected	abseiled	looked
wanted	agreed	walked
decided	stayed	smoked

8a
(E = Elena, H = Hannah)
H: Good afternoon, Power Courses. My name's Hannah, can I help you?
E: Hello, this is Miss Taffy from DCD in Cologne and I – er – would like some information about your 'Power Courses' for a team of our managers.
H: Right, would you like me to send you our latest brochure?
E: Yes, that would be great.
H: OK, could you give me the company

name and address, please?
E: Yes, that's DCD, Beethoven Straße 134.
H: Sorry, could you repeat that, please?
E: That's DCD and the street is B-E-E-T-H-O-V-E-N new word S-T-R-A-S-S-E, number 134. The postal code is 50674 in Cologne, Germany.
H: Who should I send it to?
E: Could you send it to my boss, please? That's Mr Rose – like the flower.
H: Oh, that's a nice name! I'll send out our brochure this afternoon and if you have any questions please call me again.
E: Yes, I will. Thank you very much for your help.
H: You're welcome, and thank you for calling. Bye.

H5
(F = Fast Track Fitness Centre, G = George)
F: Fast Track Fitness Centre. Can I help you?
G: This is George Jones speaking. I'd like some information about your courses, please.
F: Would you like me to send you a brochure?
G: Yes, that would be great.
F: OK. Could you give me your address, please?
G: It's 12 Humbledon View, Surrey SRX 4T8.
F: Right, I'll send it to you right away.
G: Thank you very much
F: You're welcome. Bye.
G: Bye.

Unit 3

3a
(E = Elena, G = Gordon)
G: Exclusive Cottages. Gordon Scot speaking. How can I help you?
E: This is Elena Taffy from DCD in Cologne. We're looking for some exclusive self-catering accommodation for a team of our managers to stay for one week. May I ask you some questions about your cottages?
G: Certainly, go ahead.
E: Well, I'm sure your cottages have the standard kitchen facilities, but – um – have any got more exclusive kitchen facilities?
G: Well, they all have fully-equipped kitchen facilities. You know, with oven microwave, fridge and so on. Some of the more exclusive cottages have dishwashers, dryers and small freezers, too.
E: Fine. Have any cottages got a shower and a bath?
G: Of course! All of them have both. It's standard, you see. Some are also fitted with small jacuzzis.
E: Oh, that sounds good. Have any of the cottages got a traditional old English fireplace?

G: Yes, we have some with old fireplaces.
E: Great. One last question. What about an indoor swimming pool?
G: Well, it is the UK, not Spain! No, none of them have any swimming pools, I'm afraid. Look, shall I send you one of our brochures?
E: Oh, that would be great! Could I then send you a fax with our booking request?
G: Yes, that's fine …

6

sounds v and f
1. van
2. fairy
3. very
4. view
5. fast

H3

(C = Claudia, I = Interviewer)
I: Hi Claudia, it's nice to have you in the studio today.
C: Thanks. It's good to be here. I've always wondered what it's like inside a radio studio.
I: Well, as you can see, it's nothing special! Claudia, you've lived in the UK for four years now, so you must have noticed some differences between life in Germany and life in the UK I should think.
C: Yes, that's right – I mean there are no big differences but I noticed a few things.
I: Can you give us a couple of examples?
C: Well, I suppose the obvious one is that the British are funnier – they have a great sense of humour and are always laughing at themselves – which was difficult at the beginning. I never knew if they were serious or if they were making a joke. The Germans, however, are far more efficient. When they say they will do something, well, then, they really do it.
I: What about the lifestyle?
C: In general, I believe that the lifestyle in the UK is more expensive. Food, alcohol, petrol, clothing and even going out for a meal are cheaper in Germany. Which is interesting because the high prices still don't stop the Brits from shopping or going out very often. Shops, restaurants and pubs always seem to be full!
I: Moving on to cars. Do you see any big difference?
C: Oh, yes, there's no doubt that the Germans drive bigger and I think faster cars than the Brits. Maybe that's because the Germans can drive faster on their motorways and the Brits have to drive slower.
I: OK – what about homes?
C: As the system in the UK is different it seems it is much easier to buy houses here. That means that the average British home is larger than the average

German flat. They just have more space. However, the Germans make up for this point with their holidays.
I: Oh, what do you mean?
C: Well, the Brits are busy paying for their houses and taking shorter holidays whilst the Germans seem to spend their spare money on longer and more exotic holidays – you know to the US or to the Far East. I think the average German has six weeks holiday plus all those religious holidays …
I: Ah, that's interesting. Well, Claudia that's about all we've got time for today but thanks very much for sharing your impressions with us.
C: Thanks for inviting me.

H9b

stressed syllables
furniture, **ba**lance, accommo**da**tion, **A**sia, **coun**tryside, **Tur**key, **moun**tain, **ca**bins confir**ma**tion, re**sult**, **fas**cinated, Ne**pal**, inde**pen**dent, fa**cili**ties, e**quipp**ed, ex**clu**sive

Unit 4

3a

(R = Raef, W = Dr Walter)
R: I'd like to welcome Dr Christa Walter who has come into the studio today to give us some tips on successful time-management.
W: Thank you for the invitation Raef. But let's not waste too much time with introductions and get down to business.
R: OK. What's your first tip for us then?
W: Well, you must want to change your lifestyle.
R: OK, but how?
W: Well, you could make a list of what you want to change and a list of ideas how you could change it.
R: Right.
W: You don't have to do everything on your list but you should try out different points.
R: Oh, I see, you mean each day you should try to change one thing.
W: Well, even one point each week is OK. The important point is that you mustn't forget your list completely.
R: What could I start with?
W: Well, in the morning your first task is to get up. You could try to get up a little bit earlier for example.
R: Oh dear, that's a difficult one …

6a

1. Well, it's the highest salary I've had so far and, well, you know money makes the world go round!
2. For me the people you work with make a job – and in this job I've got the friendliest colleagues you could wish for.
3. Well, this is the first time I've had a

permanent contract, so I'd have to say that this is the securest job I've ever had.
4. Er, I've just finished a two-year training course and I want to make a career. So for me, I took this job because it offered the best opportunities for promotion.

9

(sounds: silent letters b and k)

battle	**k**nee	thum**b**	snack
knowledge	job	sickness	lam**b**
bom**b**	sparkling	com**b**	**k**nife
horrible	**k**now	habit	keep

H2

(C = Cornerstone Company, M = Mike)
C: Cornerstone Company. Can I help you?
M: Hello, this is Mike Shaw from Johnstone & Johnstone. Could I speak to Colin Fleet, please?
C: Just one moment and I'll put you through.
M: Thanks.
C: Oh, I'm afraid he's talking on the other line at the moment. Would you like to hold on?
M: Yes, that's OK.
C: Hello, I'm sorry, it's still engaged. Would you like to leave a message?
M: Er, could you ask him to phone me back? He's got my number.
C: Right, I'll ask him to call you back. Thanks for your call. Bye.
M: Bye.

H6

Speaker 1
Well, I love being my own boss. There is nobody who tells me what I have to do. I like starting work at 6.00 a.m. because the day is fresh, I'm fresh and I don't have to wait for the company to open. I enjoy sitting at my own desk in the comfort of my own flat. I can take a break when I want to. But I can't stand writing invoices and I really hate waiting to be paid from different companies all the time …

Speaker 2
I hate starting work at 8.00 every day. You see we don't have a flexitime system. I also can't stand working on Saturdays. All my friends are at home and I have to work! There are good things, too, though. I love working with books – it means I'm up to date with the latest publications and I like getting a discount on the books. Oh, I enjoy talking to the customers, too.

Speaker 3
I enjoy working with people all the time. I love helping them to learn a language – it's great when you see they have learnt something new and can use it! I like looking at new coursebooks but I really can't stand preparing lessons on the weekend. And I hate photocopying. I like meeting lots of different kinds of people, too.

Unit 5

3b

- Now that Frances has started school are you going to start work again?
- Yes, I'd like to but I've decided I have to become a bit fitter in e-commerce, you know the technological business world, first.
- Oh, what are you planning to do?
- Well, I'm going to attend a computer course so that I'm up-to-date with the new software programmes.
- That's a good start!
- Yes, I want to learn how to surf the internet and to send e-mails.
- You can start by sending me e-mails if you like.
- Yes, that's a good idea. I'm also going to use an interactive German language CD-ROM so that I can improve my language skills.
- I should do that, too, my German is terrible …

8a

Dialogue 1
(B = Boss, M = Mark)
B: Come in, Mark. What did you want to see me about?
M: Well, my wife is ill and I have to collect the children from school … so may I leave work at 3.00 p.m. this afternoon?
B: Yes, of course you may, but perhaps you could stay a little longer tomorrow then.
M: Er, yes OK.

Dialogue 2
(J = Jude, P = Paul)
P: Jude, could I transfer my calls through to you while I go on my lunch break?
J: I'm afraid you can't because I'm going to a meeting in five minutes.
P: Oh!

Dialogue 3
(J = Jack, P = Phil)
P: Jack, can I take your mobile on my business trip this week as mine isn't working at the moment.
J: Sorry, but I'm going to Edinburgh tomorrow and I need it myself.

9b

(word stress)
de**vel**op, im**por**tant, co**nnect**, **in**ternet, **mo**bile, **off**ice, com**pu**ter, **comm**erce, **mo**ment, re**ply**, **choc**olate, co**mmu**ter, **coll**eague, **sal**ary, **at**mosphere, **ré**sumé

10a

"What great big ears you have, Grandma."
"All the better to hear you with," the Wolf replied.
"What great big eyes you have, Grandma," said Little Red Riding Hood.
"All the better to see you with," the Wolf replied.

He sat there watching her and smiled.
He thought, I'm going to eat this child.
Compared with her old Grandmama
She's going to taste like caviar.

Then Little Red Riding Hood said, "But Grandma,
what a lovely great big furry coat you have on.
"That's wrong!" cried the Wolf. "Have you forgot
To tell me what BIG TEETH I've got?
Ah well, no matter what you say,
I'm going to eat you anyway."

The small girl smiles.
She aims a pistol at the Wolf's head
AND bang bang bang, she shoots him dead.

A few weeks later, in the wood,
I saw Miss Riding Hood.
She said, "Hello, and please do note
My lovely furry WOLFSKIN COAT."

Unit 6

1

different sounds
1. waterfall
2. traffic noises
3. lots of people talking at the same time
4. wind/rain in trees
5. airport announcement
6. dogs barking

4a

Conversation 1
(J = Jenny, M = Mike)
M: Hi Jenny. It's Mike.
J: Oh hello, are you still in Zurich?
M: Yes, I am, but I'll be back in the office this evening. Jenny, I need someone to come into the office this weekend to do some extra work. Do you – er –think you could come?
J: I'm sorry Mike, I'm away all weekend. We're going sailing. It's a great way to switch off, you know. You should come with us some time.
M: Thanks – when I don't have to work at the weekend I will. Bye.
J: Bye.

Conversation 2
(M = Mike, S = Sue)
M: Hello Sue. It's Mike.
S: Oh no, this means trouble if you are phoning at five on a Friday afternoon. What can I do for you?
M: Hmm, are you doing anything this weekend?
S: Sorry, I can't work for you this weekend as I'm booked into a beauty clinic. I'm having massages and relaxation sessions the whole weekend. Nothing to do with work …
M: OK, OK, I get the message. See you on Monday. Bye.
S: Bye.

Conversation 3
(M = Mike, S = Sandra)
S: Hello, Mike. It's Sandra.
M: Well, hello. Nice that you called.
S: Mike, what are you doing this weekend. I'm going walking and I was wondering if you would like to come with me. You know – get out of the city for a couple of days.
M: I'd love to Sandra, but I'm working all weekend in the office I'm afraid.
S: Oh that's a pity. Another time perhaps …

6b

(sounds s or z)
pla**c**e [s], sometime**s** [z], eye**s** [z], clothe**s** [z], per**s**on [s], vi**s**it [z], **s**ink [s], me**ss**age [s], **s**ailing [s], **s**ymbolic [s], surpri**s**e [z], re**s**ult [z]

7a

You have four new messages:

'This is Brian. I'm afraid I can't make it on Monday. Could we meet on Tuesday afternoon at the same place and same time? Could you let me know if this is OK? Bye.'

'Paul here. Could we meet at 8.30 am on Tuesday instead of 9.30? Do you think we could meet at the airport as I'm flying to Hamburg at 11.00? Speak to you soon.'

'Jenny speaking. Just phoning to confirm our working lunch session on Wednesday at Pomp. Looking forward to it. Bye.'

Hi, this is Elfie speaking. I've got a problem with our appointment on Tuesday. Would it be possible to meet next Tuesday instead?

H3b

The single mum
I work full-time for the railways. The thing about being a single mum is you never have any time for yourself. I always plan to go to the gym, or even have a drink after work, but I can't. If you get any free moments, you spend it with the kids. It's OK when people say you can use your time more effectively, but you have to be in control of your own time to do that – and I'm not.

The manager
I never feel I have time to do nothing. Maybe if I didn't sleep, I could get everything done. By the time you have gone home and finished eating, it's time to think of going to bed. You then get up the next day to do everything again. I fill every hour. Doing nothing is not an option for people with a career who want to continue being successful.

The schoolboy
Things are getting faster. I quite often don't have any free time for my hobby skateboarding. When I got my skateboard I had imagined practising every evening

with my friends – but it's just impossible. I do school work every night and at the weekend. That can take the whole afternoon with some projects. My parents say I should go outside more often but they expect me to be successful at school, too.

H7

1. calm
2. cause
3. cope
4. couple
5. keep
6. course
7. cycle
8. conflict
9. continue

Unit 7

2e

The beginning is simple. We were sitting under a tree. I was kneeling on the grass and Clarissa was passing me the bottle – a 1987 Daumas Gassac.
This was the moment, this was the pinprick on the time map: I was holding out my hand for the bottle when we heard a man's shout.
We turned to look across the field and saw danger.
Next thing I was running towards it. I don't remember dropping the bottle, or hearing Clarissa calling after me.
There was the shout again. I ran faster. And there, suddenly, from different points around the field, four other men were running like me.
What was Clarissa doing? She said she walked quickly to the centre of the field. We were running towards a catastrophe. At the base of the balloon was a basket in which there was a boy. Outside of the basket was a man holding on to a rope in need of help.

3a

Dialogue 1
● Well, I met him at the train station.
■ You didn't!
● Yes, I did actually.
  He was waiting to collect me. We were going to run a workshop together for a week.
■ Oh.
● So there he was holding a bottle of sparkling wine and a sign with my name on it …
  Really!

Dialogue 2
● Actually, I was hitch-hiking around New Zealand when I met her.
■ Really!
● Yes, but she was travelling with another man.
■ Oh no!
● Anyway, we stayed in the same hostel three days later and I found out that the man was just a good friend of hers.

■ What happened then?
● Well, …

Dialogue 3
● Well, I was working in the personnel department when he came to the company.
■ Oh.
● Actually, I didn't like him when I first met him because he was very unfriendly.
■ Really?
● Yes, but I realised he wasn't unfriendly, he was just shy. So, I started talking to him.
■ What happened then?
● He asked me out to dinner.

6a

Dialogue 1
(J = Joe, K = Karen)
K: Joe, it's me, Karen. I've got two tickets for the chat show tonight. Would you like to come with me?
J: I'm afraid, I can't, I have to go to Berlin tonight on business.
K: Oh, that's a pity.
J: Yeah, another time perhaps …

Dialogue 2
(J = Jennifer, R = Rod)
J: Hello, Jennifer speaking.
R: Hello, Jennifer, this is Rod here.
J: Oh, hello.
R: Hmm, I was wondering if you would like to go out for a meal with me this evening.
J: Er, I'm sorry, I'm um, I'm washing my hair tonight.
R: All night?
J: Er, yes that's right.
R: Oh …

Dialogue 3
(P = Paul, S = Scott)
P: Scott, would you like to come to my house-warming party next Saturday?
S: Oh, I'd love to. What time?
P: Um, about eight.
S: Great, see you at eight then.

Dialogue 4
(J = Jane, L = Louise)
L: Jane, do you fancy watching that new film at the Metropolis?
J: I'd love to, but I've got to work late tonight. Maybe on the weekend?
L: OK, OK.

Dialogue 5
(G = Gill, S = Sue)
S: Hi Gill, I'm having a dinner party this Friday. Can you make it?
G: That would be lovely. Um, I'm a vegetarian though.
S: Yes, I know that – don't worry, it'll be a veggie meal.
G: Great, see you on Friday then.

H1

(I = Interviewer, S = Suspect)
I: OK, we'd like to know what you were doing in the first two weeks of May?

S: Well, I can tell you exactly as I remember it well. I was on Cyprus. I went there for three weeks and I'm sure I can find my air ticket with my name on it if you don't' believe me …
I: Oh, really! That's a long way from home. Perhaps you could give me the exact dates you were there … and yes, I do want to see your ticket, too.
S: Right … It was from the 1st May to the 22nd. I flew from Frankfurt to Pafos. We stopped at Larnaka for half of an hour but we weren't allowed to leave the plane. We then took off again for Pafos and landed a short while later. The whole flight took 2 and a half hours and I landed at 3.20 in the afternoon. At 4.00 I was sitting in the sun drinking a cool beer. Satisfied?
I: Sounds good but you still haven't told me why you went there. What were you doing for three whole weeks? Was it business or pleasure?
S: Well, if you must know, it was my annual holiday. I was walking in the hills and along the beautiful beaches. I like walking and love flowers and a friend of mine told me that Cyprus is wonderful for both in April. Did you know that Cyprus has over 45 different types of orchids?
I: No, I didn't, that's interesting. So you were walking for the whole of the three weeks then … Well, one last question, sir, and then I'll leave you alone – er, did you travel with anyone, or meet anyone there? You know at the hotel, or walking with an organised group?
S: Hm, not exactly. I have such a stressful job here, you see, that I always go on holiday alone. I'm an independent traveller. I don't like booking hotels or walking with a group, so I take a small tent and just walk from place to place … I was enjoying my own company if you like …
I: So you mean you were walking for three weeks and you didn't meet anyone?
S: No, I'm afraid not …

Unit 8

3b

(I = Interviewer, S = Senay)
I: So, I'm very happy to welcome Senay to our studio today who is going to explain some of the rituals involved in a traditional Turkish wedding. 'Shenai' is the correct pronunciation, isn't it?
S: Yes, that's perfect.
I: Thank you! So, Senay, I find the first step very interesting. It isn't the man who asks the woman's parents for permission to marry her, is it?
S: No, it isn't. His parents must ask her parents if their son can marry their daughter. It's a sign of respect.
I: That's interesting. They take gifts on this first meeting, don't they?

S: Yes, they do. The man's parents must take a particular brand of expensive chocolates and a diamond ring as gifts.

I: A diamond ring! So it's quite serious from the beginning, isn't it?

S: Yes, that's right.

I: Before the wedding, the bride-to-be holds a party for her friends, doesn't she?

S: Well, yes and no. She does have a party but it's only for her very close female friends, her female relatives – you know, sisters, aunts, cousins – and the female relatives of her future husband.

I: Oh, that's a bit like a 'Hen Night' in the UK, isn't it?

S: Well, it's only for women but they don't go out to a disco or see a male stripper like some of the women do in the UK though.

I: No, they are a bit wild in the UK sometimes! So moving on to the actual wedding reception. It has always been a tradition to give the bride gifts of silver bracelets, hasn't it?

S: Yes, the bride does get bracelets, but they must be gold as this is a symbol for wealth in their marriage.

I: Oh, I see. Well, thank you very much for sharing your traditions with us today Senay.

S: Thanks for asking me.

4b

1. You live in the city-centre, don't you? (↗)
2. That film wasn't very good, was it? (↘)
3. Frieda changed jobs last month, didn't she? (↗)
4. The Olympics hasn't been very interesting, has it? (↘)
5. You aren't vegetarian, are you? (↗)
6. You went to Greece for your holidays, didn't you? (↘)

5b

Indonesia consists of lots of small islands; **13,000** plus. While places like Bali, Lombok, and Torajaland attract many tourists each year, other places remain free of mass tourism.

There are **300** ethnic groups which speak some **365** languages and dialects. English is the first foreign language but most Indonesians can only speak **2-3** phrases. As education is expensive, few Indonesians actually go to university. As a result of little industry, lots of Indonesians are farmers. Unfortunately, the average Indonesian farmer doesn't earn much money. However, you will always find the people welcoming, friendly and willing to share what few things they have with you.

If you like the sun and enjoy being outside, there are many things to do from sunbathing in Bali to paddling in rivers, surfing off the coast, and eating over **30** different types of fruit.

Bring as little luggage as possible as you can buy most things in Indonesia. The only problem with clothes is that as the Indonesians are quite small, there are few large sizes.

6a

(S = Sam, St = Stewart)

St: Hi, Sam. You know our Japanese agent is coming to visit next week and I was wondering if you could give me some tips of what to do etc.

S: OK. Well, firstly don't be surprised if he says 'san' after your name.

St: Sorry, did you say 'san'?

S: Yes, that's right. It's his way of showing respect.

St: Can you spell that, please?

S: Yes, S-A-N.

St: Right, got it. I'd like to take him out for a traditional meal. Have you got any ideas where I should go?

S: Well, the Japanese don't usually eat big meals so unless he's really interested in trying our local food, why don't you take him to a 'sushi' bar instead.

St: Sorry, I didn't catch that. A what bar?

S: A sushi bar. That's a traditional Japanese bar. There's one near the cathedral.

St: Hey, that's a great idea. Then he won't feel so foreign and I'll get to know something about his culture, too.

S: That's right. Oh, one last tip.

St: Yes?

S: Don't be nervous if he smiles all the time but doesn't actually speak very much.

St: You said 'smile', didn't you?

S: Yes, that's right. The Japanese are not great talkers. They prefer to get to know you without using so many words. But as they are very polite, they smile very often.

St: That's OK. I think we always talk too much in any case.

S: Yes, that's true.

H6

(K = Kate, R = Roger)

R: Hello?

K: Hi Roger. Kate here. How are you?

R: Fine, thanks, Kate. And you?

K: Not so bad, thanks. Listen, shall we meet for dinner tonight?

R: Great idea! Where shall we go?

K: Well, what about Café Fleur?

R: Sorry, can you repeat that?

K: Café Fleur.

R: Oh dear. It's a bad line. Can you spell that, please?

K: It's Café F-L-E-U-R.

R: Got you, like 'flower' in English?

K: That's right. About 8.00?

R: Sorry, didn't catch that.

K: About 8.00?

R: That's fine. See you at 8.00.

K: See you. Bye.

R: Bye.

H7

Well, as I'm now 108 I've seen celebrations for two centuries now.

When we celebrated the new century in 1900, I was 7 years old. There was little of the excitement we saw this time round. I got just one box of chocolate at school to celebrate …

We had no electricity so there were none of the colourful lights we see today. I've got three daughters living in London and I spent the millennium with them. I've got five grandchildren and four great-grandchildren. I'm lucky as I'm still quite healthy. I gave up driving when I was 91.

Unit 9

2a

music piece no. 1: 'In the Mood', Glenn Miller, 'The Missing Chapters'
music piece no. 2: 'Ancient Memories', Derek Bell, 'The Harpestry'
music piece no. 3: 'El Nicoya', Santana, 'Santana's 30th Anniversary Expanded Edition'

2b

A dress flowing round
the dance floor to the music
slowly, fast, slowly.

Freckles all over,
Ginger hair but very kind
Christopher my friend.

2c

1. It smells good.
   It tastes sweet.
   It feels warm.
   It looks delicious.

   You eat it at a birthday party.
   What is it?

2. It smells horrible.
   It tastes awful.
   It feels sticky.
   It looks pink.

   You need it when you have the flu.
   What is it?

3a

(H = Ms Harrison, I = Interviewer)

I: Ms. Harrison, can you tell us the effect food choices have on our moods?

H: Food is so powerful that it alters our brain chemistry. Certain foods increase the production of neurotransmitters, like serotonin. These neurotransmitters have specific effects on our moods. If you understand this, you can choose to alter your moods with food.

I: Can you give us some examples?

H: Well, for instance, if you are worried and anxious, reach for a carbohydrate-rich snack, such as a bagel, a pretzel, low-sugar cereal, crackers or rice-cake.

This type of food will make you feel better.

I: What if you feel stressed?

H: If you are stressed or irritable, eat a plate of pasta and top it with a vegetable marinara sauce or eat a baked potato with steamed vegetables. I guarantee that you'll feel good afterwards.

I: I often feel tired and unmotivated in the evenings after work. What do you recommend?

H: A protein-rich meal will make you feel energetic. Eat a meal of chicken or fish and a salad with a small amount of dressing. If you are sleepy but need to stay up, choose a high-protein snack, such as tuna fish, beans, a hard-boiled egg, low fat cheese, non-fat yoghurt or peanut butter. You will feel marvellous.

(adapted from 'The Weekender', Times of Malta)

6a

Monday 30th October
'Sky News on the Hour' with Kevin Bart

Good Evening, the news at ten. – Psychologists at the University of Liverpool have found that smells bring back detailed memories and are more powerful than pictures or words. The researchers tested more than 100 people, using 27 smells, including oranges, boot polish, vinegar, menthol and ink.
Dr. Simon Chu, a psychology lecturer at the University of Liverpool, says that the participants were first given words, then pictures and finally they were exposed to the smells. – Smells brought back the strongest memories. The memories were clearer and more intense than the memories brought about by words or pictures. The smell of an apple is stronger than the sight of an apple. This is the first study which examines the link between memory, smell, words and pictures.

8

● Joe is **absolutely** crazy.
● You're **completely** mad.
● I had dinner with Ramon. He's **incredibly** nice. The whole evening was **simply** wonderful.
● The musical was **absolutely** great.

H6

Aromatherapy is at least 6000 years old. It began in Egypt. The Egyptians massaged their bodies with fragrant oils after bathing. The Greeks used the oils medically and wrote many books about herbal medicine. The Romans improved the medical knowledge from the Greeks and started to import products from East India and Arabia. It wasn't until the 19th century that scientists in Europe began researching the effects of essential oils. In 1937, a French chemist published a book about the healing powers of oils and

called it aromatherapy. He began his research after discovering how fast his burnt hand healed when using lavender oil. Essential oils are very expensive. 2000 kg of rose petals are needed to make 1 kilo of oil.

(adapted from www.aromafabric.com/product)

H7

An unfinished story
Joe took Monica to Paris on **their** honeymoon. He **knew** that she had never **been there**. She was very excited. At the airport they had to **wait for hours**. **Their plane** was delayed. Monica went to **buy two** postcards. She walked **through** the **waiting** lounge, went up some **stairs** till she found the **right** shop. On **her** way back, she followed the signs for British **Airways**. She was **sure** that she would find Joe in the same **place** – next to the **check**-in counter. Joe was **not there**. **One** minute passed, **two** minutes passed. She looked at **her** watch. The **plane** was leaving at **eight** minutes past **four**. She asked a man if he had **seen her** husband. She was getting nervous. **Half** an **hour** later, she saw Joe walking between **two** policemen. What had happened?

Revision 3

1c

1. Achoo! *(someone sneezes)* – Bless you.
2. Could I have a coffee, please? – Black or white?
3. When shall we meet? – Would Friday suit you?
4. Let's go out on Friday. – Sorry, I didn't catch that.
5. Just a bit of milk, please. – Say when.
6. Would you like to come to dinner on Saturday? – I can't, I'm afraid.
7. I'm sorry that flight is fully booked. – Oh no!
8. Do you want to come round for coffee on Sunday afternoon? – I'd love to.
9. More people learn French than German in Britain. – That's interesting.
10. See you later. – See you at eight then.
11. Speak to you soon. – Take care.
12. So, I just quit. – You didn't, did you?
13. So, I said I wouldn't pay for it. – You didn't.
14. Yes, I'd love some coffee. – With or without?

Unit 10

3

If
I had my life to live again, I'd try to make more mistakes.
I would relax.
I would be sillier than I have been this time.
I would take more chances.

I would take more trips.
I would climb more mountains, swim more rivers and watch more sunsets.
I would eat more ice-cream and less beans.

You see, I'm one of those people who live sensibly,
hour after hour, day after day.
Oh, I have had my moments but if I had to live again,
I'd have nothing else. Just moments, one after another.

I would walk bare-footed in the spring and stay that way till the fall.
I would play more with children.
I'd pick more daisies.

5

If I Had $1,000,000

If I had a million dollars
    If I had a million dollars
Well I'd buy you a house
    I would buy you a house
And if I had a million dollars
    If I had a million dollars
I'd buy you furniture for your house
    Maybe a nice chesterfield or an ottoman
And if I had a million dollars
    If I had a million dollars
Well I'd buy you a Ka car
    A nice reliant automobile
And if I had a million dollars
I'd buy your love

If I had a million dollars
I'd build a tree fort in our yard
If I had a million dollars
You could help, it wouldn't be that hard
If I had a million dollars
Maybe we could put a little tiny fridge in there somewhere
You know we could just go up there and like hang out
Like open the fridge and stuff

If I had a million dollars
    If I had a million dollars
Well I'd buy you a fur coat
    But not a real fur coat that's cruel
And if I had a million dollars
    If I had a million dollars
Well I'd buy you an exotic pet
    Yep, like a llama or an emu
And if I had a million dollars
    If I had a million dollars
Well I'd buy you John Merrick's remains
    Ooh, all them crazy elephant bones
And if I had a million dollars
I'd buy your love
If I had a million dollars
    We wouldn't have to walk to the store
If I had a million dollars
    We'd take a limousine 'cause it costs more
If I had a million dollars
    We wouldn't have to eat Kraft dinner
But we would eat Kraft dinner
Of course we would. We'd just eat more
And buy really expensive ketchups with it
That's right. All the fanciest – Dijon ketchup

If I had a million dollars
 If I had a million dollars
Well I'd buy you a green dress
 But not a real green dress that's cruel
And if I had a million dollars
 If I had a million dollars
Well I'd buy you some art
 A Picasso or a Garfunkel
And if I had a million dollars
 If I had a million dollars
Well I'd buy you a monkey
 Haven't you always wanted a monkey?
And if I had a million dollars
I'd buy your love

If I had a million dollars
If I had a million dollars
If I had a million dollars
If I had a million dollars
If I had a million dollars
I'd be rich

from "Born on a Pirate Ship"
by The Barenaked Ladies

6

The rich man and the poor man
Once upon a time, God the traveller felt very tired and since it was already dark, he looked for somewhere to sleep. He saw two houses opposite each other – one large and beautiful, the other small and poor. God thought to himself:
"I am sure I can stay in the big house. It obviously belongs to a rich man."
He knocked on the door. The rich man opened a window and asked the man what he wanted.
"I need somewhere to sleep."
The rich man looked at the man's shabby clothes, and since he did not seem to have any money, he shook his head and said:
"I cannot take you in. My rooms are full of seeds and if I had to take in every single person who knocked on my door, I would be just as poor as they are."
He closed the window and left the man standing outside.
So God turned his back and walked towards the poor house. The poor man immediately opened the door and asked him to come in.
"Stay with us," he said. "You cannot walk any further tonight."
The wife of the poor man welcomed him and gave him something to eat – potatoes and some goat's milk. She whispered to her husband:
"Dear husband, listen, we will make a bed of hay for ourselves tonight – the traveller can sleep in our bed and have a good rest."
The next morning, they gave their guest some bread but before God left their house, he told them:
"Because you have been so kind and so friendly, I will grant you three wishes."
The poor man replied:
"If I had three wishes, I would choose: health and something to eat every day. But I can't think of anything else."

"Wouldn't you like to live in a new house?"
"Oh, yes," said the man. "If that was possible, we would be extremely happy." God granted them their wishes, blessed them and left.

It was late when the rich man got up. He looked out of the window and could not believe his eyes. He called his wife and said:
"Where is the old house? Go over and find out what has happened."
As soon as the wife came back and told her husband, he was very angry.
"I could kill myself – the traveller was here first and I sent him away."
"Hurry!" said his wife. "Go after the traveller."

When the rich man found the traveller, he pretended to be kind and told God that he was sorry about the night before. "If you come back, you can stay with us." Then he asked God if he could also have three wishes.
"Go home, you can have your wishes, but they won't do you any good."

On the way home, the rich man told his horse:
"Calm down, Liese, I have to think."
He could not concentrate and got so angry with his horse that he shouted impatiently:
"I wish you would break your neck."
As soon as he said that, the horse dropped dead. The first wish had come true.

The rich man took the saddle over his shoulders and started walking home. The saddle was heavy and it was a hot day. He felt tired and thought of his wife, sitting in a cool room.
"If only she were sitting on this saddle." As soon as he said the last word, the saddle disappeared. The second wish had come true.

The rich man hurried home.
"Please, get me off this saddle," his wife said. And that was his third wish!
His wishes did not bring him all the riches of the world – only anger and a dead horse. But the poor man lived happily ever after in his new and beautiful house.
(translated from Grimm's Fairy Tales)

9

(sentence stress)
Time
Time is too **short** when you are **busy**.
Too **long** when you are **sad**,
too **slow** when you are **waiting**
but time –
time is too **fast** when you're **in love**.

H6

Studio reporter:
The biggest threat to health today is not cancer, nor heart disease but it's actually lack of time. This was the shock finding of a nation-wide survey in England. The survey revealed that people today are too

busy to take proper care of themselves.

In the studio today we have Doctor Singh, from the Centre for Stress Management, who is going to look at the problem of stress and its impact on our health. If you have any questions you would like to be answered by our team of doctors, please write to our magazine 'Health and Living' 'Doctor Q & A' in London NW3.

Dr. Singh:
Our survey has shown that lack of time has a huge impact on our health. Heart disease, diabetes and high blood pressure are all on the increase. People eat, drink and smoke more when they're under stress. Although you can't change your lifestyle overnight, we all need to take our health more seriously. Prevention is the key. Start by changing small things in your daily routine. It's easy once you know how. It only takes a minute to drink a glass of water. You need to drink at least 8 glasses of water a day. This will help you concentrate better and might even stop your migraines. You also need to eat five portions of fruit and vegetables a day. Drink a glass of fruit juice for breakfast, or eat fruit salad for dessert. Take a vitamin pill if you don't find the time. It doesn't take you longer than five minutes to eat an apple or an orange. Don't skip meals and avoid junk food.

If you use a computer at work, take a five-minute break every thirty minutes to exercise . Your eyes and your back need a rest. Move your head gently from side to side, shrug your shoulders and shake out your arms and legs.
Regular meditation can reduce stress and lower blood pressure. Sit comfortably with your back straight, shut your eyes and concentrate on your breathing for 10 minutes. Keep your breathing slow and deep.
It takes only 20 minutes to get more active. Exercise can help you lose weight. Try walking part of the way to work, or go for a walk at lunchtime. Join a health club and have a sauna or a complete body massage. Find 20 minutes in the evening for a relaxing bath or just lie back and relax. Put your feet up on the sofa and enjoy doing nothing.

H8

There **was** an Old **Man** of **Berlin**
Whose **form** was uncommonly **thin**;
Till he **once**, by **mistake**,
Was **mixed up** in a **cake**,
So they **baked** that Old **Man** of **Berlin**.

There **was** an Old **Man**, who when **little**
Fell casually into a **kettle**;
But, growing too **stout**,
He could **never** get out,
So he **passed** all his **life** in that **kettle**.

Tapescripts

Unit 11

4a

1. ● What did you buy?
   ■ I don't know what it's called in English. It's round; it's something like a pot in which you can cook things quickly, you know, with steam pressure. It's excellent for potatoes – they only take about 10 minutes!

2. ● I need – eh – what do you call it? It's a thing you need to cut the hair off the face!

3. ● What's that stuff?
   ■ I don't know the word in English. It's stuff to clean the frying pan. The dishwasher doesn't get it clean enough.

4. ● It's a kind of cylinder made of wood and it's used for rolling out pastry. I want to make an apple pie today. What's that in English?

5. ● How do you call that? It's a machine that takes up the dust from the carpet.

4d

Lovers lie around in it.
Broken glass is found in it.
Grass.
I like that stuff.

Tuna fish get trapped in it.
Legs come wrapped in it.
Nylon.
I like that stuff.

Eskimos and tramps chew it.
Madame Tussaud gave status to it.
Wax.
I like that stuff.

Cigarettes are lit by it.
Pensioners get happy when they sit by it.
Fire.
I like that stuff.

Well, I like that stuff.
Yes, I like that stuff.
The earth
Is made of earth.
And I like that stuff.

(adapted from Adrian Mitchell's poem)

5a

It consists of a light frame covered with thin material. You'll soon find out that a newspaper is better than a magazine and a seashore is a better place than a street. At first it will take off if you run, so you may have to try several times. Unfortunately, it falls down easily and so it takes some skill. But don't give up – it's easy to learn. Even young children can enjoy it. Once you know how, you won't meet with any difficulties. For this activity, you need lots of space. If the weather changes and it starts raining, pull it down. The rain will bring it down very fast. Too many people doing the same thing can also bring about problems. If you don't want it to blow away, a rock is a good anchor. Enjoy it, it can be very peaceful.

7

(K = Kay, Kl = Ms Kline)
K: Well, Sarah, you know, packing presents in boxes is very popular at the moment. I'll show you the two we are planning to introduce on the market. This one here is very light. It's called 'Harmony'.
Kl: How much does it weigh?
K: It weighs approximately 180 g.
Kl: What's it made of?
K: Recycled paper.
Kl: Could you tell me which colours you do?
K: We have 'Harmony' boxes in red, blue, yellow and green.
Kl: What are its dimensions?
K: As you can see, it's rectangular – it's 21 cm long, 15 cm wide and 8 cm high. The other new product is more traditional. This range is called 'Victoria'.
Kl: This is not as light. What material is it made of?
K: It's made of cardboard and weighs just over two hundred and sixty gram.
Kl: What size is it?
K: It's 30 cm in diameter and 12 cm high.
Kl: It's very pretty.
K: Yes, this box has been inspired by the round hat boxes, which were very popular in the 19th century. Today they are ideal for packing presents of all kinds. You can get the Victoria range in different patterns, striped, with dots or with stars.
Kl: Could you tell me how much they cost?
K: The retail price for Harmony is 60 pence. Victoria is more expensive. It costs £1.70.
Kl: How long does delivery take?
K: Usually between one and two weeks.

H1

1. You know I lost my job last month. I was so disappointed, but you wouldn't believe it! I have been offered an even better job by another company. As the saying goes "as one door closes, another one opens".
2. Politicians hold most of their meetings in secret – "behind closed doors". We don't really know what is going on.
3. Mary went to speak to the class teacher a number of times this month – you know – because of Mark. But the last time she was there, the teacher said she was not willing to talk to her anymore. She really "shut the door in her face".

H8

● How heavy is it?
■ It's very light – around 200g.

● What's it made of?
■ Cardboard.

● What's it used for?
■ It's mostly used for cornflakes.

● What size is it?
■ It's 30 cm high and 10 cm wide.

● What does it cost?
■ If you order more than a thousand packets, it costs 10 pence per packet.

H9b

im**mor**al, im**bal**ance, im**prob**able, im**per**sonal
in**ex**pensive, in**acc**urate, ine**ffic**ient, in**corr**ect
un**pleas**ant, un**heal**thy, un**known**, un**cer**tain

Unit 12

3a

● seventy p
● seventeen
● one hundred and eight dollars
● five hundred and fifty-five
● nine thousand nine hundred and ninety-nine pounds
● one hundred and fifty-five thousand four hundred and seventeen Euros
● a quarter
● five million nine hundred and eighty-seven thousand three hundred and seventy nine
● three quarters

3b

● ninety
● two thirds
● three hundred and thirty
● eighteen thousand eight hundred and six
● three hundred and thirteen
● seventy thousand
● one half
● forty thousand nine hundred and fourteen
● three million six hundred and sixty-five thousand seven hundred and seventeen

4b

(E = Mr Enderby, I = Interviewer)
I: Mr Enderby, you are the President of the Universal Esperanto Association. Can you tell us something about Esperanto?
E: Esperanto is an artificial language – a mix of different languages. It was invented in 1887 by Ludwig Zamenhof, a young Jewish doctor from Poland. His idea was to create an easy, international language which could be understood by the many different ethnic groups living in Poland at that time. Esperanto was first published in 1887 under the pseudonym Dr

Esperanto meaning 'one who hopes'. The name became the name of the language itself.

I: How many people speak Esperanto?

E: Nobody really knows the answer. A world-wide census has never been taken. However, according to a survey by Professor Culbert from the University of Washington, Esperanto is spoken by about two million speakers. It is also estimated that a thousand people speak Esperanto as their first language.

I: How easy is Esperanto to learn?

E: We estimate that Esperanto is up to five times as easy to learn as French, ten times as easy to learn as Russian, twenty times as easy to learn as Chinese, and infinitely easier to learn than Japanese.

About 75% of its vocabulary comes from Latin and Romance languages, especially French, about 20% comes from German and English and the rest comes from Slavic languages like Russian and Polish.

Moreover, Esperanto's grammar is very simple. There are no exceptions. There is only one article, one form of a verb, one plural form. The pronunciation is easy. Every word is pronounced exactly as it is written. In about six months you can even read Shakespeare in Esperanto.

I: Can Esperanto play a role today in a world marked by globalisation and the growing dominance of English?

E: In the beginning the idea was if you had a common language, you could avoid war. We know now that this is nonsense. The Irish speak the same language and it doesn't keep them from fighting. Yet, as you said, English has become the world language. David Crystal, the world authority on languages, says that half of the world's currently spoken 6,000 languages will die out over the next century. This means on average every two weeks a language dies somewhere in the world. The use of Esperanto will slow down the process of English taking over. In this way, Esperanto has an ethical quality about it.

I: Mr. Enderby, one last question, how often has this congress been held?

E: It has been held every year since 1905 with interruptions during the two world wars.
This year our topics include AIDS research, online data security and international aid work – all in Esperanto.

I: Mr. Enderby, thank you for this interview.

E: It was my pleasure. I would like to greet the people listening to this radio broadcast in Esperanto – "Koran saluton al vi. Espereble vi baldaŭ lernos Esperanton kaj tiam ni povos komuniki pli facile kaj egale." (A hearty hello to you. Hopefully you'll soon learn Esperanto and then we'll be able to communicate more easily and equally.)

(adapted from "The Times of Malta")

5b

Interviewer:
Do you think Esperanto is more useful than English?
Speaker 1:
Sure, you can speak to your friends from all over the world, even if you don't speak their national language.
Speaker 2:
It is easier than English. The grammar is simple. You don't have to learn any exceptions.

Interviewer:
Why do you like Esperanto?
Speaker 3:
Esperanto is easy to pronounce. There are no silent letters. You pronounce the words the way they are written.
Speaker 4:
You can write to people in a dozen countries without speaking a dozen languages.

Interviewer:
Why do you think young people should learn Esperanto?
Speaker 5:
Esperanto can be used to see the world. I love back-packing and I can stay with Esperanto speakers in more than 70 countries – for free.
Speaker 6:
Esperanto is about understanding and exploring other cultures. Our national library in England has 30,000 volumes of books in Esperanto. You can read all the works by Garcia Marquez, Shakespeare, Brecht and Dante.

Interviewer:
Why learn Esperanto when you can speak English?
Speaker 7:
English is the language of McDonald's and Coca-Cola. Esperanto doesn't belong to any country or people. It belongs equally to everybody who speaks it, acting as a bridge between cultures.

8a

Chrisler is one of the most successful companies in the world. The company was started in 1985 and produced cars for the European market. Last January, a new factory was opened and 60 more workers were hired. Our cars are now sold in over 50 countries – even in Japan. Chrisler is known for its good working conditions, high wages, flexible working hours and childcare for young mothers. Two years ago, we started language classes for our workers. They can learn English, Spanish and even Japanese. Last December, we gave $10,000 to Unicef and …

H1

English, Portugu**ese**, Hung**ar**ian, French, **Tur**kish, Japan**ese**, Nor**we**gian, Greek, **Po**lish, Chin**ese**, **Ital**ian, Dutch

H5

- twenty past ten
- thirty-first of January, ninety-nine
- half past nine
- a quarter past eleven
- ten to four
- fifth of September, two thousand
- a quarter to nine
- nineteen ninety-six

H7

1.
This is the final call for British Airways Flight BA 369 to London, boarding now at Gate 11.

2.
● Good morning. My name is Mrs. Vikki Blackwell. I've booked a room for three nights.
■ Just a moment, please. Yes, Mrs. Blackwell – a single room for 3 days. It's room 586 on the fifth floor.

3.
● What time do you serve breakfast?
■ Oh, anytime till eleven, dear. Would you like bacon and eggs or a soft-boiled egg with toast and marmalade?
● Bacon and eggs, please, and a pot of tea.

4.
● Can we have the bill, please?
■ Yes certainly – I'll bring it at once. Did you enjoy your meal?
● Yes, it was lovely.
■ Your bill, madam.
● Thank you – does it include the service charge?

5.
● How much is that altogether, please?
■ That's £76.38.
● Do you accept this credit card?
■ Certainly, madam. One moment, please.

6.
● Let's see – eh – drive further down the road till you come to a roundabout. At that roundabout, go straight across – over a bridge and it's the third on the right.
■ Thank you.

7.
● Anything to drink, Sir?
■ Yes, I'll have a lager.
● Do you want a pint?
■ No thanks. Just half a pint, please.

Unit 1

4b

for my studies
for a trip to Australia
to train my brain
to talk to my business partners

4e

I am sitting …
I am waiting …

4f

1. dinner – café
2. funnies – cartoons
3. hitch – pull
4. stockings – tights

5a

1. Dear Jo – Lots of love
2. Dear Mr Green – Best wishes

5b

possible letter

Dear Sir / Madam
I would like to take a course in general
English in the UK. I'm interested in
learning in a small group and staying with
a host family. Could you please send me
your brochure and price list.
I hope to hear from you soon.
Best wishes

6b

number of activities on offer: 6
number of English lessons in one week: 15
previous experience of the activities: no

6c

1. painting / walking / horse-riding /
   tennis / golf / climbing
2. painting: old shirt
   walking: boots / good pair of shoes
   climbing / horse-riding: comfortable
   trousers / flat shoes
   tennis: white clothing / soft shoes

7a

1b Host families
2d Self-catering
3a Shared student houses
4c Hotels

7c

rooms	housework
bedroom	cooking
kitchen	cleaning
living room	shopping
bathroom	laundry

8a

1. every morning
2. always
3. once a week
4. usually
5. in the evening

6. often
7. never
8. every night

8b

definite	indefinite
1. every morning	1. always
2. once a week	2. usually
3. in the evening	3. often
4. every night	4. never

9a

1. rucksack
2. gesundheit
3. schadenfreude
4. kindergarten
5. kitschy
6. abseil

9b

possible words
1. computer
2. manager
3. sorry
4. city
5. ticket
6. cool
7. kickboard
8. T-shirt
9. sweatshirt
10. disco

H1

1. What's your nationality?
2. What does he do?
3. What are your hobbies?
4. What pets have they got?
5. How many languages can Sylvia speak?

H2

1. trousers
2. boots
3. coat
4. jacket
5. T-shirt
6. suit
7. shirt
8. blouse
9. jumper
10. dress

missing words: socks & shoes

H3a

1. always
2. normally
3. usually
4. often
5. sometimes

H3c

1. have a snack
2. have breakfast
3. have a coffee
4. have dinner

H5

1. I'm learning English at the moment.
2. Every Sunday he plays tennis with his
   friends.

3. We work for a large international
   company.
4. Sylvia usually gets up at 8.00 am.
5. I don't eat meat or fish.
6. He has got a new job.
7. Sylvia's having a holiday in Portugal
   this week.
8. They're watching the football match
   now.
9. This month we're doing an English
   course.
10. Boris never works on Sundays.

H7

Start:
Dear Mr Smith
Dear James

Finish:
Best regards
Lots of love

H8

1f, 2d, 3a, 4e, 5c, 6b

H9

1. I'm **an** engineer for Dupont.
2. I'm **from** Sweden.
3. I **can** speak **a** little Spanish.
4. Good **to** see you again.
5. Where **do** you work?

Unit 2

1a

1. That's a nice jacket!
2. What a great flat!
3. That haircut really suits you!
4. You look really fit!

3a

1. never; 2. yes; 3. yes

3b

Partner A
Have you ever swum/ridden/done/run/
abseiled …

Partner B
Have you ever watched/driven/eaten/
spent/taken …

4a

title	speaker	action
The Red Nose Day	3	wear a red nose
The Boxing Day Dip	1	swim in the sea
Hit the Roof Day	2	abseil down a mountain

4b

1. false; 2. false; 3. false; 4. false; 5. true;
6. false

4c

1. Anthony didn't swim on Christmas
   Day. He swam on Boxing Day.
2. He didn't run to the river. He ran into
   the sea.
3. Jenny didn't wear a blue plastic nose.
   She wore a red nose.

4. She didn't collect £100 for charity. She collected £150.
5. Gill abseiled down a mountain.
6. It didn't take her 10 hours. It took her 10 minutes.

4e
1. Yesterday I wanted to go to town.
2. Have you ever been to Italy?
3. Ten years ago Mauro did a parachute jump for charity.
4. They have never run in a marathon.
5. Did you watch the Olympics on TV last night?
6. George didn't swim at the weekend because he had a cold.
7. I have flown in a helicopter before.
8. Did Enzo live here five years ago?
9. When was Boxing Day last year?
10. I decided to stay at home last weekend.

5

	[id]	[d]	[t]
1.	collected	abseiled	looked
2.	wanted	agreed	walked
3.	decided	stayed	smoked

7a
1. Early Bird Workout
2. Starter Step / Starter Aerobics
3. Spinning
4. Yoga

8
1. This is Miss Taffy from DCD.
2. I would like some information …
3. Would you like me to send …
4. Sorry, could you repeat that, please?
5. Thank you very much for your help.
6. Thank you for calling. Bye.

H1
1. to run a race
2. to ride a bike
3. to relieve stress
4. to harmonise mind & body
5. to play squash
6. to become a couch potato
7. to join a gym
8. to get fit

'to become a couch potato' is not a healthy 'activity'.

H2
1. do aerobics
2. go jogging
3. do abseiling
4. go swimming
5. go trekking
6. do exercise
7. do yoga
8. go running

H3
1. What is Red Nose Day?
2. When is Red Nose Day?
3. What is special about Red Nose Day?

4. What sort of things do people do?
5. Who gets involved?
6. Where is the money spent?

H4
1. I've been to Indonesia.
2. I went mountain climbing last weekend.
3. Have you ever ridden a camel?
4. He has run in three marathons.
5. It took him 10 hours to drive home yesterday.
6. Ten years ago we lived in Brazil.
7. We haven't swum in the Mediterranean.
8. Last year I collected £150 for charity.
9. Have they spent all their money?
10. They've never thought about going on a balloon trip.

H5
see tapescripts

H6a
1c, 2d, 3a, 4b

H7
possible suggestions
1. Why don't you take an aspirin?
2. Have you thought about doing sports at the weekend?
3. Have you tried setting your alarm clock half an hour earlier than is necessary?
4. Try taking one day free each week.
5. Why don't you get off the sofa and do something?

Unit 3

1a
1. headlights; 2. bonnet; 3. windscreen;
4. mirror; 5. indicator; 6. wing;
7. steering wheel; 8. rear lights; 9. boot;
10. petrol tank; 11. tyre; 12. wheel

1c
1. false; 2. false; 3. true

1d
1. map; 2. diagram; 3. phrase book;
4. guide book; 5. bible

1f
1. for over 30 years
2. since 1973
3. for the last 20 years
4. since 1986
5. since 1990

1. The Wheelers have written about their travels for over 30 years.
2. Since 1973 'Asia on the Cheap' has sold over half a million copies.
3. For the last 20 years the 'Lonely Planet' books have become very popular with independent travellers.
4. Since 1986 'The Lonely Planet Publications' have donated a percentage of the income from each

book to Third World Projects.
5. Since 1990 the Wheelers have produced phrase books.

2b
possible sentences
1. Mike has become fitter, healthier and more motivated.
2. Martin has become lazier, bigger and more serious / more boring.
3. Martia has become richer, smarter and more successful.

3a

		all	some	none
1.	standard kitchen facilities	✔		
2.	dishwasher		✔	
3.	shower & bath		✔	
4.	jacuzzi			✔
5.	fireplace			✔
6.	swimming pool			✔

3b
1. some; 2. any; 3. any; 4. some; 5. any

3c
Dear Mr Scot,
I'd like to make a firm booking for Strawberry Cottage for one week from 14th May to 21st May. I will send a cheque for £100 sterling as a deposit.
Could you please send me written confirmation of this booking.
Thank you in advance.
Best wishes

4b
Elaine's: bath, balcony, single, breakfast, Check, check, deposit, cancel, deposit

Ruidoso: fireplaces, fridge, stove, utensils, pillows, furniture, deposit

6
1. van; 2. fairy; 3. very; 4. view; 5. fast

7a
places: somewhere, anywhere
people: somebody, anybody
things: something, anything

7b&c
1. somewhere – swimming pool
2. something – guide book
3. anything – breakfast
4. somebody – independent traveller
5. something – deposit
6. anywhere – accommodation

H1
1. We've got some suntan lotion.
2. We haven't got any plasters.
3. Have we got any water bottles?
4. We haven't got any insect repellent.
5. We've got some accommodation.
6. Have we got any guide books?

H2

heat
1. fireplace
2. microwave
3. stove
4. oven

water
1. bath
2. dishwasher
3. fridge
4. shower

coffee machine

H3

	UK	Germany
people	funnier	more efficient
lifestyle	more expensive	cheaper
cars	slower	bigger / faster
homes	larger	smaller
holidays	shorter	longer / more exotic

H4b

	simple past	infinitive
1.	drew	draw
2.	drove	drive
3.	went	go
4.	were	be
5.	was	be
6.	knew	know
7.	brought	bring
8.	made	make

H5a

1. since last week
2. for 2 weeks
3. for a long time
4. since 1st January
5. since this morning
6. for a decade
7. since the spring
8. for 10 years

H6a

was, spent, is, has published, won, has gone, was, lives

H7

1. guide book
2. travel book
3. phrase book
4. bible
5. brochure

H8a

1. double room
2. room rates
3. written confirmation
4. advance reservation
5. receipt of payment
6. private bath

H9

furniture, balance, accommodation, Asia, countryside, Turkey, mountain, cabins confirmation, result, fascinated, Nepal, independent, facilities, equipped, exclusive

Revision Unit 1

1a

1. furniture
2. kitchen facilities
3. sports
4. accommodation
5. transport
6. nationalities

1c

1. lake
2. self-catering
3. spinning
4. shower
5. queue
6. charity
7. deposit

missing word: leisure

2

1d, 2e, 3a, 4b, 5f, 6c

3

Partner A – possible questions
1. When did Tony and his wife travel to Australia?
2. Where did they drive across?
3. How much profit did they make (on the van)?
4. Where did they go by bus and train?
5. Where did they take a boat to?
6. What did Maureen bring home at weekends?
7. What did they print? / What did they spend all their savings on?

Partner B– possible questions
1. Where did Tony and his wife travel in the 1970's?
2. How much did their mini-van cost?
3. How did they travel through Pakistan and India?
4. Where did they trek?
5. What did people ask them about?
6. What did Tony draw?

4

1. any / any
2. ever / never
3. Did / didn't
4. buy / did
5. Are / am

Unit 4

2a

1. false; 2. true; 3. false; 4. true

2b

1. lazy
2. working couples / workers
3. speed up
4. fight over
5. nothing
6. sickness

3a

must – want to change your lifestyle
don't have to – do everything on your list
mustn't – forget your list completely

3b

1. mustn't
2. don't have to
3. must
4. don't have to
5. must

4a

possible questions and answers
Partner A
1. must
   Q: What are the regulations for overtime?
   A: When you do overtime you must leave the office before 8.00p.m.

   Q: Are there any rules about private calls?
   A: When you make a private call you must first dial '0' before the number.

2. don't have to
   Q: What are the dress regulations?
   A: You don't have to wear a suit unless you are seeing a customer.

   Q: Can you tell me about the flexitime system?
   A: Well, you don't have to start and finish at the same time every day – you can choose when you start and when you finish.

3. mustn't
   Q: Can I smoke anywhere in the company?
   A: Well, you mustn't smoke in the canteen, or the cafeteria, or the meeting rooms.

   Q: What about the travel expenses regulations?
   A: Well, it's quite simple really – you mustn't claim for anything that was not for the company.

Partner B
1. must
   Q: What are the regulations for meetings?
   A: Well, you must attend weekly meetings.

   Q: Are there any rules about travel expenses?
   A: You must put in your travel expenses form in the same month as your business trip.

2. don't have to
   Q: What about holiday entitlement?
   A: You don't have to take your holiday at any special time – you can decide.

Q: Can you tell me about the flexitime system?
A: Well, you don't have to start work before 9.00 but you can come at 7.30 if you want to.

3. mustn't
Q: What are the regulations for overtime?
A: Well, you mustn't do more than 10 hours overtime in a week.

Q: What about private phone calls?
A: Well, it's quite simple really – you mustn't phone privately on company costs.

4b
possible e-mail answer
From:
To: paula-marsden@dcd.de

Dear Paula
Thanks for your e-mail. We don't really have many rules but I'll list what I can think of.
Someone in the department must be at the office from 8.30 in the morning to answer the phone for customers. You must always tell colleagues when you go on your lunch break.
We have a tea and coffee group where we all pay 15 euros a month, but you don't have to join if you don't want to. We also meet the first Thursday in the month for a drink after work, but again you don't have to come if you are busy.
There is a no-smoking policy in our department so you mustn't smoke anywhere.
See you soon.
…

5a

British	American
mobile (phone)	cell(ular) phone
colleagues	co-workers
company	enterprise
personnel department	human resources
curriculum vitae	résumé
managing director	president

6a
1. the highest salary
2. the friendliest colleagues
3. the securest job
4. the best opportunities

7c
but, although, or, however

7d
1 although
2. However
3. or
4. but

8a
possible scale
love, enjoy, like, dislike, can't stand, hate

9
words with silent letters b and k
battle
knowledge
bom**b**
horrible
knee
sparkling
know
thum**b**
com**b**
lam**b**
knife

H1

	time	depart-ments	places
1.	overtime	sales	meeting room
2.	working hours	service	reception
3.	flexitime	personnel	canteen
4.	break	marketing	office

H2
from, to, through, on, on, to, back, back, for

H3a
to smile

H3b
1. You mustn't treat customers as enemies.
2. You don't have to talk to customers within 30 seconds.
3. You must smile at the customers!
4. You don't have to give product advice if it's not appropriate.
5. You must treat customers as you'd like to be treated!

H4

	American		British
1.	downtown	a.	city centre
2.	cellular	b.	mobile
3.	co-worker	c.	colleague
4.	restrooms	d.	toilets
5.	line	e.	queue
6.	subway	f.	underground
7.	check	g.	cheque

H5
1. drawer
2. boss
3. overtime
4. break
5. flexitime
6. canteen
7. pager
8. co-workers
9. colleagues
10. reception
11. lift
12. department

missing word: working world

H6a
Speaker 1: boss of own company
Speaker 2: sales assistant in a book shop
Speaker 3: language teacher

H6b
speaker 1

love	being my own boss
enjoy	sitting at my own desk
like	starting work at 6.00 a.m.
can't stand	writing invoices
hate	waiting to be paid

speaker 2

love	working with books
enjoy	talking to the customers
like	getting a discount on the books
can't stand	working on Saturdays
hate	starting work at 8.00

speaker 3

love	helping them to learn a language
enjoy	working with people
like	looking at new coursebooks
can't stand	preparing lessons at the weekend
hate	photocopying

Unit 5

1b
comfortable – uncomfortable
convenient – inconvenient
efficient – inefficient
reliable – unreliable
expensive – inexpensive
time-consuming – time-saving

1c
upward movement: skyrocket, increase, grow
downward movement: drop, fall, decrease

2a
1. If you use a digital camera, you can easily transfer pictures to your computer.
2. If you play a DVD (digital versatile disc), you have a perfect sound and a perfect picture.
3. If you have an ISDN line, you can surf the net and phone at the same time.
4. If you use the text message service on your mobile, your message arrives in a few seconds.
5. If you have an MP3 file on your computer, you can download songs from the internet.

3b
The speaker is going to
▓ attend a computer course.
▓ learn how to surf the internet.
▓ learn how to send e-mails.
▓ use an interactive language CD-ROM.

4a

Sandra's mail: g, e, f, a, c
James' mail: d, b, j, h, i

4b

opening
With reference to your advert …
Thank you for your mail.

requesting
Could you please send me …

closing
Best wishes
Best regards

4c

possible e-mail

Dear Sir / Madam
With reference to your advert on the 'Computer World' web page, I'm interested in buying a flat screen for my computer. Could you please send me some information about different flat screens and your current price list.
I look forward to receiving the information from you.

Best regards
John Marvis

possible e-mail reply

Dear John
Thank you for your mail. I'm happy to send you all the brochures we have on flat screens. You will see that there is a big difference in the price range.
If you have any more questions, please contact me by mail or phone (0101 5689320).

Best wishes
Janice Roberts
(Marketing Manager)

6a

possible sentences
1. If you work too long at the computer, you'll get a headache.
2. If you turn off the computer without saving first, you'll lose all the new text.
3. If you don't have any paper in your printer, your printer won't print / will block.
4. If you forget your e-mail password, you won't get any new e-mails.

7a

www.visitbritain.com – tourism in Great Britain
www.hueber.de – buying language books
www.amazon.de – buying all kinds of books
www.travelclub.de – booking cheap flights and hiring cars

7b

1. As soon as possible.
2. See you.
3. easy

4. I see.
5. later
6. Oh, I see.
7. please
8. thanks
9. who, what, when, where, why
10. Write back.

8a

The speaker gets permission in dialogue 1.

8b

may, could, can

9

● •
colleague
mobile
office
commerce
moment
chocolate

• ●
reply
connect

• ● •
develop
important
computer
commuter

● • •
atmosphere
internet
salary
résumé

10a

1. A big face
2. As sweet as caviar
3. The wrong lines
4. The small pistol
5. The new coat

10c

parts of the body: ears, eyes, teeth

10d

Example:
She's got short blonde hair. She's wearing an orange sweater. She's jogging in the woods.

H1

1. lap top / palm top
2. telecommuter
3. surf
4. fax / e-mail
5. world wide web
6. crashed
7. electronic equipment
8. attend
9. e-commerce
10. dot

H2

1. If he catches the 8.20 train, he will be in Hamburg at 12.30 pm.

2. If you send me an email with the details, I will order it for you.
3. They will miss the concert if they arrive at 9.00 pm.
4. If she doesn't come tonight, I won't see her until after my holiday.
5. If the company asks you to have a home office, will you take it?
6. I'll cancel the barbecue party, if it rains tomorrow.

H3

possible sentences
1. May I open the window?
2. Excuse me, could I borrow your lighter?
3. Excuse me, could I move your rucksack so that I can sit here?
4. Can I have your car this afternoon to collect my parents from the airport, please?
5. May I use your kickboard this week, please?

H4a

c. a Japanese robot

H4b

'We are going to make as many AIBO's as the customers in Japan, the United States and Europe want.'
The heads of marketing are meeting in Tokyo next week to analyse how many additional orders for AIBO, the entertainment robot model, are expected. The Head of the European Company is staying in Tokyo for one week, too. From the beginning of April, the factories in Tokyo are shipping the goods to Europe. The Sony press relations officer added that 'Sony is going to create more different robots in the future.'

H5

Dear Sir / Madam
With reference to your advertisement in the weekly edition of 'The Electronic', I would like to have more information about your range of products. Could you please send me your latest product brochure and current price list?
I look forward to hearing from you in the near future.
Best wishes
Jennifer Hendrix

H6a

	car	body
1.	wheels	legs, feet
2.	lights	eyes
3.	boot	head, brain
4.	petrol tank	stomach
5.	horn	mouth
possible words		
6.	doors	hands
7.	indicator	back
8.	windscreen	arms
9.	mirror	ears
10.	gear stick	nose

Unit 6

1c
Lindsey: a, e, d
Nick: c, f, b

2b
verb + infinitive
plan to exercise
decide to improve
hope to stay
offer to help

verb + -ing form
finish doing
keep working
postpone booking
stop eating
imagine looking
continue being

4a
Jenny: sailing
Sue: going to a beauty clinic, relaxing
Sandra: walking
Mike: working

4c
1. leaves; 2. are visiting; 3. is taking;
4. starts; 5. am flying; 6. are going

5a
1. false; 2. false; 3. true; 4. false; 5. true

5c
1. fundamental; 2. recommendations;
3. environment; 4. combination;
5. prevent

6
[s] place, person, sink, message, sailing, symbolic
[z] sometimes, eyes, clothes, visit, surprise, result

7a
Brian: Tuesday 3:00 p.m. / same place
Paul: Tuesday 8.30 a.m. / at the airport
Elfie: next Tuesday

H1
1. meeting; 2. to go; 3. playing; 4. to look;
5. attending; 6. to jog; 7. watching;
8. living; 9. to spend; 10. smiling

H2a
living room: sofa, television, table, chair, armchair, lamp, bookcase, picture, stereo set, carpet

H2b
bedroom
1. bed; 2. lamp; 3. wardrobe;
4. cupboard; 5. curtains

kitchen
1. fridge; 2. oven; 3. chair; 4. sink;
5. dishwasher

bathroom
1. bath; 2. shower; 3. basin; 4. mirror;
5. toilet

study
1. desk; 2. computer; 3. printer; 4. phone;
5. shelves

H3a
possible sentences
1. You should get some fresh air.
2. You ought to do some stretching exercises.
3. You should listen to some calm music.
4. You ought to go to bed earlier.
5. You should drink some peppermint tea.
6. You ought to try yoga.

H3b
1. The single mum never has any time for herself.
2. The manager never has time to do nothing.
3. The schoolboy doesn't have any free time for his hobby skateboarding.

H4
1. to cope with stress
2. to be calm
3. to let off steam
4. to relax the muscles
5. to focus the mind

H5a
1. The train arrives at 3 p.m.
2. What are you doing tonight?
3. My sister is coming to visit next Friday.
4. The flight arrives in Düsseldorf at 13.15.
5. The conference starts at 9.30 a.m. with an opening talk by Professor Hill.
6. Phil and Charlie are sailing in the Netherlands this weekend.
7. I'm having a party next Friday.
8. Does the ferry depart at 11.20 tomorrow?
9. We aren't visiting friends this weekend after all because our car has broken down.
10. Don't forget that the meeting begins at 2.30 this afternoon!

H6
healthy, medicine, energy, diet, emotional, imbalanced, colour, harmonise, conventional

H7
1. calm; 2. cause; 3. cope; 4. couple;
5. keep; 6. course; 7. cycle; 8. conflict;
9. continue

Revision 2

1
The verbs
A: to arrange a meeting
B: to be calm
C: to commute from home to work
D: to disagree with an opinion
E: to enter a room (to come in)
F: to fax a letter (electronically)
G: to go to the cinema
H: to hurry when you are late
I: to invest money at the bank
J: to jog in the park
K: to keep working (not to stop)
L: to let off steam
M: to meet friends at the weekend

The nouns
N: There's nobody here yet.
O: What's your opinion on this subject?
P: With my palm top I can type on the train.
Q: The queen is the head of GB.
R: refridgerator
S: I've got a stomach-ache.
T: My toes are on the end of my feet!
U: The underground in Paris is called the Metro.
V: The flowers look nice in that vase.
W: A massage gives a feeling of well-being.
X: Joker!
Y: Yoga is a relaxing sport.
Z: A zebra is an animal which has black and white stripes.

2
1. The Eurotrain leaves at 6.45 tomorrow.
2. I don't think there will be a unified Europe in the future.
3. This weekend I'm just going to relax.
4. Are you attending the meeting on Friday morning?
5. In ten years time the mobile will be the only form of phone.
6. In my new job I won't work at the weekend.
7. In June I'm flying to Jamaica.
8. Will the Euro exist in 20 years' time?

3
1d, 2c, 3a, 4e, 5b

4
1. call; 2. repeat; 3. phone; 4. forward;
5. e-mail; 6. thanks; 7. best; 8. memo;
9. flexitime; 10. holiday entitlement;
11. telecommuter

missing word: appointment

5a
telecommute, internet, e-mails, stress, feng shui, working time, overtime, live, live

Unit 7

1b
1. a novel; 2. a detective story;
3. a children's book

1c
1. crowded; 2. bus ride; 3. brake; 4. stare;
5. unusual; 6. midnight

2a

Baba was taking Ammu to the hospital (1) when the car broke down (2).

Chee saw a man (2) walking down the road (1).

The man was walking down the center of the road (1) while carrying a whisky bottle (1).

2b

1. Sandra was making the salad while Mauro was cooking the pasta.
2. Pedro was steering the boat while Rosa was holding the sails.
3. The children were swimming in the sea while their mother was lying on the beach.
4. I was phoning on the mobile while Phil was surfing the internet.
5. We were having a party while our neighbours were trying to sleep.

2e

were sitting, was passing, was holding, heard, look, was running, ran, were running, was … doing, was … holding

3a

1. at the train station
2. in New Zealand
3. at work

3b

filler words: Well / Actually / So
words to show interest: Really / Oh / Oh no / What happened then?

4a

1. weather report
2. children's programme
3. film
4. news
5. comedy programme
6. commercials
7. quiz
8. chat shows
9. documentary programmes
10. soap operas

5b

1. You have to stay in the house.
2. You needn't be an actress or actor.
3. You have to agree that the viewers can watch every moment of your life.
4. You needn't be a pop singer.
5. You need to be an extrovert.
6. You need to have lots of self-confidence.

6a

1. no; 2. no; 3. yes; 4. no; 5. yes

6b

Would you like to …?
Do you fancy …?

I'm afraid, I can't …
I'm sorry, I'm …

That would be lovely.
I'd love to.

6e

An invitation
We would like to invite you to our English workshop weekend on Saturday 26th June. The workshop will last two days and all meals and drinks will be included. Please let us know in writing if you wish to attend.

An acceptance
I would like to accept your invitation to the English workshop on Saturday 26th June. Could you inform me of the costs of the workshop and if you could provide accommodation. Would it be possible to send us a map and a description of how to get to the school? …

A declination
… I'm afraid I can't come to the English workshop on Saturday 26th June as I'm on a business trip. However, if you hold another workshop later on in the year, I will be very interested in receiving more details. …

H1a

Where? – Cyprus.
When? – First three weeks in May.
Why? – Annual holiday.
Who with? – Nobody.

H1b

1. false; 2. false; 3. true; 4. false; 5. false;
6. false

H2a

1. While the detectives were talking to the reporter, the police team was looking for the criminal.
2. When the elephant arrived all the other animals were talking.
3. The peace talks broke down last night.
4. Batman was speaking to Robin in a quiet voice when the Joker appeared.
5. Every film star I met in Hollywood had a guru.
6. Mozart died at the age of 35 in 1791.

H2b

1. detective story
2. children's book
3. newspaper
4. comic
5. magazine
6. history / biography

H3

factual
1. chat; 2. quiz; 3. news; 4. weather; 5. documentary

fictional
1. comedy; 2. soap; 3. film

mixture of both
1. children's programme; 2. commercial

H4

have to, have to, need, needn't, needn't, need

H5

possible sentences
1. I'd love to, but I've got no money at the moment.
2. I'm afraid, I can't. I'm afraid of heights.
3. That would be lovely/great.
4. I'm sorry, I can't. I'm going to the cinema on Saturday.
5. I'd love to.

H6

1d, 2f, 3a, 4e, 5c, 6b

H7

Dear Roberto
I'm writing to confirm our appointment on the morning of June 29th. I arrive by train at 6.00 in the evening. I'm staying at the Sitges Hotel and would be happy to accept your dinner invitation that evening. Could you let me know when and where we should meet for dinner. I'm looking forward to seeing you next week.
Best regards / Best wishes
Lucia

H8

1. application   to apply
2. invitation   to invite
3. cancellation   to cancel
4. information   to inform
5. a walk   to walk
6. an eclipse   to eclipse
7. sleep   to sleep
8. actor/actress   to act

Unit 8

1c

1. Italians; 2. Swiss; 3. Spanish; 4. British;
5. French; 6. Germans

2

1d. India; 2a. Turkey; 3b. Malaysia;
4c. Jamaica; 5e. China

3a

1. false; 2. true; 3. true; 4. false

3c

1. is it?; 2. don't they?; 3. isn't it?;
4. doesn't she?; 5. hasn't it?

4b

1. voice goes up; 2. voice goes down;
3. up; 4. down; 5. up; 6. down

5a

13,000
300
365
2-3
30

5d
1. many; 2. much; 3. little; 4. few;
5. much; 6. little; 7. many; 8. few

6a
1. Don't be surprised if he says 'san' after your name.
2. Why don't you take him to a sushi bar?
3. Don't be nervous if he smiles all the time but doesn't speak.

6b
Sorry, did you say 'san'?
Can you spell that, please?
Sorry, I didn't catch that
You said 'smile', didn't you?

H1a
1. bride; 2. groom; 3. parents-in-law;
4. aunt; 5. niece

H1b
1. uncle; 2. grandmother; 3. son;
4. brothers; 5. nephews

H2a
1. You don't know a good street café, do you?
2. August is a rainy season in Australia, isn't it?
3. You didn't hear my music last night, did you?
4. He has a northern dialect, hasn't he?
5. You went to a sushi bar last week, didn't you?
6. You have flown on a long distance flight, haven't you?
7. He looks like a film star, doesn't he?
8. They haven't been here before, have they?

H3a
1d, 2b, 3e, 4a, 5c, 6g, 7f

H4
little, much, few, many, many, few, many, little

H5

	verb		noun
1.	to present	1.	presentation
2.	to meet	2.	meeting
3.	to discuss	3.	discussion
4.	to market	4.	marketing
5.	to produce	5.	production
6.	to begin	6.	beginning

H6
see tapescripts

H7
1.	108	his age
2.	seven	his age in 1900
3.	one	box of chocolates in 1900 celebrations
4.	three	daughters
5.	five	grandchildren
6.	91	gave up driving

Unit 9

1a
picture 1: delicious, exotic, tasty
picture 2: soft, classical, relaxing
picture 3: pleasant, strong, sweet
picture 4: regular, healthy, fit

1b
1. strong; 2. mild; 3. salty; 4. careful

1. food; 2. sport; 3. smell; 4. music

2b
A haiku poem consists of seventeen syllables in three lines of five, seven and five.

2c
It smells good.
It tastes sweet.
It feels warm.
It looks delicious.
– a birthday cake

It smells horrible.
It tastes awful.
It feels sticky.
It looks pink.
– a cough mixture

3a

what you should eat	how you will feel
worried?	
a bagel, a pretzel, cereal, crackers, rice-cake	better
stressed?	
pasta with marinara sauce, baked potato and steamed vegetables	good
tired?	
chicken, fish, salad	energetic
sleepy?	
tuna fish, beans, hard-boiled egg, yoghurt, peanut butter	marvellous

3c
possible answer
It is called 'Moody Moves' because movement, e.g. dancing, can change your mood.

3d

adjectives	adverbs	verbs + adverbs
regular	powerfully	changes powerfully
happy	regularly	workout regularly
optimistic	quickly	walk quickly
useful	slowly	start slowly
favourite	gently	move gently
fast	gradually	warm up gradually
slow	freely	dance freely
good	gently	bring down gently

6

main points	details
psychologists	from the University of Liverpool
smells	more powerful than pictures or words
27 smells	oranges, boot polish, vinegar, menthol, ink
Dr. Simon Chu	a psychology lecturer at the University of Liverpool
smell of an apple	is stronger than the sight of an apple
link	between memory, smell, words and pictures

7
possible summaries & headlines
Wait and smell
Heathrow Airport introduced artificial smells of fresh grass and sea air in the arrivals lounge of British Airways. The scents came from capsules hidden at floor level. The idea is to reduce stress since the lounge is used by 70,000 business travellers a year. The use of aromas is also popular in supermarkets.

Calm down with seaside scents
Scents of seaside can be introduced in the Underground to cut down the stress of the travellers. Scientists say that scents can also calm down football hooligans in stadiums. This idea is based on aromatherapy.

8
see tapescripts

H1
possible sentences
1. Last Sunday the weather was warm.
2. She is such a friendly person.
3. The pizza was delicious.
4. Last night, the Hitchcock film on TV was very exciting.
5. Have a relaxing time!
6. The bride looked beautiful.
7. I bought a comfortable armchair.
8. Spain was wonderful.

H2
possible sentences
1. He drives carefully.
2. The children opened the classroom door noisily.
3. I speak French badly.
4. The President won the election easily.
5. She held the baby gently.
6. The thief ran away quickly.
7. My sister plays the piano well.

H3a
1. carefully; 2. good, well; 3. early, bad, late;
4. fluently; 5. strange

H3b
1. adjective; 2. adjective; 3. adverb;
4. adjective; 5. adverb; 6. adverb

H4

1. Mary spent a quiet morning in the office. (adjective)
2. Philip spoke to his boss quietly. (adverb)
3. The young couple seemed very happy. (adjective)
4. The children played happily in the garden. (adverb)
5. My father gave me an angry look. (adjective)
6. First he looked amazed, then he started shouting angrily. (adverb)

H5a

beautiful
useful useless
tasteful tasteless
peaceful
endless
helpful helpless
careful careless

H5b

possible answers

beautiful actress
useless book
tasteless dinner
peaceful day
endless fun
helpful secretary
careless driver

H6b

ancient – very, very old
art – the way of doing something
healing – making healthy
power – energy
essential oil – natural oil
distilled – heated to make pure
bark of tree – the outer part of a tree
fragrance – a sweet smell

H6c

possible answers

main points	details
Egyptians	massaged their bodies with oils
Greeks	wrote many books about herbal medicine
Romans	imported products from East India and Arabia
scientists in Europe	began researching the effects of oils
a French chemist	published the first book about aromatherapy

H7

An unfinished story

Joe took Monica to Paris on their honeymoon. He knew that she had never been there. She was very excited. At the airport they had to wait for hours. Their plane was delayed. Monica went to buy two postcards. She walked through the waiting lounge, went up some stairs till she found the right shop. On her way back, she followed the signs for British Airways. She was sure that she would find Joe in the same place – next to the check-in counter. Joe was not there. One minute passed, two minutes passed. She looked at her watch. The plane was leaving at eight minutes past four. She asked a man if he had seen her husband. She was getting nervous. Half an hour later, she saw Joe walking between two policemen. What had happened?

H8a

adverbs	adjectives
highly	qualified
extremely	pretty
bitterly	cold
elegantly	dressed
seriously	ill
surprisingly	easy

H8b

1. highly qualified
2. extremely pretty
3. bitterly cold
4. elegantly dressed
5. seriously ill
6. surprisingly easy

Revision 3

1a

1e, 2f, 3n, 4g, 5m, 6a, 7l, 8j, 9b, 10d, 11c, 12k, 13i, 14h

1b

1. Achoo! (someone sneezes)
2. Could I have a coffee, please?
3. When shall we meet?
4. Let's go out on Friday.
5. Just a bit of milk, please.
6. Would you like to come to dinner on Saturday?
7. I'm sorry, that flight is fully booked.
8. Do you want to come round for coffee on Sunday afternoon?
9. More people learn French than German in Britain.
10. See you later.
11. Speak to you soon.
12. So, I just quit.
13. So, I said I wouldn't pay for it.
14. Yes, I'd love some coffee.

2a

Day 1: drank, didn't hear, got, bought, had to pay, arrived
Day 2: survived, is
Day 3: was playing, fell, smashed
Day 4: was travelling, looked
Day 5: don't, bought, watching, realised, didn't understand
Day 6: was taking, ran, was running, were screaming, was
Day 7: stayed

Unit 10

1

Across

2: second – one of 60 parts which make a minute
6: year – a period of 12 months
7: century – a period of 100 years
9: clock – it tells you the time; it is usually found on the wall of a house
10: hour – a period of 60 minutes

Down

1: minute – one of 60 parts which make an hour
3: day – a period of 24 hours
4: watch – it tells you the time; it is usually worn on the wrist
5: week – a period of 7 days
8: month – a period of 30 or 31 days

2c

(B = Barbara, S = Sheila)

B: I'm too busy at the moment. I don't have enough time for myself.
S: You're right. You look very tired. You're working too hard.
B: I'm working too many hours, but I'm saving to buy a new car. I still don't have enough money.
S: I know you are old enough to look after yourself, but I worry about you. You smoke too many cigarettes and you don't eat enough vegetables.
B: Don't worry about me! I'm healthy enough.

3a

mountains, rivers, sunsets, ice-cream, beans, fall (autumn), children, daisies

3b

I would relax, I would be sillier, I'd try to make more mistakes, I would take more chances, I would take more trips, I would climb more mountains, I would swim more, I would watch more sunsets, I would eat more ice-cream, I would walk bare-footed, I would play more with children, I'd pick more daisies

5a

furniture
house
emu
car
Picasso painting
woollen coat is wrong (fur coat)
monkey
grey dress is wrong (green dress)

5b
"If I had a million dollars, we wouldn't have to walk to the store."
"If I had a million dollars, we wouldn't have to eat Kraft dinner."

6a
possible answers
magic, prince and princess, wishes, castle, king and queen, good and bad fairy

The three wishes are:
poor man: health, something to eat every day, a new house
rich man: his horse should break his neck, his wife should sit on the saddle, his wife should get off the saddle

7b&c
Ms Edgell uses the following services: cleaner, gardener, dog-sitter, party service, interior decorator.
(not on the list: car washer, dog washer, present service)

7e
Americans haven't got time for themselves. (line 1)
They buy themselves time. (line 1)
She doesn't do anything herself. (line 3)
Americans spend more income on themselves. (line 11)

1. He only thinks of himself.
2. Maria is old enough to take care of herself.
3. They have no time for themselves.
4. Tell me about yourself.
5. Sometimes I talk to myself.

8
These responses are from a standard British point of view.

1a + 1b This is not very polite.
1c   This is the most acceptable response.
2   This depends on which country you are in. British and American people normally shake hands only on first meetings and introductions. Embracing or kissing might be common in other cultures.
2a   This is acceptable in formal situations.
2b   This is not acceptable in formal situations – although it is becoming more and more fashionable.
2c   This is not expected in European countries.
2d   Acceptable.
3a   This is not necessary but it is usually a nice gesture.
3b   Gifts are not normally expected.
3c   Only acceptable if the business colleagues are good friends.

4a   Only acceptable if it is done politely.
4b   Acceptable.
4c   There is no need to eat it if you really cannot.
4d   Not acceptable; it is clear that the guest is not telling the truth.

9
see tapescripts

H1
1. She's not old enough.
2. It isn't hot enough.
3. It isn't strong enough.
4. It isn't big enough.
5. It isn't clean enough.

H2
1. If she ate less, she would lose weight.
2. I might save some money if I had an extra job.
3. He would feel better if he stopped smoking.
4. If they had more time, they would come to visit us.
5. If you studied harder, you could pass the exam.

H3a
1. It will be better, if you go outside and get some fresh air.
2. Mr. Dunmore would take a year off if he won the lottery.
3. You will be late if you don't hurry.
4. Malta would be the ideal holiday place if it wasn't so hot.
5. If I were you, I would study harder.
6. If I go to France this Summer, I will visit the Louvre.

H3b
● The first conditional refers to a possible future action – something which may or may not happen.
▲ In the second conditional the action is less likely to happen.

H4
pay
say

H5a
house: large, beautiful, new, small, poor, big, old
man: rich, kind, poor, friendly
clothes: shabby

H5b
house: comfortable, dream, elegant, spacious, cosy
man: proud, brave, hard-working, happy, busy
clothes: second-hand, trendy, warm, fashionable

H6
length of time	tips
1 minute	drink a glass of water, fruit juice, take a vitamin pill
5 minutes	eat fruit salad, an apple or an orange, take a break to exercise
10 minutes	meditate
20 minutes	go for a walk, take a sauna, a massage, a bath, relax and do nothing

H7
possible answers
She should join a health club and do regular exercises. She could also try to go out with her friends more often. You might want to surprise her with a holiday somewhere where she can relax. If I were you, I'd try to persuade her to work and to smoke less.

H8
see tapescripts

H9
Time to go. – We should leave now.
Time is up. – The time allowed for something is over.
Time flies! – Time passes very quickly.
Time is money – Don't waste your time.
Dead on time! – Absolutely punctual.
Behind the times. – No longer modern in one's ideas.

H10a
food	places	people
French fries	youth hostel	film star
baked beans	police station	baby-sitter
mineral water	health centre	pen friend
chewing gum	post office	bank manager
tea bag	lost property	bus driver

H10b
possible answers
swimming pool
table tennis
junk food
zebra crossing
T-shirt
dining room
make-up
science fiction
air conditioner

Unit 11

1a
	sentence number
colour	3
description	4
material	1
size	2

2a
natural
neutral

attractive
fashionable
aggressive
bright
coloured

3a

shapes from top to bottom
oval, square, round, oblong

4a

1. pressure cooker; 2. shaver; 3. detergent;
4. rolling pin; 5. vacuum cleaner

4b

(3) It's stuff to …
(4) It's a kind of …
(5) It's a machine …
(2) It's a thing you need …
(1) It's something like …

4c

Across
1 scales
2 cooker
6 teapot
7 plug
10 sieve
11 toaster

Down
1 saucepan
3 kettle
4 polish
5 grater
8 glue
9 broom

4d

grass
nylon
wax
fire

5a

tennis, jogging, golf, climbing, skiing,
motor racing, cycling, baseball, riding,
beach volleyball, swimming, sailing,
canoeing

kite-flying

5b

find out; take off; falls down; give up; meet
with; pull down; bring down; bring about;
blow away

6a

take: away, back, in, off, on, out, down
give: away, back, in
put: away, back, in, off, on, out, down
switch: on, off

6b

1. Hello, you're early. Come in and sit
    down.
2. I told Jan to come back at 10.00.
3. I'm feeling hot. I'll take off my coat.
4. Write down the name in my notebook.
    I forget names quickly.
5. You have to sign here and fill in your
    date of birth.
6. Darcy had to put down the suitcase. It
    was too heavy for him.

6c

Turn down a job/TV/cooker/radio/lights.
Turn off the lights/TV/cooker/radio.
Turn up the radio/TV/lights.
Turn over the page.

7

	Product 1	Product 2
Name	Harmony	Victoria
Weight	180 g	260 g
Material	recycled paper	cardboard
Description	red, blue, yellow, green	striped, with dots or stars
Shape	rectangular	round
Dimensions	21cm long, 15cm wide, 8 cm high	30 cm diameter, 12 cm high
Price	60 p	£1.70
Delivery	1-2 weeks	1-2 weeks

The products are boxes in which presents
are packed (gift boxes).

H1

1. As one door closes, another one opens.
2. The meeting was held behind closed
    doors.
3. She shut the door in her face.

H2

plastic
steel
aluminium
wood
glass
iron

H3a

1. I drink wine. However, I don't drink
    beer.
2. Although the weather was terrible, we
    went for a long walk.
3. She went to the supermarket.
    However, she forgot to buy milk.
4. She cannot speak German, although
    she lived in Austria for 10 years.
5. He bought a new car, although he
    couldn't afford it.
6. I thought Mary was older than George.
    However, I was wrong.

H3b

possible sentences
1. Although I was very hungry, I didn't eat
    anything.
2. His English is not very good, although
    he studied it for 10 years.
3. She didn't feel well. However, she still
    went to work.
4. Jane said that the musical was very
    good. However, I didn't like it.
5. Although it was raining, we had a very
    good time.

H4

1. Mr. Lipsey phoned while you were out.
    OK, I'll ring him up.
2. She threw away all his letters into the
    waste paper bin.
3. They had to pay the money back (or:
    pay back the money).
4. The radio is too loud. I'll switch it off.
5. My husband cut down the old cherry
    tree in the corner of the garden.
6. It's so dark. Please turn the lights on
    (or: turn on the lights).

H5

Susanne found out that her brother was in
Vienna. She asked him to come back. Her
parents wanted to see him. She fixed up a
meeting at a motorway restaurant. He
turned up two hours late, made up a story
of losing his passport and said that he had
to go away for some time. Susanne's
parents broke down. I think they will never
stop looking for him.

H6

1. She looked at them in amazement.
2. He waited for her all evening.
3. The dog belongs to them.
4. He always agrees with them.
5. She paid for him.

H7b

1. The city of Niagara Falls wanted to
    build a bridge across the valley in 1847.
2. They had the technology to build the
    bridge.
3. Homan Walsh, a 10-year-old boy,
    crossed the river by ferry.
4. His kite flew high over the cliffs but did
    not come down at night, when the
    winds dropped.
5. There was an ice storm and Homan
    could not cross back to get his kite.
6. After 8 days, the weather was better
    and he returned home.
7. He was successful the second time.
8. Homan was given ten dollars which
    was a lot of money at that time.
9. Leonardo da Vinci had also planned
    the use of kites in bridge construction.

H8

1. How heavy is it?
2. What's it made of?
3. What's it used for?
4. What size is it?
5. What does it cost?

H9a

impatient, impossible, impractical
informal, intolerant, independent
unhappy, unusual, unable, unlucky

H9b

see tapescripts

Unit 12

1

English is spoken as the mother tongue in the following countries:
USA, Canada, Great Britain, Ireland, Australia, New Zealand, South Africa, several Caribbean countries

English is spoken as a second or official language in over 70 countries, such as:
Ghana, Nepal, Uganda, Sri Lanka, Philippines, Kenya, India

2b

1.5 billion
1/4 (a quarter)
400 million
70
100
1996

2c

1. English is spoken by 400 million native speakers.
2. English is used as an official language by the Indian government.
3. English is taught as a foreign language in over 100 countries.
4. French was replaced by English in Algerian schools.

2d

Countries using English as a first language:
USA, Canada, Great Britain, Ireland, Australia, New Zealand, South Africa

Countries using English as a second language:
India, Singapore, Gibraltar, Malta, Nigeria

Countries using English as a foreign language:
China, Russia, Germany, Brazil, Egypt

3b

90	2/3	330
18,806	313	70,000
1/2	40,914	3,665,717

4

Esperanto Quiz
1. What is Esperanto? (a.)
2. When was it invented? (b.)
3. How many people speak it? (c.)
4. Where does Esperanto's vocabulary come from? (c.)
5. Can you read Shakespeare in Esperanto? (a.)
6. What is the role of Esperanto today? (b.)

4c

1. Esperanto was invented by Ludwig Zamenhof.
2. Esperanto was published in 1887.
3. A world-wide census has never been taken.
4. Esperanto is spoken by two million speakers.
5. Every word is pronounced exactly as it is written.
6. The congress has been held every year since 1905.

4d

present simple passive:
is spoken, is pronounced

past simple passive:
was invented, was published

present perfect passive:
has been held, has been taken

5b

Communication: Speaker 1, Speaker 4
Travel: Speaker 5
Culture: Speaker 6, Speaker 7
Easy to learn: Speaker 2, Speaker 3

6a

(Bed & Breakfast): Breakfast is served between 6.30 and 9.30 a.m.
(airport): Dear Smoker, you are entering a non-smoking passenger terminal. Smoking is not allowed.
(bar): Under-18s will not be served beer.
(department store): Credit cards are accepted.
(restaurant): English is spoken here.
(hotel): Our guests are kindly asked not to smoke in bed.
(hospital): Visitors are asked to leave before 7.00 p.m.
(street): Cars will be towed away.

6b

You can have breakfast between 6.30 and 9.30 a.m.
You can't (mustn't) smoke here.
You can't (mustn't) drink beer.
You can pay by credit card.
We can speak English.
You can't (mustn't) smoke in bed.
You can't (mustn't) stay here after 7.00 p.m.
You can't (mustn't) park here.

6c

1. In a zoo.
2. In a park.
3. In the Underground.
4. On a train.
5. In the entrance of a house.
6. In the streets.
7. In the entrance of a house.

6d

1. You shouldn't ride your bike.
2. You shouldn't turn left.
3. You shouldn't drink and drive.
4. You should use the other side of the road.
5. You should reduce speed now.
6. You should keep to the path.
7. You should pay at the exit.

7a

Black or white? – you ask if somebody wants coffee with or without milk
Cheers! – you drink to somebody's health
After you! – you wish to be polite and let somebody pass before you
Say when! – you want to know how much to pour when serving a drink, for example, how much water with a glass of whisky
With or without? – you ask if somebody wants coffee with sugar and/or milk
Bless you! – you say this when somebody sneezes
Take care! – you say this when somebody goes on a journey or when somebody leaves

8a

Dear Sandy
Yesterday the managing director of Chrisler gave a press conference. This is what I found out about them.
The company was started in 1985. At first the cars were produced for the European market only. In January, a new factory was opened and 60 workers were hired. The cars are now sold in over 50 countries. The company has good working conditions – high wages, and even childcare. Language classes in English, Spanish and Japanese were started two years ago. The company must be successful! Last December, they gave UNICEF $10,000.
I hope this information was useful.
I look forward to seeing you next week.
Best wishes
Angela:)

8b

produce cars
open a factory
hire workers
sell cars

a bad wage
hard company

H1b

-ish	-ese	-ian	other
English	Portuguese	Hungarian	French
Turkish	Japanese	Norwegian	Greek
Polish	Chinese	Italian	Dutch

H2b

Headline 1 = article b
Headline 2 = article a

H2c

1. A new language law is (was, has been) introduced.
2. The mother tongue is protected from Anglicisms.

Passive constructions:
The word Coca-Cola has been changed in Russian.
It is written as Coca-Colu.

A new law has been passed in Poland.
All import documents are translated into Polish.

Both articles are about the influence of the English language in Russia and in Poland.

H3

The Play 'Copenhagen' is produced by 'The Royal National Theatre'.
It is directed by Michael Blakemore.

The book 'English Elements 3' is published by Hueber.

The 'sofa' is designed by Ikea. / It's designed in Sweden.

The Smart car is sold in Germany.

The T-shirt is made in Turkey. / It's made of 100% cotton.

H4a

has invented
is called
is published
started
receives
has written
is spoken

H4b

active verbs: has invented, started, receives, has written

passive verbs: is called, is published, is spoken

H5

see tapescripts

H6

1. Don't drive so fast!
2. Don't smoke!
3. Don't walk on the grass!
4. Don't litter!
5. Don't talk to the driver!

H7

1. airport; 2. hotel; 3. Bed & Breakfast;
4. restaurant; 5. department store;
6. street; 7. pub

H8

possible explanations
Visitors can complain at the office between nine and eleven daily.
Ladies are asked not to take children with them into the bar.
A woman dressed in trousers mustn't (is not allowed to) enter the temple.

Revision 4

1

wages	income
company	firm
scent	perfume/smell
employee	worker
commuter	traveller

2

managing director – a person who controls the business operations of a company
fairy tale – a story for children
haiku – a Japanese poem of seventeen syllables
aromatherapy – the art of healing with essential oils
global language – English is a global language because it is spoken all over the world

3

lazy	hard-working
necessary	unnecessary
polite	impolite
light	heavy / dark
tired	energetic

4

inform	information
describe	description
connect	connection
explain	explanation
govern	government

5

ad**ver**tisement
ho**tel**
comfortable
thir**teen**
edu**ca**tion

6

forei**g**ner
vege**t**able
bri**gh**t
clim**b**
psychologist

7

(possible answers)
take: out, up, off, in, away, on, down
put: up, in, off, down, out, away, back
give: in, up, away, back
turn: in, off, on, down, over, up
switch: on, off

Das Wörterverzeichnis enthält alle neuen Wörter der Units in alphabetischer Reihenfolge. Die Beispielsätze in der mittleren Spalte setzen das zu lernende Wort in einen Zusammenhang. Das erleichtert das Lernen der wichtigsten Vokabeln.

Lautschrift und Beispielwörter:

[:]   Ein Doppelpunkt bedeutet, dass ein vorhergehender Laut lang ausgesprochen wird.
[']   Betonungszeichen oben: Die Hauptbetonung liegt auf der folgenden Silbe.
[,]   Betonungszeichen unten: Die Nebenbetonung liegt auf der folgenden Silbe.
[‿]   Ein Bogen unter Lauten bedeutet, dass die Laute zusammengezogen werden bei der Aussprache.

Die Lautschrift folgt Jones, English Pronouncing Dictionary, 15th edition.

[ʌ]	bus	[bʌs]	[ɪ]	it	[ɪt]	[ŋ]	young	[jʌŋ]
[ɑ]	last	[lɑːst]	[ɪə]	here	[hɪə]	[r]	friend	[frend]
[aɪ]	my	[maɪ]	[i:]	please	[pliːz]	[s]	sir	[sɜː]
[aʊ]	how	[haʊ]				[z]	busy	['bɪzɪ]
[æ]	back	[bæk]	[ɒ]	not	[nɒt]	[θ]	both	[bəʊθ]
			[ɔ]	boy	[bɔɪ]	[ð]	that	[ðæt]
[e]	next	[nekst]	[ɔ:]	all	[ɔːl]	[ʃ]	shop	[ʃɒp]
[eɪ]	name	[neɪm]				[ʒ]	television	['telɪvɪʒn]
[eə]	where	[weə]	[ʊ]	book	[bʊk]	[v]	visit	['vɪzɪt]
[ə]	member	['membə]	[ʊə]	tourist	[tʊərɪst]	[w]	well	[wel]
[əʊ]	own	[əʊn]	[u:]	who	[hu:]	[tʃ]	church	[tʃɜːtʃ]
[ɜ]	word	[wɜːd]				[dʒ]	Germany	['dʒɜːmənɪ]

Unit 1

accommodation [əˌkɒmə'deɪʃn]	What types of ~ are there?	Unterkunft
already [ɔːl'redi]	I ~ know Silke.	schon
adverts ['ædvɜːts]	Look at the ~ in the newspaper.	Annoncen
according to [ə'kɔːdɪŋ tʊ]	Stand in order ~ your names.	laut /gemäß
again [ə'ɡen]	Nice to see you ~.	wieder
anything else [ˌenɪθɪŋ 'els]	Do you need ~?	noch etwas
attend [ə'tend]	I ~ an English course.	teilnehmen an
available [ə'veɪləbl]	Here's a list of ~ hotels.	verfügbar, zur Verfügung stehen
bathroom ['bɑːθrʊm]		Badezimmer
bedroom ['bedrʊm]		Schlafzimmer
below [bɪ'ləʊ]	Look at the words ~.	unten, unter, unterhalb
Best wishes! [best 'wɪʃɪz]		Viele Grüße!
Bless you! ['bles jʊ]		Gesundheit!
boots [buːts]	Bring some ~ for walking.	Stiefel
brain [breɪn]	I want to train my ~.	Gehirn
choice [tʃɔɪs]	You have a ~ of hotels.	Auswahl
choose [tʃuːz]	Which course would you ~?	wählen, auswählen
cleaning ['kliːnɪŋ]	You should do your own ~.	putzen, reinigen
climbing ['klaɪmɪŋ]	One of the sports is ~.	Klettern
clothing ['kləʊðɪŋ]	What ~ do I need?	Kleidung
comfortable ['kʌmfətəbl]	Bring ~ clothes.	bequem
complete [kəm'pliːt]	~ this sentence.	vervollständigen
confidence ['kɒnfɪdəns]	We can give you ~ in speaking.	Selbstvertrauen
cooking ['kʊkɪŋ]	You can do your own ~.	kochen
counter ['kaʊntə]		Tresen
daughter ['dɔːtə]	He's got a ~.	Tochter
different ['dɪfrənt]	This word has ~ meanings.	unterschiedlich, -e
difficulties ['dɪfɪkəltiz]	Are you having any ~?	Schwierigkeiten
divorced [dɪ'vɔːst]	He is ~.	geschieden
encourage [ɪn'kʌrɪdʒ]	We ~ you to learn.	unterstützen /ermutigen
equipment [ɪ'kwɪpmənt]	What ~ do I need?	Ausrüstung
explain [ɪk'spleɪn]	Can you ~ this word?	erklären
facilities [fə'sɪlətiz]	There are washing ~.	Einrichtungen, Möglichkeiten
favourite ['feɪvrɪt]	In the evening I play my ~ CD.	Lieblings-
flat [flæt]	You need ~ shoes.	flach
forget [fə'ɡet]	Don't ~ to take your Word Bank.	vergessen
full-board [ˌfʊl'bɔːd]	This hotel offers ~.	Vollpension
funnies ['fʌniz]	~ is American English for 'cartoons'.	Cartoon, Witzzeichnung
get to know [ˌɡet tə 'nəʊ]	~ the other people in the class.	kennen lernen
habit ['hæbɪt]	What are your learning ~s?	Gewohnheit, -en
half-board [ˌhɑːf'bɔːd]	This host family offers ~.	Halbpension

hitch [hɪtʃ]	She's ~ing up her skirt.	hochziehen
host family ['həʊst ˌfæmɪli]	He is staying with a ~.	Gastfamilie
housework ['haʊswɜːk]	There is a lot of ~.	Hausarbeit
improve [ɪm'pruːv]	You can ~ your English.	verbessern
increase [ɪn'kriːs]	Your speaking skills can ~.	(sich) erhöhen
instead of [ɪn'sted əv]	Say 'Bless you' ~ 'Gesundheit'.	anstelle von
introduce [ˌɪntrə'djuːs]	May I ~ myself?	vorstellen
join in [ˌdʒɔɪn 'ɪn]	~ with family life.	beteiligen / mitmachen
just [dʒʌst]	~ for fun!	nur, bloß
knowledge ['nɒlɪdʒ]	How is your ~ of English?	Kenntnisse
laundry ['lɔːndri]	You can do your ~.	Wäsche
linen ['lɪnɪn]	There is new ~ every week.	Bettwäsche
living room ['lɪvɪŋ rʊm]	This is a big ~.	Wohnzimmer
leisure ['leʒə]	There are ~ activities.	Freizeit
Lots of love! [ˌlɒts əv 'lʌv]		Herzliche Grüße!
never ['nevə]	I ~ forget my books.	niemals
offer ['ɒfə]	What do they ~?	anbieten
outside [aʊt'saɪd]	You can do activities ~.	draußen
own [əʊn]	They have their ~ bedrooms.	eigene
particular [pə'tɪkjʊlə]	Do you want any ~ course?	besondere, -n
pet [pet]	I have one ~.	Haustier
penfriend ['penfrend]	I write to my ~ every week.	Brieffreund
possible ['pɒsɪbl]	Is that ~?	möglich, machbar
pour [pɔː]		gießen, einschenken
previous ['priːviəs]	Do I need any ~ experience?	vorherige, vorhergegangene
provide [prə'vaɪd]	We ~ bed linen.	zur Verfügung stellen, bereitstellen
pub [pʌb]	I have a drink in the ~.	Gaststätte, Lokal
push in [pʊʃ 'ɪn]	Please don't ~.	vordrängeln
questionnaire [ˌkwestʃə'neə]	Look at the ~.	Fragebogen
queue [kjuː]	Do you stand in a ~?	Schlange
reason ['riːzn]	He has a good ~ for learning.	Grund
remember [rɪ'membə]	~ your word bank.	sich erinnern, denken an
responsible [rɪ'spɒnsəbl]	You are ~ for your shopping.	verantwortlich
self-catering [self'keɪtərɪŋ]	I would like ~ accommodation.	Selbstverpflegung
share [ʃeə]	We ~ the rooms in the house.	teilen
shirt [ʃɜːt]	You need an old ~ for painting.	Hemd
similar ['sɪmɪlə]	The words have ~ meanings.	ähnlich, -e
shoe [ʃuː]	You need good ~s.	Schuh
short [ʃɔːt]	I write ~ e-mails.	kurz
size [saɪz]	What's your shoe ~?	Größe
skill [skɪl]	You have good listening ~s.	Fähigkeit, -en
stockings ['stɒkɪŋz]		Strümpfe
strange [streɪndʒ]	I had a ~ feeling.	komisch /merkwürdig
survey ['sɜːveɪ]	I'm doing a ~.	Umfrage
tights [taɪts]		Strümpfe
trousers ['traʊzəz]		Hose
whole [həʊl]	Talk to the ~ class.	gesamt
wrong [rɒŋ]	Which sentence is ~?	falsch

Unit 2

abseil ['æbseɪl]	I had agreed to ~ down.	abseilen
across [ə'krɒs]	We ran ~ the sand.	über
adventurous [əd'ventʃərəs]	I want to do something ~.	abenteuerlich
ago [ə'gəʊ]	That was three years ~.	vor
balloon ride [bə'luːn raɪd]	I want to go on a ~.	Ballonfahrt
body ['bɒdi]	This exercises your ~.	Körper
Boxing Day ['bɒksɪŋ deɪ]	He went swimming on ~.	Zweiter Weihnachtsfeiertag
breathing ['briːðɪŋ]	Yoga helps you with correct ~.	Atmen
care [keə]	There is personal ~.	Betreuung
careful ['keəfʊl]	Be ~ with the tenses.	vorsichtig
charity ['tʃærəti]	This was a ~ race.	Wohltätigkeits-
celebrate ['selɪbreɪt]	We went to the pub to ~.	feiern
cheer [tʃɪə]	They came to ~ us.	zujubeln / anfeuern
change [tʃeɪndʒ]		Veränderung
collect [kə'lekt]	I ~ lots of money.	sammeln
completely [kəm'pliːtli]	You are ~ wrong.	total, vollständig

couch potato [ˌkaʊtʃ pə'teɪtəʊ]	Are you afraid of becoming a ~?	jmd., die/der gern auf dem Sofa sitzt, um zu entspannen (evtl. dabei isst und fernsieht)
crazy ['kreɪzi]	Was I ~?	verrückt
crowd [kraʊd]	There was a ~ of 3,000 people.	Menschenmenge
crisps [krɪsps]	Some people like eating ~.	Kartoffelchips
decide [dɪ'saɪd]	~ which is correct.	entscheiden
department [dɪ'pɑːtmənt]	Which ~ do you work for?	Abteilung
describe [dɪ'skraɪb]	~ a sport.	beschreiben
description [dɪ'skrɪpʃn]	Read the class ~.	Beschreibung
dip [dɪp]		hier: Kurzbad; kurz eintauchen
donate money to [dəʊ'neɪt]		Geld stiften, spenden
download ['daʊnləʊd]	You can ~ from the internet.	etwas runterladen
early ['ɜːli]	She goes to bed ~.	früh
early bird ['ɜːlibɜːd]	Are you an ~?	Frühaufsteher
Easter ['iːstə]		Ostern
enjoy [ɪn'dʒɔɪ]	I ~ sports.	genießen
environment [ɪn'vaɪrənmənt]	You can work in a different ~.	Umgebung
ever ['evə]	Have you ~ been to Spain?	jemals
exercise ['eksəsaɪz]	Yoga ~s breathing.	üben
exercise ['eksəsaɪz]	~ is good for you.	etwa: Bewegung tut gut.
expression [ɪk'spreʃn]	Find the right ~.	Ausdruck
festivity [fes'tɪvəti]	Which ~ do you prefer?	Feier / Festivität
fill in [fɪl 'ɪn]	~ the missing words.	ausfüllen, eintragen
flat [flæt]	You've got a great ~.	Wohnung
flight [flaɪt]	I want to book a ~.	Flug
get up [ˌget 'ʌp]	He ~s up at 8.00 am.	aufstehen
gentle ['dʒentl]	Yoga is a ~ sport.	sanft
give up [ˌgɪv 'ʌp]	He's ~ing up smoking.	aufgeben
Greek [griːk]	Crete is a ~ island.	griechisch
guess [ges]	Can you ~ the answer?	raten
gym [dʒɪm]	Have you been to a ~?	Fitnesszentrum
harmonise ['hɑːmənaɪz]	Yoga ~s mind and body.	harmonisieren, ausgleichen
hate [heɪt]	She ~s rain.	hassen
helicopter ['helɪkɒptə]	Have you ever flown in a ~?	Hubschrauber
hop [hɒp]	You can ~ or run.	hüpfen
incentive [ɪn'sentɪv]		Anreiz, Ansporn
indoor [ɪn'dɔː]		drinnen
introduction [ˌɪntrə'dʌkʃn]	This is a good ~.	Einführung
island ['aɪlənd]	He's been to a Greek ~.	Insel
lazy ['leɪzi]	That was a ~ weekend.	faul
lift [lɪft]	Take the ~ up one floor.	Aufzug
marketing ['mɑːkətɪŋ]	This is the ~ team.	Werbung, Werbe-
match [mætʃ]	~ the correct words.	zuordnen
member ['membə]	Are you a ~ of a club?	Mitglied
mind [maɪnd]	Yoga relaxes your ~.	Geist
mountain ['maʊntɪn]		Berg
needs [niːdz]	They have special exercise ~.	Bedarf /Bedürfnisse
nose [nəʊz]	She had a red ~.	Nase
outdoor [aʊt'dɔː]		draußen
oysters ['ɔɪstəz]	Have you ever eaten ~ ?	Austern
parachute jump ['pærəʃuːt ˌdʒʌmp]	Have you ever done a ~?	Fallschirmsprung
pay compliments [ˌpeɪ 'kɒmplɪmənts]	He paid her a compliment.	Komplimente machen
postal code ['pəʊstl kəʊd]	What is your ~?	Postleitzahl
prefer [prɪ'fɜː]	I ~ badminton.	vorziehen
pronunciation [prəˌnʌnsɪ'eɪʃn]	Remember the ~.	Aussprache
race [reɪs]	He ran in a ~.	Rennen
raise money for [ˌreɪz 'mʌni]	He ~d money for charity.	Geld sammeln, aufbringen
relieve [rɪ'liːv]	Yoga can ~ stress.	lindern, abbauen
repeat [rɪ'piːt]	Can you ~ that, please?	wiederholen
report [rɪ'pɔːt]	~ back to the class.	berichten
resistance [rɪ'zɪstəns]	You have the ~ of the water.	Widerstand
rewards [rɪ'wɔːdz]	~ are essential.	Belohnung, -en
roof [ruːf]	Look at the ~.	Dach
safe [seɪf]	This is a ~ sport.	sicher
sales [seɪlz]	She is the ~ manager.	Vertrieb-
sea [siː]	He swam in the ~.	Meer
show [ʃəʊ]	Let me ~ you around.	zeigen

skip [skɪp]	You can ~ or run.	hüpfen / springen
sleepy ['sli:pi]	This brings your ~ body to life.	schläfrig
smile [smaɪl]	She had a ~ on her face.	Lächeln
something ['sʌmθɪŋ]		etwas
specific [spə'sɪfɪk]	They have ~ needs.	bestimmte
spend [spend]	How did you ~ your weekend?	verbringen
spend money on [spend 'mʌni]		Geld ausgeben für
spinning ['spɪnɪŋ]		Rad fahren im Fitnesszentrum
stationary ['steɪʃənri]	You can ride on ~ bikes.	feststehend
suggestion [sə'dʒestʃn]	Can you make a ~?	Vorschlag
suit [su:t]	That jacket ~s you.	passen
support [sə'pɔ:t]	The supervisor will ~ you.	unterstützen
take [teɪk]	It ~s me 10 minutes.	brauchen
terrible ['terɪbl]	I looked ~.	schrecklich
tired ['taɪəd]	I'm always ~.	müde
together [tə'geðə]	Work ~ in groups.	zusammen
track [træk]	You're on the right ~.	Spur, Weg
wear [weə]	I had to ~ the red nose the whole day.	tragen, aufsetzen
Wedding Day ['wedɪŋ ˌdeɪ]	What happened on your ~?	Hochzeitstag
weight [weɪt]	You can lose ~.	Gewicht
whatever [wɒt'evə]	You can cycle ~ the weather.	egal was, was auch immer
workplace ['wɜ:kpleɪs]	Where is your ~?	Arbeitsplatz
workout ['wɜ:kaʊt]	This is the best time to ~.	trainieren

Unit 3

advance [əd'vɑ:ns]	You should book in ~ .	im voraus
anybody ['enibɒdi]		(irgend)jemand, niemand, keiner
anything ['eniθɪŋ]		(irgend)etwas
anywhere ['eniweə]		(irgend)wo
arrival [ə'raɪvl]	Please pay on ~.	Ankunft
balcony ['bælkəni]	Every bedroom has a ~.	Balkon
bonnet ['bɒnɪt]		Motorhaube
booking ['bʊkɪŋ]	I'd like to make a firm ~.	Buchung
boot [bu:t]		Kofferraum
brake [breɪk]		Bremse
breathe [bri:ð]		atmen
busy ['bɪzi]	He's ~.	beschäftigt
cancel ['kænsl]	Don't forget to ~ in time.	stornieren
cancellation [ˌkænsə'leɪʃn]	~ must be 7 days before.	Stornierung
check-in ['tʃekɪn]	~ is after three o'clock.	sich anmelden
check-out ['tʃekaʊt]	~ is before ten o'clock.	sich abmelden
confirmation [ˌkɒnfə'meɪʃn]	Please send us a written ~.	Bestätigung
destination [ˌdestɪ'neɪʃn]	What's your ~?	Zielort
deposit [dɪ'pɒzɪt]	Please send us a ~.	Anzahlung
diagram ['daɪəgræm]	They drew their own ~.	Diagramm
dishwasher ['dɪʃwɒʃə]	Is there a ~ in the kitchen?	Geschirrspüler
dissatisfied [ˌdɪ'sætɪsfaɪd]	She is more ~.	unzufrieden
draw [drɔ:]	Can you ~?	zeichnen
drier ['draɪə]	The kitchen has a ~.	Trockner
enquire [ɪn'kwaɪə]		nachfragen
equipped [ɪ'kwɪpt]		ausgestattet
experience [ɪk'spɪəriəns]	What's you're ~?	Erfahrung
failure ['feɪljə]	~ to cancel means loss of deposit.	Versäumnis, Nichtbeachtung
fascinated ['fæsɪneɪtɪd]		fasziniert
fireplace ['faɪəpleɪs]	Have you got a cottage with a ~?	Kamin
for over 30 years [ˌθɜ:ti 'jɪəz]		seit über 30 Jahren
freezer ['fri:zə]	There's a ~ in the kitchen.	Tiefkühltruhe
guide book ['gaɪd bʊk]	They wrote a ~.	(Reise-)führer
headlights ['hedlaɪts]		Scheinwerfer
hitchhike ['hɪtʃhaɪk]	They ~d across Europe.	per Anhalter reisen
independent travellers [ˌɪndɪpendənt 'trævələz]	~ love their guide books.	Individualreisende
indicators ['ɪndɪkeɪtəz]		Blinker
include [ɪn'klu:d]		beinhalten
journey ['dʒɜ:ni]	Their ~ lasted one year.	Reise
lodge cabin [lɒdʒ 'kæbɪn]		Blockhaus
lonely ['ləʊnli]		einsam
loss [lɒs]	This will mean ~ of your deposit.	Verlust

map [mæp]	They drew their own ~.	(Land-)karte
microwave ['maɪkrəʊweɪv]	The kitchen has a ~.	Mikrowelle
mirror ['mɪrə]		Spiegel
neck [nek]	You're breathing down my ~.	Hals
personal space [ˌpɜ:snl 'speɪs]		*hier:* der Platz, den man sich in Abstand zu anderen (unbekannten) Menschen wünscht
petrol tank ['petrəl ˌtæŋk]		Benzintank
phrase books ['freɪz bʊks]	They produce ~.	Sprachführer
pillows ['pɪləʊz]	Each bed has ~.	Kopfkissen
printing ['prɪntɪŋ]	The ~ costs were high.	Druck-
produce [prə'dju:s]		produzieren
profit ['prɒfɪt]	The books made a large ~.	Gewinn
publication [ˌpʌblɪ'keɪʃn]	The book was ready for ~.	Veröffentlichung
realise ['rɪəlaɪz]	He ~d he could start a business.	bemerken
rear lights [rɪə 'laɪts]		Rücklichter
receipt [rɪ'si:t]	On ~ of your booking.	nach Erhalt
request [rɪ'kwest]	Please send us your booking ~.	Anfrage
require [rɪ'kwaɪə]	We ~ written confirmation.	benötigen
reservation [ˌrezə'veɪʃn]	Please make a ~.	Reservierung
savings ['seɪvɪŋz]		Ersparnisse
serious ['sɪəriəs]	He has become more serious.	ernsthaft
shower ['ʃaʊə]	Each bathroom has a ~.	Dusche
since 1986 [sɪns]		seit 1986
smart [smɑ:t]		schlau, flott, schick
somebody ['sʌmbədi]		(irgend)jemand
something ['sʌmθɪŋ]		(irgend)etwas
somewhere ['sʌmweə]		(irgend)wo
steering wheel ['stɪərɪŋ wi:l]		Lenkrad
stove [stəʊv]	There's a ~ in the kitchen.	Herd
successful [sək'sesfʊl]	The books were very ~.	erfolgreich
tall [tɔ:l]	She is very ~.	groß
toe [təʊ]	You're standing on my ~.	Zeh
trail [treɪl]		Pfad
traveller's companion [ˌtrævələz kəm'pænjən]		Reisebegleiter
travels ['trævəlz]		Reisen
trek [trek]	I want to ~ in Nepal.	trecken, wandern
triplets ['trɪpləts]		Drillinge
typewriter ['taɪpraɪtə]	She wrote it on a ~.	Schreibmaschine
tyre ['taɪə]		Reifen
umbrella [ʌm'brelə]		Regenschirm
unusual [ʌn'ju:ʒl]		ungewöhnlich
up-to-date [ˌʌptə'deɪt]		aktuell
utensil [ju:'tənsl]	They have all the cooking ~s.	Utensilien
van [væn]	They drove in a ~.	Lieferwagen
vary ['veəri]		sich unterscheiden, abweichen von
vast [vɑ:st]		riesig, weit
view [vju:]	From there you can enjoy a fantastic ~.	Aussicht
well-known [ˌwel'nəʊn]		bekannt
well-researched [ˌwelrɪ'sɜ:tʃt]	The books are ~.	gründlich recherchiert
windscreen ['wɪnskri:n]		Windschutzscheibe
wing [wɪŋ]		Kotflügel
wooden ['wʊdn]	There are lots of ~ chairs in the lodge cabin.	Holz-

Unit 4

ad [æd]	Look at this ~ .	Annonce
advice [əd'vaɪs]	Can you give me some ~?	Rat(-schlag)
allow [ə'laʊ]	It is not ~ed to smoke here.	erlauben
although [ɔ:l'ðəʊ]	~ it was raining, she went out.	obwohl
apply [ə'plaɪ]	Please ~ in writing.	bewerben
battle ['bætl]		kämpfen
best [best]	This is the ~ department.	der, die, das beste
better ['betə]	This job is ~ than the last one.	besser
biscuits ['bɪskɪts]		Kekse
boredom ['bɔ:dəm]	~ is one reason for eating.	Langeweile
boost [bu:st]	This can ~ your energy.	aufputschen
branch [brɑ:ntʃ]	This is the biggest ~ office.	Filiale

break [breɪk]	He has a ~ every day.	Pause
canteen [kæn'ti:n]	Do you eat in the ~?	Kantine
can't stand [ˌkɑ:nt 'stænd]		nicht ausstehen können
cellular phone (U.S.) [ˌseljʊlə 'fəʊn]		Mobiltelefon, Handy
comb [kəʊm]		Kamm
co-worker [ˌkəʊ'wɜ:kə]		Kollege, Kollegin
curriculum vitae [kərɪkjələm 'vi:taɪ]		Lebenslauf
day off [deɪ 'ɒf]	She takes a ~ every month.	freier Tag
diary ['daɪəri]	Write a ~.	Tagebuch
dislike [dɪs'laɪk]	What do you ~?	nicht mögen
do's & don'ts [ˌdu:z n 'dəʊnts]	The ~ of time-management.	was man tun und nicht tun will/soll
drawer ['drɔ:ə]	What's in your office ~?	Schublade
driving licence ['draɪvɪŋ ˌlaɪsəns]	Have you got a ~?	Führerschein
dunk [dʌŋk]		eintunken
during ['djʊərɪŋ]		während
enterprise (U.S.) ['entəpraɪz]	This is a large ~.	Firma
excuse [ɪk'skju:z]	Do you ~ yourself for being late?	entschuldigen
fight [faɪt]		Kampf
flexitime ['fleksɪtaɪm]	Their company has ~.	Gleitzeit
forever [fə'revə]	Are you ~ apologising?	immer, ewig
goal planning ['gəʊl ˌplænɪŋ]		Zielplanung
heading ['hedɪŋ]	Look at the ~s.	Titel, Überschrift
herbal tea [ˌhɜ:bl 'ti:]		Kräutertee
holiday entitlement	How many days ~ do you have?	Urlaubstage
['hɒlɪdeɪ ɪnˌtaɪtlmənt]		
horrible ['hɒrɪbl]		schrecklich
hurry ['hʌri]	Do you have '~ sickness'?	Eile, Hektik
jam [dʒæm]	Do you like ~?	Marmelade
laptop ['læptɒp]		Laptop
latest ['leɪtəst]		neueste, -r, -s
link [lɪŋk]		verbinden
manage ['mænɪdʒ]	Do you ~ your time well?	zurechtkommen
memo(randum) [ˌmeməˈrændəm]	Read this ~.	Mitteilung
mouldy ['məʊldi]		verschimmelt
must [mʌst]	You ~ be at work on time	müssen
mustn't ['mʌsnt]	You ~ smoke in the office.	nicht dürfen
munch [mʌntʃ]	Do you ~ biscuits in your break?	mampfen
nothing ['nʌθɪŋ]		nichts
odd [ɒd]	They have ~ eating habits.	komisch / seltsam
onion ['ʌnjən]		Zwiebel
opportunity [ˌɒpə'tju:nəti]	This project is a good ~ for me.	Gelegenheit
optional ['ɒpʃənl]		wahlweise, freiwillig
overtime ['əʊvətaɪm]	Do you do ~?	Überstunden
pen [pen]		Kugelschreiber
pencil ['pensl]		Bleistift
personal mission statement		persönliche Zielsetzung
[ˌpɜ:snl 'mɪʃn ˌsteɪtmənt]		
personnel department		Personalabteilung
[pɜ:sə'nel dɪpɑ:tmənt]		
prefer [prɪ'fɜ:]	I ~ tea to coffee.	vorziehen
promotion [prə'məʊʃn]	There are chances of ~.	Beförderung
ready-made meals [ˌredɪmeɪd 'mi:lz]		Fertiggerichte
regulations [ˌregjə'leɪʃnz]	These are the new company ~.	Vorschriften
remote control [rɪˌməʊt kən'trəʊl]		Fernbedienung
remind [rɪ'maɪnd]	Just a quick note to ~ you.	erinnern
reply [rɪ'plaɪ]	~ to her e-mail.	beantworten, erwidern
résumé ['rezju:meɪ]		Lebenslauf
rotting ['rɒtɪŋ]	There's ~ food in the cupboard.	verfault
salary ['sæləri]	He has a high ~.	Gehalt
secret ['si:krɪt]	What are your ~ eating habits?	geheim
secure [sɪ'kjʊə]	This is a ~ position.	sicher
sell-by date ['selbaɪˌdeɪt]	This food is past its ~.	Verfallsdatum
sickness ['sɪknəs]	Do you have 'hurry ~'?	Krankheit
snack counter ['snæk ˌkaʊntə]		Regal mit Süßigkeiten
sparkling wine [ˌspɑ:klɪŋ 'waɪn]	Drink ~ to boost your energy.	Sekt
speed up [spi:d 'ʌp]		beschleunigen
suffer from ['sʌfə frəm]	I ~ from stress.	leiden
suggestion [sə'dʒestʃən]	Can you make any ~s?	Vorschlag
thumb [θʌm]		Daumen

travel expenses ['trævl ɪkˌspensɪz]	Don't forget your ~.	Reisekosten
understanding [ˌʌndə'stændɪŋ]	Thank you for your ~.	Verständnis
unemployed [ˌʌnɪm'plɔɪd]	He is ~.	arbeitslos
unrefrigerated [ˌʌnrɪ'frɪdʒəreɪtɪd]		ungekühlt
vacation [veɪ'keɪʃn]	Where are you going for your ~?	Urlaub
worker ['wɜːkə]		Arbeiter
work tools ['wɜːk tuːlz]	I work with the latest ~.	Werkzeug
worse [wɜːs]	This is ~ than before.	schlimmer
worst [wɜːst]	This is the ~ job I've had.	schlimmste, -r, -s

Unit 5

abbreviation [əˌbriː:vi'eɪʃn]	What's this ~?	Abkürzung
account manager [ə'kaʊnt ˌmænɪdʒə]		Buchhalter
advantage [əd'vɑː:ntɪdʒ]	What's the ~?	Vorteil
agree [ə'griː]	Do you ~?	einverstanden sein
Best regards! [ˌbest rɪ'gɑː:dz]		Viele Grüße!
borrow ['bɒrəʊ]	Could I ~ your car?	leihen
business trip ['bɪznɪs trɪp]	He went on a ~.	Geschäftsreise
cheap [tʃiː:p]	You can get ~ flights.	billig
coat [kəʊt]		Mantel
collect [kə'lekt]	I have to ~ the children.	abholen
commute [kə'mjuːt]	Do you ~ to work?	pendeln
connect [kə'nekt]		verbinden
convenient [kən'viː:niənt]	Working at home is very ~.	bequem
crash [kræʃ]	My computer ~ed yesterday.	hier: abstürzen
crash diet ['kræʃ ˌdaɪət]	~s are not good for you.	Radikaldiät
decrease [dɪ'kriː:s]		sinken
develop [dɪ'veləp]		entwickeln
digital camera [ˌdɪdʒɪtl 'kæmrə]		digitaler Photoapparat
disadvantage [ˌdɪsəd'vɑː:ntɪdʒ]	What is the ~?	Nachteil
disagree [ˌdɪsə'griː:]	Do you ~?	nicht einverstanden sein
disciplined ['dɪsɪplɪnd]	She is very ~.	diszipliniert
disc [dɪsk]	Don't lose your ~.	Diskette
drop [drɒp]		sinken, fallen lassen
ears [ɪəz]		Ohren
eyes [aɪz]		Augen
e-commerce ['iː: ˌkɒmɜ:s]		elektronischer Handel
efficient [ɪ'fɪʃnt]	This process is ~.	effizient
electronic organiser [ˌɪlektrɒnɪk 'ɔ:gənaɪzə]	Do you use an ~?	elektronischer Kalender
employee [ɪm'plɔɪiː:]		Arbeitnehmer
employer [ɪm'plɔɪə]		Arbeitgeber
error ['erə]	Learn to live with ~s.	Fehler
expensive [ɪk'spensɪv]	A car can be ~.	teuer
exhibition [ˌeksɪ'bɪʃn]	I'm going to the new art ~.	Ausstellung
face [feɪs]		Gesicht
familiarise [fə'mɪliəraɪz]	~ yourself with the internet.	vertraut machen
fine [faɪn]	That's ~ by me.	in Ordnung.
grow [grəʊ]		wachsen
hazards ['hæzədz]		Risiken, Gefahren
head [hed]		Kopf
hire ['haɪə]		mieten
inefficient [ˌɪnɪ'fɪʃnt]	Some colleagues are ~.	ineffizient
insecure [ˌɪnsɪ'kjʊə]	Are you ~?	unsicher
isolation [ˌaɪsə'leɪʃn]		Vereinsamung
keep up [kiː:p 'ʌp]	~ with the electronic age!	mithalten
level ['levl]	My productivity ~ is better.	Niveau
Little Red Riding Hood [ˌlɪtl red 'raɪdɪŋ hʊd]		Rotkäppchen
look forward to ['fɔ:wəd]	I ~ meeting you.	sich freuen auf
may [meɪ]		dürfen
millennium [mɪ'leniəm]		Jahrtausend
nobody ['nəʊbɒdi]		niemand
of course [əv 'kɔ:s]		natürlich
oil [ɔɪl]	Don't forget to check the ~!	Öl
own [əʊn]		eigene
owner ['əʊnə]	Find the ~.	Besitzer

password ['pɑːswɜːd]	Don't forget your ~.	Kennwort
permission [pə'mɪʃn]	Ask for ~.	Erlaubnis
personally ['pɜːsnəli]	Well, ~ I think it's not OK.	persönlich
practise ['præktɪs]		üben
price list ['praɪs lɪst]	Could you send me a ~?	Preisliste
predictions [prɪ'dɪkʃnz]	~ for the future.	Vorhersage
power cut ['paʊə kʌt]	There was a ~.	Stromausfall
printer ['prɪntə]	The ~ is broken.	Drucker
rather ['rɑːðə]	They send e-mails ~ than letters.	lieber als
redistribute [ˌriːdɪ'strɪbjuːt]	~ the papers.	umverteilen
reference ['refrəns]		Bezug
refuse [rɪ'fjuːz]	Accept or ~.	ablehnen
reliable [rɪ'laɪəbl]	This system is very ~.	zuverlässig
reply [rɪ'plaɪ]	Please ~ to my e-mail.	antworten
request [rɪ'kwest]		wünschen, bitten um
save [seɪv]	Don't forget to ~.	speichern
sharp [ʃɑːp]	Your pictures are ~.	scharf
skyrocket ['skaɪrɒkɪt]		in die Höhe schießen
snowy ['snəʊi]	The streets are ~.	schneereich
software ['sɒftweə]	This is modern ~.	Software
stress [stres]		Betonung
surf [sɜːf]	You can ~ the internet.	surfen
sure [ʃʊə]	I'm not so ~.	sicher
taste [teɪst]		schmecken
teeth [tiːθ]		Zähne
telecommuter ['telɪkəˌmjuːtə]		jmd., der/die zu Hause am Bildschirm arbeitet und nicht pendelt (nur die Daten „pendeln")
text message ['tekst ˌmesɪdʒ]	Send a ~ on your mobile.	Textnachricht am Telefon (SMS)
time-consuming ['taɪm kənˌsjuːmɪŋ]	Commuting by tram is very ~.	zeitaufwendig
time-saving ['taɪm ˌseɪvɪŋ]		zeitsparend
traffic jam ['træfɪk dʒæm]	There are a lot of ~s.	Stau
transfer [træns'fɜː]	Could I ~ my calls to your phone?	durchstellen
true [truː]	That could be ~.	wahr
turn off [tɜːn 'ɒf]	~ the computer.	ausschalten
uncomfortable [ʌn'kʌmfətəbl]		unbequem
unreliable [ˌʌnrɪ'laɪəbl]	The system is ~.	unzuverlässig
up-to-date [ˌʌptə'deɪt]	The equipment is ~.	auf dem neuesten Stand
weight [weɪt]	I want to lose ~.	Gewicht

Unit 6

advisor [əd'vaɪzə]	She is a good ~ .	Berater
age-old ['eɪdʒ əʊld]	It's an ~ practice.	uralt
appointment [ə'pɔɪntmənt]	You have an ~ with him at 6.00.	Termin
arrangement [ə'reɪndʒmənt]		Verabredung
backache ['bækeɪk]	He gets ~s.	Rückenschmerzen
calm [kɑːm]		ruhig
cause [kɔːz]	It can ~ side effects	verursachen
celebrity party [sə'lebrəti ˌpɑːti]		Prominentenparty
check-ups ['tʃekʌps]		Kontroll-
close contact [ˌkləʊs 'kɒntækt]	You have ~ with him.	enger Kontakt
common sense [ˌkɒmən 'sens]	It is ~.	gesunder Menschenverstand
continue [kən'tɪnjuː]		weiterführen
cope with stress [ˌkəʊp wɪθ 'stres]	How do you ~?	Stress bewältigen
couple ['kʌpl]		ein Paar
cycle of energy [ˌsaɪkl əv 'enədʒi]		Energiekreis
Cyprus ['saɪprəs]	I'm flying to ~.	Zypern
dates [deɪts]		Verabredungen
dizzy ['dɪzi]	Do you sometimes feel ~?	schwindlig
dye [daɪ]	He is ~ing his hair blonde.	färben
enter ['entə]		hier: eindringen
exhausted [ɪg'zɔːstɪd]	I felt ~.	erschöpft
environment [ɪn'vaɪrənmənt]		Umgebung / Umwelt
facial ['feɪʃl]	At the club you can have a ~.	Gesichtsbehandlung
fiancee [fi'ɑːnseɪ]	He has a ~.	Verlobte
flat [flæt]		Wohnung
follower ['fɒləʊə]		Anhänger
fruit juice ['fruːt dʒuːs]	He likes to drink ~.	Obstsaft

hairdresser ['heədresə]	He has an appointment at his ~.	Friseur
harbour ['hɑːbə]	The boat leaves the ~ at 6.00.	Hafen
head-to-toe [ˌhed tə 'təʊ]	It's a ~ massage.	Kopf bis Fuß (wörtl.: Zehe)
healthy ['helθi]	Stay ~.	gesund
imagine [ɪ'mædʒɪn]	~ looking this good in 20 years!	sich vorstellen
intuition [ˌɪntjuˈɪʃn]		Intuition
instead of [ɪnˈstəd əv]		anstatt
invest [ɪn'vest]		investieren
ironic humour [aɪˌrɒnɪk 'hjuːmə]	The British like ~.	ironischer Humor
let off steam [stiːm]	I play squash to ~.	Dampf ablassen
logical thinking [ˌlɒdʒɪkl 'θɪŋkɪŋ]	It is ~.	logische Denkweise
make it ['meɪk ɪt]		schaffen
massage ['mæsɑːdʒ]	He has a ~ every week.	Massage
masseur ['mæ'sɜː]	He has a ~.	Masseur
mailbox ['meɪlbɒks]	Leave a message on the ~.	Mailbox
mental ['mentl]		geistig, mental
message ['mesɪdʒ]	Please leave a ~.	Nachricht
mind [maɪnd]	It relaxes your ~.	Geist
miserable ['mɪzərəbl]	If you put on weight you feel ~.	elend
muscles ['mʌslz]	It relaxes your ~.	Muskeln
ought to ['ɔːt tə]	You ~ do this.	sollen
perhaps [pə'hæps]		vielleicht
psychiatrist [saɪˈkaɪətrɪst]		Psychiater
postpone [pəs'pəʊn]	Don't ~ booking.	verschieben
powerful ['paʊəfʊl]	It is a ~ treatment.	kräftig
pressure ['preʃə]		Druck
prevent [prɪ'vent]		verhindern
put on weight [weɪt]	If you eat too much, you will ~.	zunehmen
recommendations [ˌrekəmən'deɪʃnz]		Empfehlungen
reduce [rɪ'djuːs]	This can ~ stress.	reduzieren
refreshed [rɪ'freʃt]	He felt ~.	erfrischt
relatives ['relətɪvz]	I'm visiting my ~.	Verwandte
relieve [rɪ'liːv]	It ~s stress.	lindern
rigid ['rɪdʒɪd]		steif
rush [rʌʃ]	I have to ~ every day.	hetzen
self-irony [ˌself'aɪrəni]	The British like ~.	Selbstironie
should [ʃʊd]		sollen
sink [sɪŋk]		Spülbecken
stretching exercises ['stretʃɪŋ ˌeksəsaɪzɪs]	We start with ~.	Dehnübungen
sail [seɪl]		segeln
side-effects ['saɪd ɪˌfekts]	This treatment has ~.	Nebenwirkungen
shares [ʃeəz]	He buys lots of ~.	Aktien, Anteile
stomach-ache ['stɒmək ˌeɪk]	Do you get ~?	Bauchschmerzen
switch off [swɪtʃ 'ɒf]	It helps me to ~.	abschalten
taste [teɪst]		Geschmack
tension ['tenʃn]	She suffers from ~ headaches.	Spannungs-
timetable ['taɪmteɪbl]	Make a ~.	Zeitplan
tranquillity [ˌtræn'kwɪləti]	You have the feeling of ~.	Ruhe und Gelassenheit
treatment ['triːtmənt]	It's a good ~.	Behandlung
trouble ['trʌbl]		Ärger
well-being [wel'biːɪŋ]	It's a feeling of ~.	Wohlergehen
wonderful ['wʌndəfʊl]	You feel ~.	wunderbar

Unit 7

accept [ək'sept]	I ~ your invitation!	annehmen
accident ['æksɪdənt]		Unfall
actor ['æktə]	He would like to be an ~.	Schauspieler
actress ['æktrəs]		Schauspielerin
actually ['æktʃʊəli]	~, I met him last week.	eigentlich
afraid [ə'freɪd]	I'm ~ I can't come.	befürchten
after that [ˌɑːftə 'ðæt]	~, I met her regularly.	danach
alarm [ə'lɑːm]		Wecker
anyway ['eniweɪ]		sowieso
art [ɑːt]	Let's go to the ~ exhibition.	Kunst
basket ['bɑːskɪt]	The balloon had a large ~.	Korb
brake [breɪk]		bremsen

bus ride ['bʌs raɪd]	They had free ~s.	Busfahrt
catastrophe [kə'tæstrəfi]		Katastrophe
century ['sentʃəri]	This was the new ~.	Jahrhundert
chat [tʃæt]	I've got tickets for the ~ show.	Talkshow
chain of events [,tʃeɪn əv ɪ'vents]		Kette von Ereignissen
comedy ['kɒmədi]	I like ~ programmes.	Komödie
commercials [kə'mɜːʃlz]	He hates the ~.	Werbung
confidence ['kɒnfɪdəns]	Story-telling can increase your ~.	(Selbst-)vertrauen
crowded ['kraʊdɪd]	The bus was ~.	überfüllt
danger ['deɪndʒə]	He was in ~.	Gefahr
day trip [deɪ 'trɪp]	They went on a ~.	Tagesausflug
decline [dɪ'klaɪn]	~ the invitation.	ablehnen
declination [,deklɪ'neɪʃn]		Ablehnung
detective stories [dɪ'tektɪv ,stɔːrɪz]	He enjoys ~.	Kriminalgeschichten
documentary [,dɒkjə'mentəri]	I prefer ~ programmes.	Reportage
eclipse [ɪ'klɪps]	Did you see the ~?	Sonnenfinsternis
everything ['evrɪθɪŋ]		alles
exhibitionist [,eksɪ'bɪʃənɪst]	Are you an ~?	Exhibitionist
factual ['fæktʃʊəl]	I want some ~ information.	sachlich
field [fiːld]	I ran across the ~.	Feld, Wiese
flea market ['fliː ,mɑːkɪt]	Would you like to go to a ~?	Flohmarkt
give up [gɪv 'ʌp]		aufgeben
happen ['hæpn]	What ~ed then?	passieren
historical books [hɪ,stɒrɪkl 'bʊks]	She enjoys reading ~.	Geschichtsbücher
house-warming ['haʊswɔːmɪŋ]	I'm having a ~ party.	Einweihungs-
include [ɪn'kluːd]		beinhalten
invite [ɪn'vaɪt]		einladen
invitation [,ɪnvɪ'teɪʃn]	Thanks for the ~!	Einladung
kneel [niːl]	She was ~ing on the grass.	knien
last [lɑːst]	How long does it ~?	dauern
lie [laɪ]		liegen
lovely ['lʌvli]	That would be ~.	schön
midnight ['mɪdnaɪt]	It was almost ~.	Mitternacht
mountain ['maʊntɪn]	Would you like to go the ~s?	Berg
neighbour ['neɪbə]		Nachbarn
need [niːd]	You ~ to be an extrovert.	*hier:* müssen
news [njuːz]	I always watch the ~.	Nachrichten
numerous ['njuːmərəs]		zahlreich
novels ['nɒvlz]	They prefer reading ~.	Romane
pinprick ['pɪnprɪk]	It was a ~ in time.	Nadelstich
pistol ['pɪstl]	She had a ~.	Pistole
pity ['pɪti]	That's a ~!	Schade!
poem ['pəʊɪm]	Do you like reading ~s?	Gedicht
possible ['pɒsɪbl]	Would it be ~?	möglich
programme ['prəʊgræm]	Which ~s do you prefer?	Sendung
really ['rɪəli]		wirklich
receive [rɪ'siːv]	You will ~ 1 million dollars.	bekommen
rock-climbing ['rɒkklaɪmɪŋ]	Shall we go ~ on Saturday?	klettern
rope [rəʊp]		Seil
run [rʌn]	We are ~ing a workshop.	leiten
sail [seɪl]		Segel
self-confidence [self'kɒnfɪdəns]	You need lots of ~!	Selbstbewusstsein
show [ʃəʊ]	We will ~ this on TV.	zeigen
shy [ʃaɪ]	Don't be ~.	schüchtern
simply ['sɪmpli]		einfach
sign [saɪn]	He had a ~ with my name on it.	Schild
soap opera ['səʊp ,ɒprə]	I hate ~s!	Seifenoper
stare [steə]	He was ~ing at something.	starren
steer [stɪə]	She was ~ing the boat.	steuern
sunny ['sʌni]	Tomorrow will be ~.	sonnig
suddenly ['sʌdnli]		plötzlich
together [tə'geðə]	We did the workshop ~.	zusammen
torch [tɔːtʃ]		Taschenlampe
trade fair ['treɪd feə]		Messe
unfriendly [,ʌn'frendli]	He wasn't ~.	unfreundlich
unusual [,ʌn'juːʒl]	He was an ~ boy.	ungewöhnlich
vegetarian [,vedʒɪ'teəriən]	Are you a ~?	Vegetarier
viewer ['vjuːə]	The ~s can watch everything.	Zuschauer
well [wel]		nun

wildlife ['waɪldlaɪf]		Tierwelt
wizard ['wɪzəd]	He was a ~.	Zauberer

Unit 8

able to ['eɪbl]	They aren't ~ have fun.	in der Lage sein
appropriate [ə'prəʊpriət]	Find the ~ question tag.	angemessen, passend
as [æz]		da
attract [ə'trækt]	Indonesia ~s many tourists.	anlocken, anziehen
aunt [ɑ:nt]	Her ~s are coming to the party.	Tante
average ['ævrɪdʒ]		Durchschnitt-
behaviour [bɪ'heɪvjə]		Verhalten
between [bɪ'twi:n]	Listen to the conversation ~ the two men.	zwischen
bracelets ['breɪsləts]	She is wearing ~ on her arm.	Armreifen
bride [braɪd]		Braut
bride-to-be [ˌbraɪd tə 'bi:]		zukünftige Braut
catch [kætʃ]	I'm sorry I didn't ~ that.	*hier:* nicht verstanden
change [tʃeɪndʒ]		ändern
check [tʃek]	Can I ~ that, please?	prüfen
clarify ['klærɪfaɪ]	We need to ~ some points.	klären
cliché ['kli:ʃeɪ]		Klischee
coast [kəʊst]	You can surf off the ~.	Küste
contact partner ['kɒntækt ˌpɑ:tnə]	He's your ~.	Ansprechpartner
consist of [kən'sɪst]		bestehen aus
cousin ['kʌzn]	She's my ~.	Cousine / Cousin
double-decker [ˌdʌbl'dekə]	There are still ~ buses in London.	Doppeldecker
earn [ɜ:n]		verdienen
education [ˌedjʊ'keɪʃn]	They don't have much ~.	Ausbildung
evil ['i:vl]		böse
explanation [ˌeksplə'neɪʃn]	Look at the ~s.	Erklärung
farmer ['fɑ:mə]	There are lots of ~s.	Bauer
female ['fi:meɪl]		weiblich
few [fju:]	There are only a ~ sizes.	wenige
fork [fɔ:k]		Gabel
funeral ['fju:nərəl]		Beerdigung
gifts [gɪfts]	They bring ~ with them.	Geschenke
groom [gru:m]	The ~'s parents give presents.	Bräutigam
happiness ['hæpɪnəs]	This will bring ~.	Glück
however [haʊ'evə]		jedoch
humour ['hju:mə]		Humor
humorous ['hju:mərəs]	It's a ~ way of writing.	humorvoll
Hen Night ['hen naɪt]		eine Feier ‚nur' mit weiblichen Gästen, die für die Braut vor der Hochzeit arrangiert wird
itinerary [ɪ'tɪnərəri]	Look at the ~.	Reisedaten, Reiseroute
joy [dʒɔɪ]		Freude
key product ['ki: ˌprɒdʌkt]	This is a ~ for this market.	Schlüsselprodukt
knowledge ['nɒlɪdʒ]	Test your ~.	Wissen
let in [let 'ɪn]		eingelassen
little ['lɪtl]	Bring as ~ luggage as possible.	wenig
luggage ['lʌgɪdʒ]	She has a lot of ~.	Gepäck
many ['meni]	How ~ cheques do we need?	viele
much [mʌtʃ]	You don't need too ~ money.	viel
nephew ['nevju:]		Neffe
niece [ni:s]		Nichte
observe [əb'zɜ:v]		achten auf etwas, beobachten
offended [ə'fendɪd]	Please don't be ~!	beleidigt
paddle ['pædl]	You can ~ in the rivers.	paddeln
parents-in-law ['peərənts ɪn ˌlɔ:]	Have you met my ~?	Schwiegereltern
peas [pi:z]	Do you like eating ~?	Erbsen
polite [pə'laɪt]	They are very ~.	höflich
properly ['prɒpəli]	They can't eat ~.	richtig
protect [prə'tekt]		be-, schützen
prospective [prə'spektɪv]		zukünftig
queue [kju:]	They don't know how to ~.	Schlange stehen
remain [rɪ'meɪn]	It ~s free of tourists.	bleiben
rainy ['reɪni]	This is the ~ season.	regnerisch
repeat [rɪ'pi:t]	Can you ~ that, please?	wiederholen
ridiculous [rɪ'dɪkjələs]	It's ~!	lächerlich

ritual ['rɪtjuəl]	It's a ~ for them.	Ritual
river ['rɪvə]	There are boat trips on the ~.	Fluss
sacred ['seɪkrɪd]	This is ~.	heilig
sales conditions ['seɪlz kən,dɪʃnz]	They need to talk about the ~.	Verkaufsbedingungen
sales department ['seɪlz dɪ,pɑːtmənt]	This is the ~.	Vertrieb
sales outlet ['seɪlz ,aʊtlət]	They will visit the ~.	Verkaufsaußenstelle
share [ʃeə]		teilen
size [saɪz]	They only have small ~s.	Größe (Kleidung)
soul [səʊl]	It's the seat of the ~.	Seele
spirits ['spɪrɪts]		Geister
staff [stɑːf]	They have a large ~.	Mitarbeiterstab
surprised [sɜ:'praɪzd]	Are you ~?	überrascht
symbolise ['sɪmbəlaɪz]	It ~s freedom.	symbolisiert
talker ['tɔːkə]	They are not great ~s.	Redner
touch [tʌtʃ]	Don't ~ it!	berühren
travel critic ['trævl ,krɪtɪk]	He's a ~.	kritischer Reiseberichterstatter
unfortunately [ʌn'fɔːtʃnətli]		leider
upside down [,ʌpsaɪd 'daʊn]	It's ~.	andersherum
wealth [welθ]		Reichtum
wedding reception ['wedɪŋ rɪ,sepʃn]	The ~ starts at 3.30.	Hochzeitsempfang
while [waɪl]		während
windmills ['wɪndmɪlz]	There are lots of ~ in Holland.	Windmühlen

Unit 9

absolutely [,æbsə'luːtli]	He is ~ mad.	wirklich, vollkommen
aggression [ə'greʃn]	He was full of ~.	Aggressivität
ancient ['eɪntʃnt]		uralt
aniseed ['ænɪsiːd]		Anis
arrival [ə'raɪvl]	What time is your ~?	Ankunft
arrow ['ærəʊ]	Can you draw an ~?	Pfeil
artificial [,ɑːtɪ'fɪʃl]		künstlich
at least [ət 'liːst]	Jog for ~ 30 minutes!	mindestens
bagel ['beɪgl]	I ate three ~s	kleines, rundes Brötchen
bark [bɑːk]		Baumrinde
besides [bɪ'saɪdz]	~ novels, he wrote short stories.	abgesehen von, außerdem
block [blɒk]	There's a ~ of flats.	Block
blood [blʌd]	~ is red.	Blut
body ['bɒdi]	Warm-up your ~!	Körper
bored [bɔːd]	We are never ~.	gelangweilt
brain [breɪn]	You think with your ~.	Gehirn
break [breɪk]	What time is your ~?	Pause
calm down [kɑːm 'daʊn]	Calm down!	Beruhigen Sie sich!
capsule ['kæpsjuːl]	The medicine was in a ~.	Kapsel
celebrate ['selɪbreɪt]	Did you ~ your birthday?	feiern
change [tʃeɪndʒ]	She can ~ the colour.	wechseln
choice [tʃɔɪs]	They were given a ~.	Auswahl
claim [kleɪm]	Scientists ~ that the world temperature is increasing.	Anspruch erheben, behaupten
competitive [kəm'petətɪv]		Wettbewerb-
completely [kəm'pliːtli]		völlig
connection [kə'nekʃn]	There is a ~ between the two rooms.	Verbindung
count [kaʊnt]	She can ~ till 100.	zählen
crazy ['kreɪzi]	She is really ~.	verrückt
create [kri'eɪt]	We ~d a new style.	schaffen, entwickeln
customer ['kʌstəmə]	We had many ~s.	Kunde
cut down [kʌt 'daʊn]	We ~ on overtime.	reduzieren
delicious [dɪ'lɪʃəs]	The food was ~.	köstlich
discovery [dɪ'skʌvəri]	He made a fantastic ~.	Entdeckung
effective [ɪ'fektɪv]	She learns in an ~ way.	effektiv
elevator ['eləveɪtə]	We took the ~.	Aufzug
else [els]	What ~ can you do?	noch
employee [ɪm'plɔɪiː]	We have a new ~.	Mitarbeiter
exchange [ɪks'tʃeɪndʒ]	We ~d cars.	tauschen
exercise ['eksəsaɪz]	I do my ~s in the morning.	Gymnastik
experience [ɪk'spɪəriəns]	What is your personal ~?	Erfahrung
extension [ɪk'stenʃn]		Erweiterung, Ausdehnung
flow [fləʊ]	The dress ~s around.	fließen
flow [fləʊ]	Blood ~s through the veins.	fließen
food consultant ['fuːd kən,sʌltənt]		Ernährungsberater, -in

fragrance ['freɪgrəns]		Duft, Wohlgeruch
freckle ['frekl]	He has ~s on his face.	Sommersprosse
gentle ['dʒentl]	She's a ~ child.	sanft
ginger ['dʒɪndʒə]	The boy has ~ hair.	rötlich
gist [dʒɪst]	I understood the ~ of the article.	wesentliche
gradually ['grædʒuəli]	Warm-up ~!	langsam, nach und nach
great [greɪt]	The musical was ~.	großartig
headline ['hedlaɪn]	I only read the ~s.	Überschrift
heal [hi:l]	You can ~ most illnesses.	heilen
hearing ['hɪərɪŋ]		Hörvermögen
heart rate ['hɑ:t reɪt]	Bring down your ~!	Herzschlag
heat [hi:t]	We ~ed the room.	heizen
homophones ['hɒməfəʊnz]		Wörter, die gleich klingen, aber unterschiedlich geschrieben werden
human ['hju:mən]	We are all ~ beings.	menschlich
image ['ɪmɪdʒ]	A picture is a visual ~.	Bild
increase [ɪn'kri:s]	The number ~d.	zunehmen
incredibly [ɪn'kredɪbli]	He is ~ nice.	unglaublich
junk food [dʒʌŋk]	Teenagers often eat ~.	ungesundes Essen
leather ['leðə]	Shoes are made of ~.	Leder
line [laɪn]	Write along the ~.	Linie
lounge [laʊndʒ]	The arrivals ~ was full of people.	Warteraum
low [ləʊ]	The morale was ~.	niedrig
mad [mæd]	She is completely ~.	verrückt
memory ['meməri]	I have a good ~.	Gedächtnis, Erinnerungsvermögen
memories ['meməriz]		Erinnerungen
mood [mu:d]	I was in a bad ~.	Laune, Stimmung
noisy ['nɔɪzi]		geräuschvoll
pace [peɪs]	Increase the ~!	Geschwindigkeit
physical ['fɪzɪkl]	I do something ~ everyday.	körperlich
pleasant ['pleznt]	He is a ~ person.	angenehm
popularity [ˌpɒpjə'lærəti]	They enjoyed the ~.	Bekanntheitsgrad
powerful ['paʊəfʊl]	The man was ~.	kräftig, mächtig
Primary School ['praɪməri ˌsku:l]	The boy goes to ~.	Grundschule
problem-solving ['prɒbləm ˌsɒlvɪŋ]		Problemlösung
purpose ['pɜ:pəs]	What is the ~ of doing that?	Zweck
quality ['kwɒləti]	It was made of good ~.	Qualität
realise ['rɪəlaɪz]	I ~d that I was late.	bemerken
reduce [rɪ'dju:s]	You can ~ tension.	verringern
release [rɪ'li:s]	He was ~d.	freigeben, entlassen
remind [rɪ'maɪnd]	I will ~ you about it.	erinnern
researcher [rɪ'sɜ:tʃə]	He always wanted to be a ~.	Forscher
resources [rɪ'sɔ:sɪz]	He's the human ~ manager.	Ressourcen
riddle ['rɪdl]	That was a difficult ~.	Rätsel
rough [rʌf]		rauh, hart
rush hour ['rʌʃ ˌaʊə]	The traffic was terrible in the ~.	Hauptverkehrszeit
scent [sent]	They created a new ~.	Duft, Parfum
scientist ['saɪəntɪst]	He became a ~.	Wissenschaftler
sight [saɪt]	He has good eye ~.	Sehvermögen
smell [smel]	I can never ~ things.	riechen
smell [smel]		Geruch, Geruchssinn
spicy ['spaɪsi]	The curry was ~.	würzig
spokesperson ['spəʊkspɜ:sn]	She was the company ~.	Sprecher
stadium ['steɪdiəm]	The ~ was full.	Stadium
step [step]	There were many ~s.	Stufen
suffix ['sʌfɪks]		Wortendung
suggestion [sə'dʒestʃn]	She had a good ~.	Vorschlag
summary ['sʌməri]	I wrote a short ~.	Zusammenfassung
taste [teɪst]	It ~s good.	schmecken
tasty ['teɪsti]	The food was ~.	schmackhaft
tension ['tenʃn]	You should reduce ~.	Spannung
touch [tʌtʃ]		Tastsinn
underground ['ʌndəgraʊnd]	I take the ~ to work.	U-Bahn
unpleasant [ʌn'pleznt]	Garlic is ~ to smell.	unangenehm
use [ju:s]	The ~ of leather is important.	Verwendung
well-being [wel'bi:ɪŋ]	I had a feeling of ~.	Wohlergehen
whether ['weðə]	~ it is slow or fast, it does you good.	ob
working environment ['wɜ:kɪŋ ɪnˌvaɪrənmənt]	There's a good ~.	Arbeitsklima

| workout ['wɜ:kaʊt] | I have a ~ every week. | Krafttraining |
| worried ['wʌrɪd] | He looks ~. | besorgt |

Unit 10

across [ə'krɒs]	I know all the words ~.	waagerecht
angry ['æŋgri]	He was ~.	verärgert
available [ə'veɪləbl]		zur Verfügung stehen
bare-foot ['beəfʊt]	The children played ~ed.	barfuß
bean [bi:n]	~s are healthy.	Bohne
bow [baʊ]		verbeugen
brave [breɪv]		mutig, unerschrocken
business ['bɪznɪs]	He's in the hotel ~.	Geschäft
busy ['bɪzi]	I have a ~ life.	beschäftigt
butler ['bʌtlə]	James is her ~.	Butler
chance [tʃɑ:ns]	She has many ~s.	Chance
cheek [tʃi:k]	He kissed her on her ~.	Wange
circle ['sɜ:kl]	~ all the adjectives!	einkreisen
clause [klɔ:z]	A ~ is a part of a sentence.	Satzteil
climb [klaɪm]	She ~ed Mount Everest.	besteigen, klettern
clue [klu:]	The ~s were easy.	Hinweis
complain [kəm'pleɪn]	He always ~s.	beschweren
conditional [kən'dɪʃənl]	~ sentences are difficult.	*hier:* Bedingungs-
cook [kʊk]	My father is an excellent ~.	Koch
cosy ['kəʊzi]		behaglich, gemütlich
daily chores [,deɪli 'tʃɔ:z]	She has no time for the ~.	Hausarbeit
daisy ['deɪzi]	I picked a ~.	Gänseblümchen
decorate ['dekəreɪt]	He wanted to ~ the house.	streichen/tapezieren
describe [dɪ'skraɪb]	Can you ~ the room?	beschreiben
desirable [dɪ'zaɪrəbl]	Peace is ~.	wünschenswert
disappointed ['dɪsəpɔɪntɪd]	The mother was ~.	enttäuscht
dog walker ['dɒg ,wɔ:kə]	He earns money as a ~.	jmd., der/die Hunde ausführt
economist [ɪ'kɒnəmɪst]	She became an ~.	Betriebswirt
embarrassed [ɪm'bærəst]	The girl was ~.	verlegen
emphasize ['emfəsaɪz]	You can ~ that word.	betonen
emu ['i:mu]	I saw an ~ in the zoo.	Emu
enjoy [ɪn'dʒɔɪ]	I can ~ life.	genießen
enough [ɪ'nʌf]	I have ~ time.	genug
fairy tale ['feəri ,teɪl]		Märchen
firm [fɜ:m]	She hired a ~ to clean her house.	Firma
fix [fɪks]	He ~es things in the house.	in Ordnung bringen
frightened ['fraɪtənd]	I'm ~ in the dark.	sich fürchten
furniture ['fɜ:nɪtʃə]	We bought new ~ for the house.	Möbel
gardener ['gɑ:dnə]	He hired a ~.	Gärtner
get lost [get 'lɒst]	She got lost in the city.	sich verlaufen
grant [grɑ:nt]	The man was ~ed three wishes.	gewähren
healthy ['helθi]	I eat ~ food.	gesund
highlight ['haɪlaɪt]	~ the nouns in green!	markieren
hire ['haɪə]	She ~d a baby-sitter	einstellen
imagine [ɪ'mædʒɪn]	Can you ~ the situation?	sich vorstellen
income ['ɪŋkʌm]	I spend all my ~.	Einkommen
interior designer [ɪn,tɪəriə dɪ'zaɪnə]	She became an ~.	Innenarchitekt
introduce [,ɪntrə'dju:s]	He was ~d to the president.	vorstellen
invisible [ɪn'vɪzəbl]	I read a story about an ~ man.	unsichtbar
knowledge ['nɒlɪdʒ]	He has no ~ of Chinese.	Wissen
laundry ['lɔ:ndri]	I have no time for the ~.	Wäsche
lawn [lɔ:n]	He cut the ~.	Rasen
lucky ['lʌki]	You are ~.	Glück haben
majority [mə'dʒɒrəti]	The ~ were males.	Mehrheit
mention ['menʃn]	She ~ed that she was married.	erwähnen
mistake [mɪ'steɪk]	I always make ~s in maths.	Fehler
monkey ['mʌŋki]	The ~s are in the zoo.	Affe
nanny ['næni]	She still remembers her ~.	Kindermädchen
necessary ['nesəsri]	It's ~ to arrive before nine.	nötig, notwendig
note [nəʊt]	He always takes ~s in English.	Notizen
nowadays ['naʊədeɪz]	This is a problem ~.	heutzutage
outside [aʊt'saɪd]	She went ~.	außen, draußen
personal ['pɜ:snl]	Don't ask too many ~ questions.	persönlich
pick [pɪk]	I'd ~ more daisies.	pflücken

plant [plɑ:nt]	We ~ed some flowers.	Pflanzen
pleased [pli:zd]	The teacher was ~.	erfreut
poverty ['pɒvəti]	They live in ~.	Armut
press [pres]	He's ~ed for time.	unter Zeitdruck stehen
proper ['prɒpə]	This is the ~ way.	richtig
provide [prə'vaɪd]	The hotel ~s a baby-sitter.	zur Verfügung stellen
puzzle ['pʌzl]	This is a good ~.	Rätsel
questionnaire [ˌkwestʃə'neə]	I hate ~s.	Fragebogen
recommend [ˌrekə'mend]	She ~ed her son for the job.	empfehlen
regular ['reqjələ]	I practise the piano ~ly.	regelmäßig
relax [rɪ'læks]	I can ~ with music.	entspannen
response [rɪ'spɒns]	He gave no ~.	Antwort
river ['rɪvə]	The Thames is a ~ in England.	Fluss
save [seɪv]	Did you ~ enough money?	sparen
sensible ['sensəbl]	He's a ~ boy.	vernünftig
service ['sɜ:vɪs]	The ~ in the hotel was very good.	Service
shake [ʃeɪk]	They always ~ their hands.	schütteln
silly ['sɪli]	She is very ~.	albern
snap [snæp]	Don't ~ your fingers.	schnippen
spacious ['speɪʃəs]		geräumig
strategy ['strætədʒi]	Highlighting is a good ~.	Strategie
sunset ['sʌnset]	I watched the ~.	Sonnenuntergang
take care [ˌteɪk 'keə]	She takes care of the boy.	aufpassen auf
themselves [ðəm'selvz]	They don't have time for ~.	sich selbst
too many [tu: 'meni]		zu viele
trip [trɪp]	We took a ~ to Lucerne.	Ausflug
vegetables ['vedʒtəblz]	I only eat ~.	Gemüse
waste [weɪst]	Don't ~ your time!	verschwenden
woollen ['wʊlən]	I wore a ~ coat.	aus Wolle
worry ['wʌri]	I ~ about you.	sich Sorgen machen
wrap [ræp]	She likes to ~ presents.	einpacken
yourself [jə'self]	You need time for ~.	dich selbst

Unit 11

above [ə'bʌv]	The lamp was ~ the door.	über, oberhalb
behind [bɪ'haɪnd]	She hid ~ the door.	hinter
below [bɪ'ləʊ]	Choose a word from ~!	unten, unterhalb
blinds [blaɪndz]	We have ~ in the windows.	Rollo
bright [braɪt]	The room is ~.	hell
broom [bru:m]		Besen
cardboard ['kɑ:dbɔ:d]		Pappe
care [keə]	Choose your colour with ~!	Umsicht
cheerful ['tʃɪəfʊl]	The girl is ~.	fröhlich
chew [tʃu:]	He is always ~ing.	kauen
choose [tʃu:z]	I can never ~.	wählen
coat [kəʊt]	The door needs a ~ of paint.	hier: Anstrich
coloured ['kʌləd]	It's all ~.	bunt
consider [kən'sɪdə]	He's ~ed to be a genius.	betrachten
consist of [kən'sɪst əv]	It ~s of many words.	bestehen aus
cooker ['kʊkə]	We bought a new ~.	Herd
crack [kræk]	The paint will ~ in the sun.	rissig werden
curtain ['kɜ:tn]	The ~s are green.	Gardinen
curved [kɜ:vd]	The line is ~.	gebogen
dark [dɑ:k]	Her new dress is ~ blue.	dunkel
delivery [dɪ'lɪvri]		Lieferung
detergent [dɪ'tɜ:dʒnt]		Reinigungsmittel
dirty ['dɜ:ti]	The children are always ~.	schmutzig
dot [dɒt]	The box has blue ~s.	Punkte
draw [drɔ:]	She can ~ well.	zeichnen
drawing ['drɔ:ɪŋ]	She sold her ~s.	Zeichnung
earth [ɜ:θ]	We live on the ~.	Erde
fashionable ['fæʃnəbl]	They like ~ clothes.	modisch
frame [freɪm]	The ~ is made of wood.	Rahmen
fresh [freʃ]	The paint is ~.	frisch
frosted ['frɒstɪd]	The glass is ~.	mattiert
gateway ['geɪtweɪ]	He passed through the ~ .	Tor
generally ['dʒenrəli]	~, I like to be alone.	im Allgemeinen
glue [glu:]		Klebstoff

grater ['greɪtə]		Reibe
guess [ges]	Can you ~ the meaning?	raten
impression [ɪm'preʃn]	She left a good ~.	Eindruck
kite [kaɪt]		Drachen
label ['leɪbl]	The dress has a ~.	Etikett
latest ['leɪtɪst]	This was their ~ product.	neueste, -r, -s
lie [laɪ]	I ~ in bed.	liegen
light [laɪt]		leicht
limit ['lɪmɪt]	You must set the ~.	Grenze
lovers ['lʌvəz]	Romeo and Julia were ~.	Liebende
material [mə'tɪəriəl]	Wood is a ~.	Rohstoff
object ['ɒbdʒɪkt]	What's the name of the ~?	Gegenstand
oblong ['ɒblɒŋ]	The drawing is ~.	rechteckig
outdoor ['aʊtdɔ:]	Football is an ~ activity.	im Freien
oval ['əʊvl]		oval
pale [peɪl]	Pink is a ~ colour.	blass
particularly [pə'tɪkjələli]	You find crime ~ in cities.	insbesondere
peel [pi:l]	The paint will ~ in the sun.	abblättern
pensioner ['penʃənə]	He just became a ~.	Rentner
personality [,pɜ:sə'næləti]	He has a good ~.	Persönlichkeit
plain [pleɪn]	The dress is ~.	einfach
plug [plʌg]		Stecker
polish ['pɒlɪʃ]	She likes to ~ her car.	polieren
popular ['pɒpjələ]	Yellow is a ~ colour.	beliebt
pressure cooker ['preʃə ,kʊkə]		Dampfdruckkochtopf
privacy ['prɪvəsi]	~ is very important.	Privatsphäre
protect [prə'tekt]	They ~ their house.	schützen
rectangular [,rek'tæŋgjələ]	It had a ~ shape.	rechteckig
rolling pin ['rəʊlɪŋ ,pɪn]		Nudelrolle
rustic ['rʌstɪk]	The gate is ~.	rustikal
scales [skeɪlz]		Waage
shape [ʃeɪp]	The ~ of an orange is round.	Form
shaver ['ʃeɪvə]		Rasierapparat
sieve [sɪv]		Sieb
similar ['sɪmələ]	This poem is ~ to yours.	ähnlich
size [saɪz]	What is your shoe ~?	Größe
smart [smɑ:t]	It looks ~.	schick
sophisticated [sə'fɪstɪkeɪtɪd]	Blue is a ~ colour.	elegant
square [skweə]	The box is ~.	quadratisch
star [stɑ:]	The box had orange ~s.	Stern
steel [sti:l]	The door is made of ~.	Stahl
striped [straɪpt]	The box was ~.	gestreift
stuff [stʌf]	I hate that ~.	Zeug
suitcase ['su:tkeɪs]	The ~ was heavy.	Koffer
take off [teɪk 'ɒf]	The plane takes off soon.	starten
toy [tɔɪ]		Spielzeug
tramp [træmp]	I saw a ~ at the station.	Landstreicher
trap [træp]	They tried to ~ him.	einfangen
treat [tri:t]	I ~ him nicely.	behandeln
vacuum cleaner ['vækju:m ,kli:nə]		Staubsauger
water melon ['wɔ:tə ,melən]	A ~ is red on the inside.	Wassermelone
wax [wæks]		Wachs
weights & measurements [,weɪts n 'meʒəmənts]		Gewichte & Maße
wooden ['wʊdn]	I like ~ doors.	aus Holz
wrought iron [,rɔ:t 'aɪən]	The window is made of ~.	Schmiedeeisen

Unit 12

advertisements [əd'vɜ:tɪsmənts]		Werbeanzeigen
allow [ə'laʊ]	Smoking is not ~ed.	erlauben
annual ['ænjuəl]	It's an ~ conference.	jährlich
artificial [,ɑ:tɪ'fɪʃl]	Esperanto is an ~ language.	künstlich
aspect ['æspekt]	The story has different ~.	Aspekt
bar [bɑ:]	The ~ has just opened.	Bar
beware [bɪ'weə]	~ of the dog!	Vorsicht, bissiger Hund!
billion ['bɪliən]	One ~ people speak English.	Milliarde
census ['sensəs]	The ~ was world-wide.	Volkszählung
cheers [tʃɪəz]	~!	Prost!

childcare ['tʃaɪldkeə]	We need ~ in the company.	Kinderbetreuung
colony ['kɒləni]	Malta was a British ~ .	Kolonie
commerce ['kɒməs]	Austria's ~ is growing.	Handel
common ['kɒmən]	It's ~ly used.	gewöhnlich
construction [kən'strʌkʃn]	Notice the passive ~.	Satzbau
convert [kən'vɜːt]	~ the information!	umwandeln
disregard [ˌdɪsrɪ'gɑːd]	~ what is not important!	ignorieren
during ['djʊərɪŋ]	I met him ~ the conference.	während
education [ˌedʒʊ'keɪʃn]	In Germany ~ is free.	Schulbildung
expand [ɪk'spænd]	The company is ~ing.	expandieren
expression [ɪk'spreʃn]	I like that ~.	Ausdruck
extract ['ekstrækt]	Read this short ~!	Auszug
feed [fiːd]	Don't ~ the animals!	füttern
fluent ['fluːənt]	They are ~ in English.	fließend
former ['fɔːmə]	Algeria is a ~ French colony.	ehemalig
furthermore [ˌfɜːðə'mɔː]	~, English is easy to learn	außerdem
global ['gləʊbl]	English is a ~ language.	global
government ['gʌvnmənt]	English is the language of the ~.	Regierung
growth [grəʊθ]	The ~ of English is amazing.	Wachstum
hire ['haɪə]	We ~d a new worker.	einstellen
increase [ɪn'kriːs]	The number is ~ing.	zunehmen
invent [ɪn'vent]	It was ~ed in 1958.	erfinden
keep off [kiːp 'ɒf]	~ the grass!	nicht betreten
lean out [liːn 'aʊt]	Don't ~ of the window.	hinauslehnen
look forward to [ˌlʊk 'fɔːwəd]	I ~ seeing you.	sich freuen auf
main [meɪn]	English is the ~ language.	Haupt-
managing director	He is the ~ of Shell.	Geschäftsführer
[ˌmænɪdʒɪŋ dɪ'rektə]		
map [mæp]	Malta is on the ~.	Landkarte
market ['mɑːkɪt]	We produce for the world ~.	Markt
meal [miːl]	I had a good ~.	Essen, Mahlzeit
media ['miːdiə]		Medien
million ['mɪljən]	She has a ~ dollars.	Million
mind the gap [ˌmaɪnd ðə 'gæp]	Mind the gap!	Ansage in der U-Bahn: 'Beachten Sie den Abstand zwischen Zug und Bahnsteig!'
mother tongue [ˌmʌðə 'tʌŋ]	German is my ~.	Muttersprache
mysterious [mɪ'stɪəriəs]	He is a ~ person.	rätselhaft
name [neɪm]		(be-)nennen
native speaker [ˌneɪtɪv 'spiːkə]	There are many ~s of English.	Muttersprachler
official [ə'fɪʃl]	English is the ~ language.	offiziell
path [pɑːθ]	Keep to the ~.	Pfad, Weg
peace [piːs]	It brings about ~.	Frieden
polite [pə'laɪt]	She is very ~ .	höflich
population [ˌpɒpjə'leɪʃn]	The ~ of the world is growing.	Bevölkerung
pronounce [prə'naʊns]	English is difficult to ~.	aussprechen
publish ['pʌblɪʃ]	The book was ~ed.	herausgeben, veröffentlichen
reduce [rɪ'djuːs]	~ speed!	reduzieren
rephrase [ˌriː'freɪz]	~ your sentences!	anders ausdrücken
replace [ˌriː'pleɪs]	English has ~d French.	ersetzen
score [skɔː]	You ~ one point.	erzielen
serve [sɜːv]	Lunch is ~d at one o'clock.	auftragen
sieve		Sieb
sign [saɪn]	You can see many road ~s.	Schild
slow down [sləʊ 'daʊn]	He needs to ~ .	langsam werden
socially ['səʊʃəli]		gesellschaftlich
speech [spiːtʃ]	He gave a ~.	Rede
successful [sək'sesfəl]	The company is ~.	erfolgreich
take care [teɪk 'keə]	~!	Pass' gut auf dich auf!
tick [tɪk]	~ the correct answer!	Häkchen setzen
tidy ['taɪdi]	Keep Malta tidy!	sauber
tow away [ˌtəʊ ə'weɪ]	The car was ~ed.	abschleppen
underline [ˌʌndə'laɪn]	~ all the verb forms!	unterstreichen
useful ['juːsfʊl]	It's ~ to speak Spanish.	nützlich
wage [weɪdʒ]	He has a high ~.	Lohn
widely ['waɪdli]		weit verbreitet
without [wɪ'ðaʊt]	I like tea ~ milk.	ohne
working conditions	We have good ~.	Arbeitsverhältnisse
['wɜːkɪŋ kən'dɪʃnz]		
world-wide [wɜːld'waɪd]	You can buy the book ~.	weltweit

A

abbreviation *(Unit 5)*
able to *(Unit 8)*
above *(Unit 11)*
abseil *(Unit 2)*
absolutely *(Unit 9)*
accept *(Unit 7)*
accident *(Unit 7)*
accommodation *(Unit 1)*
according to *(Unit 1)*
account manager *(Unit 5)*
across *(Unit 2, 10)*
actor *(Unit 7)*
actress *(Unit 7)*
actually *(Unit 7)*
ad *(Unit 4)*
advance *(Unit 3)*
advantage *(Unit 5)*
adventurous *(Unit 2)*
advertisements *(Unit 12)*
adverts *(Unit 1)*
advice *(Unit 4)*
advisor *(Unit 6)*
afraid *(Unit 7)*
after that *(Unit 7)*
again *(Unit 1)*
age-old *(Unit 6)*
aggression *(Unit 9)*
ago *(Unit 2)*
agree *(Unit 5)*
alarm *(Unit 7)*
allow *(Unit 4, 12)*
already *(Unit 1)*
although *(Unit 4)*
ancient *(Unit 9)*
angry *(Unit 10)*
aniseed *(Unit 9)*
annual *(Unit 12)*
anybody *(Unit 3)*
anything else *(Unit 1)*
anything *(Unit 3)*
anyway *(Unit 7)*
anywhere *(Unit 3)*
apply *(Unit 4)*
appointment *(Unit 6)*
appropriate *(Unit 8)*
arrangement *(Unit 6)*
arrival *(Unit 3, 9)*
arrow *(Unit 9)*
art *(Unit 7)*
artificial *(Unit 9, 12)*
as *(Unit 8)*
aspect *(Unit 12)*
at least *(Unit 9)*
attend *(Unit 1)*
attract *(Unit 8)*
aunt *(Unit 8)*
available *(Unit 1, 10)*
average *(Unit 8)*

B

backache *(Unit 6)*
bagel *(Unit 9)*
balcony *(Unit 3)*
balloon ride *(Unit 2)*

bar *(Unit 12)*
bare-foot *(Unit 10)*
bark *(Unit 9)*
basket *(Unit 7)*
bathroom *(Unit 1)*
battle *(Unit 4)*
bean *(Unit 10)*
bedroom *(Unit 1)*
behaviour *(Unit 8)*
behind *(Unit 11)*
below *(Unit 1, 11)*
besides *(Unit 9)*
Best regards! *(Unit 5)*
Best wishes! *(Unit 1)*
best *(Unit 4)*
better *(Unit 4)*
between *(Unit 8)*
beware *(Unit 12)*
billion *(Unit 12)*
biscuits *(Unit 4)*
Bless you! *(Unit 1)*
blinds *(Unit 11)*
block *(Unit 9)*
blood *(Unit 9)*
body *(Unit 2, 9)*
bonnet *(Unit 3)*
booking *(Unit 3)*
boost *(Unit 4)*
boot *(Unit 3)*
boots *(Unit 1)*
bored *(Unit 9)*
boredom *(Unit 4)*
borrow *(Unit 5)*
bow *(Unit 10)*
Boxing Day *(Unit 2)*
bracelets *(Unit 8)*
brain *(Unit 1, 9)*
brake *(Unit 3, 7)*
branch *(Unit 4)*
brave *(Unit 10)*
break *(Unit 4, 9)*
breathe *(Unit 3)*
breathing *(Unit 2)*
bride *(Unit 8)*
bride-to-be *(Unit 8)*
bright *(Unit 11)*
broom *(Unit 11)*
bus ride *(Unit 7)*
business trip *(Unit 5)*
business *(Unit 10)*
busy *(Unit 3, 10)*
butler *(Unit 10)*

C

calm down *(Unit 9)*
calm *(Unit 6)*
can't stand *(Unit 4)*
cancel *(Unit 3)*
cancellation *(Unit 3)*
canteen *(Unit 4)*
capsule *(Unit 9)*
cardboard *(Unit 11)*
care *(Unit 2, 11)*
careful *(Unit 2)*
catastrophe *(Unit 7)*
catch *(Unit 8)*
cause *(Unit 6)*
celebrate *(Unit 2, 9)*
celebrity party *(Unit 6)*

cellular phone (U.S.) *(Unit 4)*
census *(Unit 12)*
century *(Unit 7)*
chain of events *(Unit 7)*
chance *(Unit 10)*
change *(Unit 2, 8, 9)*
charity *(Unit 2)*
chat *(Unit 7)*
cheap *(Unit 5)*
check *(Unit 8)*
check-in *(Unit 3)*
check-out *(Unit 3)*
check-ups *(Unit 6)*
cheek *(Unit 10)*
cheer *(Unit 2)*
cheerful *(Unit 11)*
cheers *(Unit 12)*
chew *(Unit 11)*
childcare *(Unit 12)*
choice *(Unit 1, 9)*
choose *(Unit 1, 11)*
circle *(Unit 10)*
claim *(Unit 9)*
clarify *(Unit 8)*
clause *(Unit 10)*
cleaning *(Unit 1)*
cliché *(Unit 8)*
climb *(Unit 10)*
climbing *(Unit 1)*
close contact *(Unit 6)*
clothing *(Unit 1)*
clue *(Unit 10)*
coast *(Unit 8)*
coat *(Unit 5, 11)*
collect *(Unit 2, 5)*
colony *(Unit 12)*
coloured *(Unit 11)*
comb *(Unit 4)*
comedy *(Unit 7)*
comfortable *(Unit 1)*
commerce *(Unit 12)*
commercials *(Unit 7)*
common sense *(Unit 6)*
common *(Unit 12)*
commute *(Unit 5)*
competitive *(Unit 9)*
complain *(Unit 10)*
complete *(Unit 1)*
completely *(Unit 2, 9)*
conditional *(Unit 10)*
confidence *(Unit 1, 7)*
confirmation *(Unit 3)*
connect *(Unit 5)*
connection *(Unit 9)*
consider *(Unit 11)*
consist of *(Unit 8, 11)*
construction *(Unit 12)*
contact partner *(Unit 8)*
continue *(Unit 6)*
convenient *(Unit 5)*
convert *(Unit 12)*
cook *(Unit 10)*
cooker *(Unit 11)*
cooking *(Unit 1)*
cope with stress *(Unit 6)*
cosy *(Unit 10)*

couch potato *(Unit 2)*
count *(Unit 9)*
counter *(Unit 1)*
couple *(Unit 6)*
cousin *(Unit 8)*
co-worker *(Unit 4)*
crack *(Unit 11)*
crash diet *(Unit 5)*
crash *(Unit 5)*
crazy *(Unit 2, 9)*
create *(Unit 9)*
crisps *(Unit 2)*
crowd *(Unit 2)*
crowded *(Unit 7)*
curriculum vitae *(Unit 4)*
curtain *(Unit 11)*
curved *(Unit 11)*
customer *(Unit 9)*
cut down *(Unit 9)*
cycle of energy *(Unit 6)*
Cyprus *(Unit 6)*

D

daily chores *(Unit 10)*
daisy *(Unit 10)*
danger *(Unit 7)*
dark *(Unit 11)*
dates *(Unit 6)*
daughter *(Unit 1)*
day off *(Unit 4)*
day trip *(Unit 7)*
decide *(Unit 2)*
declination *(Unit 7)*
decline *(Unit 7)*
decorate *(Unit 10)*
decrease *(Unit 5)*
delicious *(Unit 9)*
delivery *(Unit 11)*
department *(Unit 2)*
deposit *(Unit 3)*
describe *(Unit 2, 10)*
description *(Unit 2)*
desirable *(Unit 10)*
destination *(Unit 3)*
detective stories *(Unit 7)*
detergent *(Unit 11)*
develop *(Unit 5)*
diagram *(Unit 3)*
diary *(Unit 4)*
different *(Unit 1)*
difficulties *(Unit 1)*
digital camera *(Unit 5)*
dip *(Unit 2)*
dirty *(Unit 11)*
disadvantage *(Unit 5)*
disagree *(Unit 5)*
disappointed *(Unit 10)*
disc *(Unit 5)*
disciplined *(Unit 5)*
discovery *(Unit 9)*
dishwasher *(Unit 3)*
dislike *(Unit 4)*
disregard *(Unit 12)*
dissatisfied *(Unit 3)*
divorced *(Unit 1)*
dizzy *(Unit 6)*
do's & don'ts *(Unit 4)*

documentary *(Unit 7)*
dog walker *(Unit 10)*
donate money to *(Unit 2)*
dot *(Unit 11)*
double-decker *(Unit 8)*
download *(Unit 2)*
draw *(Unit 3, 11)*
drawer *(Unit 4)*
drawing *(Unit 11)*
drier *(Unit 3)*
driving licence *(Unit 4)*
drop *(Unit 5)*
dunk *(Unit 4)*
during *(Unit 4, 12)*
dye *(Unit 6)*

E

early bird *(Unit 2)*
early *(Unit 2)*
earn *(Unit 8)*
ears *(Unit 5)*
earth *(Unit 11)*
Easter *(Unit 2)*
eclipse *(Unit 7)*
e-commerce *(Unit 5)*
economist *(Unit 10)*
education *(Unit 8, 12)*
effective *(Unit 9)*
efficient *(Unit 5)*
electronic organiser *(Unit 5)*
elevator *(Unit 9)*
else *(Unit 9)*
embarrassed *(Unit 10)*
emphasize *(Unit 10)*
employee *(Unit 5, 9)*
employer *(Unit 5)*
emu *(Unit 10)*
encourage *(Unit 1)*
enjoy *(Unit 2, 10)*
enough *(Unit 10)*
enquire *(Unit 3)*
enter *(Unit 6)*
enterprise (U.S.) *(Unit 4)*
environment *(Unit 2, 6)*
equipment *(Unit 1)*
equipped *(Unit 3)*
error *(Unit 5)*
ever *(Unit 2)*
everything *(Unit 7)*
evil *(Unit 8)*
exchange *(Unit 9)*
excuse *(Unit 4)*
exercise *(Unit 2, 9)*
exhausted *(Unit 6)*
exhibition *(Unit 5)*
exhibitionist *(Unit 7)*
expand *(Unit 12)*
expensive *(Unit 5)*
experience *(Unit 3, 9)*
explain *(Unit 1)*
explanation *(Unit 8)*
expression *(Unit 2, 12)*
extension *(Unit 9)*
extract *(Unit 12)*
eyes *(Unit 5)*

F

face *(Unit 5)*
facial *(Unit 6)*
facilities *(Unit 1)*
factual *(Unit 7)*
failure *(Unit 3)*
fairy tale *(Unit 10)*
familiarise *(Unit 5)*
farmer *(Unit 8)*
fascinated *(Unit 3)*
fashionable *(Unit 11)*
favourite *(Unit 1)*
feed *(Unit 12)*
female *(Unit 8)*
festivity *(Unit 2)*
few *(Unit 8)*
fiancee *(Unit 6)*
field *(Unit 7)*
fight *(Unit 4)*
fill in *(Unit 2)*
fine *(Unit 5)*
fireplace *(Unit 3)*
firm *(Unit 10)*
fix *(Unit 10)*
flat *(Unit 1, 2, 6)*
flea market *(Unit 7)*
flexitime *(Unit 4)*
flight *(Unit 2)*
flow *(Unit 9)*
fluent *(Unit 12)*
follower *(Unit 6)*
food consultant
    (Unit 9)
for over 30 years
    (Unit 3)
forever *(Unit 4)*
forget *(Unit 1)*
fork *(Unit 8)*
former *(Unit 12)*
fragrance *(Unit 9)*
frame *(Unit 11)*
freckle *(Unit 9)*
freezer *(Unit 3)*
fresh *(Unit 11)*
frightened *(Unit 10)*
frosted *(Unit 11)*
fruit juice *(Unit 6)*
full-board *(Unit 1)*
funeral *(Unit 8)*
funnies *(Unit 1)*
furniture *(Unit 10)*
furthermore *(Unit 12)*

G

gardener *(Unit 10)*
gateway *(Unit 11)*
generally *(Unit 11)*
gentle *(Unit 2, 9)*
get lost *(Unit 10)*
get to know *(Unit 1)*
get up *(Unit 2)*
gifts *(Unit 8)*
ginger *(Unit 9)*
gist *(Unit 9)*
give up *(Unit 2, 7)*
global *(Unit 12)*
glue *(Unit 11)*
goal planning *(Unit 4)*

government *(Unit 12)*
gradually *(Unit 9)*
grant *(Unit 10)*
grater *(Unit 11)*
great *(Unit 9)*
Greek *(Unit 2)*
groom *(Unit 8)*
grow *(Unit 5)*
growth *(Unit 12)*
guess *(Unit 2, 11)*
guide book *(Unit 3)*
gym *(Unit 2)*

H

habit *(Unit 1)*
hairdresser *(Unit 6)*
half-board *(Unit 1)*
happen *(Unit 7)*
happiness *(Unit 8)*
harbour *(Unit 6)*
harmonise *(Unit 2)*
hate *(Unit 2)*
hazards *(Unit 5)*
head *(Unit 5)*
heading *(Unit 4)*
headlights *(Unit 3)*
headline *(Unit 9)*
head-to-toe *(Unit 6)*
heal *(Unit 9)*
healthy *(Unit 6, 10)*
hearing *(Unit 9)*
heart rate *(Unit 9)*
heat *(Unit 9)*
helicopter *(Unit 2)*
Hen Night *(Unit 8)*
herbal tea *(Unit 4)*
highlight *(Unit 10)*
hire *(Unit 5, 10, 12)*
historical books
    (Unit 7)
hitch *(Unit 1)*
hitchhike *(Unit 3)*
holiday entitlement
    (Unit 4)
homophones *(Unit 9)*
hop *(Unit 2)*
horrible *(Unit 4)*
host family *(Unit 1)*
house-warming
    (Unit 7)
housework *(Unit 1)*
however *(Unit 8)*
human *(Unit 9)*
humorous *(Unit 8)*
humour *(Unit 8)*
hurry *(Unit 4)*

I

image *(Unit 9)*
imagine *(Unit 10)*
imagine *(Unit 6)*
impression *(Unit 11)*
improve *(Unit 1)*
incentive *(Unit 2)*
include *(Unit 3, 7)*
income *(Unit 10)*
increase *(Unit 1, 9, 12)*
incredibly *(Unit 9)*

independent travellers
    (Unit 3)
indicators *(Unit 3)*
indoor *(Unit 2)*
inefficient *(Unit 5)*
insecure *(Unit 5)*
instead of *(Unit 1, 6)*
interior designer
    (Unit 10)
introduce *(Unit 1, 10)*
introduction *(Unit 2)*
intuition *(Unit 6)*
invent *(Unit 12)*
invest *(Unit 6)*
invisible *(Unit 10)*
invitation *(Unit 7)*
invite *(Unit 7)*
ironic humour *(Unit 6)*
island *(Unit 2)*
isolation *(Unit 5)*
itinerary *(Unit 8)*

J

jam *(Unit 4)*
join in *(Unit 1)*
journey *(Unit 3)*
joy *(Unit 8)*
junk food *(Unit 9)*
just *(Unit 1)*

K

keep off *(Unit 12)*
keep up *(Unit 5)*
key product *(Unit 8)*
kite *(Unit 11)*
kneel *(Unit 7)*
knowledge
    (Unit 1, 8, 10)

L

label *(Unit 11)*
laptop *(Unit 4)*
last *(Unit 7)*
latest *(Unit 4, 11)*
laundry *(Unit 1, 10)*
lawn *(Unit 10)*
lazy *(Unit 2)*
lean out *(Unit 12)*
leather *(Unit 9)*
leisure *(Unit 1)*
let in *(Unit 8)*
let off steam *(Unit 6)*
level *(Unit 5)*
lie *(Unit 2, 7)*
lift *(Unit 2)*
light *(Unit 11)*
limit *(Unit 11)*
line *(Unit 9)*
linen *(Unit 1)*
link *(Unit 4)*
Little Red Riding Hood
    (Unit 5)
little *(Unit 8)*
living room *(Unit 1)*
lodge cabin *(Unit 3)*
logical thinking
    (Unit 6)
lonely *(Unit 3)*

look forward to
    (Unit 5, 12)
loss *(Unit 3)*
Lots of love! *(Unit 1)*
lounge *(Unit 9)*
lovely *(Unit 7)*
lovers *(Unit 11)*
low *(Unit 9)*
lucky *(Unit 10)*
luggage *(Unit 8)*

M

mad *(Unit 9)*
mailbox *(Unit 6)*
main *(Unit 12)*
majority *(Unit 10)*
make it *(Unit 6)*
manage *(Unit 4)*
managing director
    (Unit 12)
many *(Unit 8)*
map *(Unit 3, 12)*
market *(Unit 12)*
marketing *(Unit 2)*
massage *(Unit 6)*
masseur *(Unit 6)*
match *(Unit 2)*
material *(Unit 11)*
may *(Unit 5)*
meal *(Unit 12)*
media *(Unit 12)*
member *(Unit 2)*
memo(randum)
    (Unit 4)
memories *(Unit 9)*
memory *(Unit 9)*
mental *(Unit 6)*
mention *(Unit 10)*
message *(Unit 6)*
microwave *(Unit 3)*
midnight *(Unit 7)*
millennium *(Unit 5)*
million *(Unit 12)*
mind the gap *(Unit 12)*
mind *(Unit 2, 6)*
mirror *(Unit 3)*
miserable *(Unit 6)*
mistake *(Unit 10)*
monkey *(Unit 10)*
mood *(Unit 9)*
mother tongue
    (Unit 12)
mouldy *(Unit 4)*
mountain *(Unit 2, 7)*
much *(Unit 8)*
munch *(Unit 4)*
muscles *(Unit 6)*
must *(Unit 4)*
mustn't *(Unit 4)*
mysterious *(Unit 12)*

N

name *(Unit 12)*
nanny *(Unit 10)*
native speaker
    (Unit 12)
necessary *(Unit 10)*
neck *(Unit 3)*

need *(Unit 7)*
needs *(Unit 2)*
neighbour *(Unit 7)*
nephew *(Unit 8)*
never *(Unit 1)*
news *(Unit 7)*
niece *(Unit 8)*
nobody *(Unit 5)*
noisy *(Unit 9)*
nose *(Unit 2)*
note *(Unit 10)*
nothing *(Unit 4)*
novels *(Unit 7)*
nowadays *(Unit 10)*
numerous *(Unit 7)*

O

object *(Unit 11)*
oblong *(Unit 11)*
observe *(Unit 8)*
odd *(Unit 4)*
of course *(Unit 5)*
offended *(Unit 8)*
offer *(Unit 1)*
official *(Unit 12)*
oil *(Unit 5)*
onion *(Unit 4)*
opportunity *(Unit 4)*
optional *(Unit 4)*
ought to *(Unit 6)*
outdoor *(Unit 11)*
outdoor *(Unit 2)*
outside *(Unit 1)*
outside *(Unit 10)*
oval *(Unit 11)*
overtime *(Unit 4)*
own *(Unit 1, 5)*
owner *(Unit 5)*
oysters *(Unit 2)*

P

pace *(Unit 9)*
paddle *(Unit 8)*
pale *(Unit 11)*
parachute jump
    (Unit 2)
parents-in-law *(Unit 8)*
particular *(Unit 1)*
particularly *(Unit 11)*
password *(Unit 5)*
path *(Unit 12)*
pay compliments
    (Unit 2)
peace *(Unit 12)*
peas *(Unit 8)*
peel *(Unit 11)*
pen *(Unit 4)*
pencil *(Unit 4)*
penfriend *(Unit 1)*
pensioner *(Unit 11)*
perhaps *(Unit 6)*
permission *(Unit 5)*
personal mission
    statement *(Unit 4)*
personal space *(Unit 3)*
personal *(Unit 10)*
personality *(Unit 11)*
personally *(Unit 5)*

personnel department *(Unit 4)*
pet *(Unit 1)*
petrol tank *(Unit 3)*
phrase books *(Unit 3)*
physical *(Unit 9)*
pick *(Unit 10)*
pillows *(Unit 3)*
pinprick *(Unit 7)*
pistol *(Unit 7)*
pity *(Unit 7)*
plain *(Unit 11)*
plant *(Unit 10)*
pleasant *(Unit 9)*
pleased *(Unit 10)*
plug *(Unit 11)*
poem *(Unit 7)*
polish *(Unit 11)*
polite *(Unit 8, 12)*
popular *(Unit 11)*
popularity *(Unit 9)*
population *(Unit 12)*
possible *(Unit 1, 7)*
postal code *(Unit 2)*
postpone *(Unit 6)*
pour *(Unit 1)*
poverty *(Unit 10)*
power cut *(Unit 5)*
powerful *(Unit 6, 9)*
practise *(Unit 5)*
predictions *(Unit 5)*
prefer *(Unit 2, 4)*
press *(Unit 10)*
pressure cooker *(Unit 11)*
pressure *(Unit 6)*
prevent *(Unit 6)*
previous *(Unit 1)*
price list *(Unit 5)*
Primary School *(Unit 9)*
printer *(Unit 5)*
printing *(Unit 3)*
privacy *(Unit 11)*
problem-solving *(Unit 9)*
produce *(Unit 3)*
profit *(Unit 3)*
programme *(Unit 7)*
promotion *(Unit 4)*
pronounce *(Unit 12)*
pronunciation *(Unit 2)*
proper *(Unit 10)*
properly *(Unit 8)*
prospective *(Unit 8)*
protect *(Unit 8, 11)*
provide *(Unit 1, 10)*
psychiatrist *(Unit 6)*
pub *(Unit 1)*
publication *(Unit 3)*
publish *(Unit 12)*
purpose *(Unit 9)*
push in *(Unit 1)*
put on weight *(Unit 6)*
puzzle *(Unit 10)*

Q

quality *(Unit 9)*
questionnaire *(Unit 1)*
questionnaire *(Unit 10)*

queue *(Unit 1, 8)*

R

race *(Unit 2)*
rainy *(Unit 8)*
raise money for *(Unit 2)*
rather *(Unit 5)*
ready-made meals *(Unit 4)*
realise *(Unit 3, 9)*
really *(Unit 7)*
rear lights *(Unit 3)*
reason *(Unit 1)*
receipt *(Unit 3)*
receive *(Unit 7)*
recommend *(Unit 10)*
recommendations *(Unit 6)*
rectangular *(Unit 11)*
redistribute *(Unit 5)*
reduce *(Unit 6, 9, 12)*
reference *(Unit 5)*
refreshed *(Unit 6)*
refuse *(Unit 5)*
regular *(Unit 10)*
regulations *(Unit 4)*
relatives *(Unit 6)*
relax *(Unit 10)*
release *(Unit 9)*
reliable *(Unit 5)*
relieve *(Unit 2, 6)*
remain *(Unit 8)*
remember *(Unit 1)*
remind *(Unit 4, 9)*
remote control *(Unit 4)*
repeat *(Unit 2, 8)*
rephrase *(Unit 12)*
replace *(Unit 12)*
reply *(Unit 4, 5)*
report *(Unit 2)*
request *(Unit 3, 5)*
require *(Unit 2)*
researcher *(Unit 9)*
reservation *(Unit 3)*
resistance *(Unit 2)*
resources *(Unit 9)*
response *(Unit 10)*
responsible *(Unit 1)*
résumé *(Unit 4)*
rewards *(Unit 2)*
riddle *(Unit 9)*
ridiculous *(Unit 8)*
rigid *(Unit 6)*
ritual *(Unit 8)*
river *(Unit 8, 10)*
rock-climbing *(Unit 7)*
rolling pin *(Unit 11)*
roof *(Unit 2)*
rope *(Unit 7)*
rotting *(Unit 4)*
rough *(Unit 9)*
run *(Unit 7)*
rush hour *(Unit 9)*
rush *(Unit 6)*
rustic *(Unit 11)*

S

sacred *(Unit 8)*
safe *(Unit 2)*
sail *(Unit 6, 7)*
salary *(Unit 4)*
sales conditions *(Unit 8)*
sales department *(Unit 8)*
sales outlet *(Unit 8)*
sales *(Unit 2)*
save *(Unit 5, 10)*
savings *(Unit 3)*
scales *(Unit 11)*
scent *(Unit 9)*
scientist *(Unit 9)*
score *(Unit 12)*
sea *(Unit 2)*
secret *(Unit 4)*
secure *(Unit 4)*
self-catering *(Unit 1)*
self-confidence *(Unit 7)*
self-irony *(Unit 6)*
sell-by date *(Unit 4)*
sensible *(Unit 10)*
serious *(Unit 3)*
serve *(Unit 12)*
service *(Unit 10)*
shake *(Unit 10)*
shape *(Unit 11)*
share *(Unit 1, 8)*
shares *(Unit 6)*
sharp *(Unit 5)*
shaver *(Unit 11)*
shirt *(Unit 1)*
shoe *(Unit 1)*
short *(Unit 1)*
should *(Unit 6)*
show *(Unit 2, 7)*
shower *(Unit 3)*
shy *(Unit 7)*
sickness *(Unit 4)*
side-effects *(Unit 6)*
sieve *(Unit 11)*
sight *(Unit 9)*
sign *(Unit 7, 12)*
silly *(Unit 10)*
similar *(Unit 1, 11)*
simply *(Unit 7)*
since 1986 *(Unit 3)*
sink *(Unit 6)*
size *(Unit 1, 8, 11)*
skill *(Unit 1)*
skip *(Unit 2)*
skyrocket *(Unit 5)*
sleepy *(Unit 2)*
slow down *(Unit 12)*
smart *(Unit 3, 11)*
smell *(Unit 9)*
smile *(Unit 2)*
snack counter *(Unit 4)*
snap *(Unit 10)*
snowy *(Unit 5)*
soap opera *(Unit 7)*
socially *(Unit 12)*
software *(Unit 5)*
somebody *(Unit 3)*
something *(Unit 2, 3)*
somewhere *(Unit 3)*

sophisticated *(Unit 11)*
soul *(Unit 8)*
spacious *(Unit 10)*
sparkling wine *(Unit 4)*
specific *(Unit 2)*
speech *(Unit 12)*
speed up *(Unit 4)*
spend money on *(Unit 2)*
spend *(Unit 2)*
spicy *(Unit 9)*
spinning *(Unit 2)*
spirits *(Unit 8)*
spokesperson *(Unit 9)*
square *(Unit 11)*
stadium *(Unit 9)*
staff *(Unit 8)*
star *(Unit 11)*
stare *(Unit 7)*
stationary *(Unit 2)*
steel *(Unit 11)*
steer *(Unit 7)*
steering wheel *(Unit 3)*
step *(Unit 9)*
stockings *(Unit 1)*
stomach-ache *(Unit 6)*
stove *(Unit 3)*
strange *(Unit 1)*
strategy *(Unit 10)*
stress *(Unit 5)*
stretching exercises *(Unit 6)*
striped *(Unit 11)*
stuff *(Unit 11)*
successful *(Unit 3, 12)*
suddenly *(Unit 7)*
suffer from *(Unit 4)*
suffix *(Unit 9)*
suggestion *(Unit 2, 4, 9)*
suit *(Unit 2)*
suitcase *(Unit 11)*
summary *(Unit 9)*
sunny *(Unit 7)*
sunset *(Unit 10)*
support *(Unit 2)*
sure *(Unit 5)*
surf *(Unit 5)*
surprised *(Unit 8)*
survey *(Unit 1)*
switch off *(Unit 6)*
symbolise *(Unit 8)*

T

take care *(Unit 10, 12)*
take off *(Unit 11)*
take *(Unit 2)*
talker *(Unit 8)*
tall *(Unit 3)*
taste *(Unit 5, 6, 9)*
tasty *(Unit 9)*
teeth *(Unit 5)*
telecommuter *(Unit 5)*
tension *(Unit 6, 9)*
terrible *(Unit 2)*
text message *(Unit 5)*
themselves *(Unit 10)*
thumb *(Unit 4)*
tick *(Unit 12)*
tidy *(Unit 12)*

tights *(Unit 1)*
time-consuming *(Unit 5)*
time-saving *(Unit 5)*
timetable *(Unit 6)*
tired *(Unit 2)*
toe *(Unit 3)*
together *(Unit 2, 7)*
too many *(Unit 10)*
torch *(Unit 7)*
touch *(Unit 8, 9)*
tow away *(Unit 12)*
toy *(Unit 11)*
track *(Unit 2)*
trade fair *(Unit 7)*
traffic jam *(Unit 5)*
trail *(Unit 3)*
tramp *(Unit 11)*
tranquillity *(Unit 6)*
transfer *(Unit 5)*
trap *(Unit 11)*
travel critic *(Unit 8)*
travel expenses *(Unit 4)*
traveller's companion *(Unit 3)*
travels *(Unit 3)*
treat *(Unit 11)*
treatment *(Unit 6)*
trek *(Unit 3)*
trip *(Unit 10)*
triplets *(Unit 3)*
trouble *(Unit 6)*
trousers *(Unit 1)*
true *(Unit 5)*
turn off *(Unit 5)*
typewriter *(Unit 3)*
tyre *(Unit 3)*

U

umbrella *(Unit 3)*
uncomfortable *(Unit 5)*
underground *(Unit 9)*
underline *(Unit 12)*
understanding *(Unit 4)*
unemployed *(Unit 4)*
unfortunately *(Unit 8)*
unfriendly *(Unit 7)*
unpleasant *(Unit 9)*
unrefrigerated *(Unit 4)*
unreliable *(Unit 5)*
unusual *(Unit 3, 7)*
upside down *(Unit 8)*
up-to-date *(Unit 3, 5)*
use *(Unit 9)*
useful *(Unit 12)*
utensil *(Unit 3)*

V

vacation *(Unit 4)*
vacuum cleaner *(Unit 11)*
van *(Unit 3)*
vary *(Unit 3)*
vast *(Unit 3)*
vegetables *(Unit 10)*
vegetarian *(Unit 7)*
view *(Unit 3)*
viewer *(Unit 7)*

W

wage *(Unit 12)*
waste *(Unit 10)*
water melon *(Unit 11)*
wax *(Unit 11)*
wealth *(Unit 8)*
wear *(Unit 2)*
Wedding Day *(Unit 2)*
wedding reception
   (Unit 8)
weight *(Unit 2, 5)*
weights & measure-
   ments *(Unit 11)*
well *(Unit 7)*
well-being *(Unit 6, 9)*
well-known *(Unit 3)*
well-researched
   (Unit 3)
whatever *(Unit 2)*
whether *(Unit 9)*
while *(Unit 8)*
whole *(Unit 1)*
widely *(Unit 12)*
wildlife *(Unit 7)*
windmills *(Unit 8)*
windscreen *(Unit 3)*
wing *(Unit 3)*
without *(Unit 12)*
wizard *(Unit 7)*
wonderful *(Unit 6)*
wooden *(Unit 3, 11)*
woollen *(Unit 10)*
work tools *(Unit 4)*
worker *(Unit 4)*
working conditions
   (Unit 12)
working environment
   (Unit 9)
workout *(Unit 2, 9)*
workplace *(Unit 2)*
world-wide *(Unit 12)*
worried *(Unit 9)*
worry *(Unit 10)*
worse *(Unit 4)*
worst *(Unit 4)*
wrap *(Unit 10)*
wrong *(Unit 1)*
wrought iron *(Unit 11)*

Y

yourself *(Unit 10)*

Acknowledgements

The authors and publishers are grateful to the following copyright owners for permission to reproduce artwork, photographs, illustrations and texts. It has not been possible to identify the sources of all the material used and in such cases the publishers would welcome information from copyright owners.

Illustrations on pages 13, 25, 43, 50, 63, 71, 79, 89, 126, 132, 133, 167: Reinhard Wendlinger, München

Cover: *top:* Bavaria Bildagentur, Gauting / *bottom:* London / Isle of Dogs, Canary Wharf, Edmund Nägele, F.R.P.S

page 10: Gerd Pfeiffer, München   **page 11:** IFA Bilderteam, Int. Stock, München   **page 12:** *top:* photodisc; European Centre of English Language Studies, Malta   **page 14 & 128:** The Park Language Centre, Sheffield (logo and extract)   **page 18:** The Stock Market (Jeff Zaruba), Düsseldorf   **page 19:** Pennine Way, Yorkshire, BTA, Frankfurt/M.   **page 20:** *top:* Jackie Sykes, Köln; "Red Nose Day", copyright: Comic Relief   **page 21:** The Stock Market (Nancy Brown), Düsseldorf   **page 23 & 130:** The Sunderland Health & Racquet Club, Sunderland, UK   **page 24:** IFA Bilderteam, it-stock, München   **page 26:** *top:* Micro Compact Car smart GmbH (A2000F7031 und A2000F7032), Renningen; *bottom:* MHV Archiv (Erna Friedrich)   **page 27:** MHV Archiv (Erna Friedrich)   **page 28:** *top:* The Stock Market (Charles Gupton), Düsseldorf; *middle:* 2x IFA Bilderteam, Int. Stock, München; *middle right:* The Stock Market (Nancy Ney), Düsseldorf   **page 29:** Rüdiger Modell, München   **page 30:** *left:* Elaine's Bed&Breakfast, Cedar Crest, New Mexico; *right:* Ruidoso, New Mexico   **page 31:** *top left:* Rüdiger Modell, München; *top middle:* Eishotel,Marc Oliver-Schulz; *top right:* MHV Archiv (Erna Friedrich); *middle left:* IFA Bilderteam (Jung), München; *middle right:* Jackie Sykes, Köln; *bottom:* MHV Archiv (Erna Friedrich)   **page 36-37:** Look (Jan Greune), München   **page 37:** IFA Bilderteam, it/tpl, München

page 41: 2x Rüdiger Modell, München   **page 42:** photodisc   **page 44:** IFA Bilderteam, it-stock, München; *bottom:* Holger Latzel, München;   **page 45:** Holger Latzel, München   **page 51:** 3x IFA Bilderteam (*left:* Heron, 2x it-stock), München   **page 52:** The Stock Market (Tom&DeeAnn McCarthy), Düsseldorf; *bottom:* IFA Bilderteam (Franka), München   **page 53:** photodisc   **page 56:** Cartoon "Fans Utd" by David Haldane, published by The Funday Times   **page 57:** IFA Bilderteam (Bail&Spiegel), München   **page 58:** Holger Latzel, München   **page 62:** "The God of Small Things" by Arundhati Roy, from Harper Collins Publishers; "Harry Potter" by J. K. Rowling, from Bloomsbury Publishing Plc; "Coyote Waits" by Tony Hillerman, from Penguin Books Ltd.   **page 64:** Jacket Cover from "Enduring Love" by Ian McEwan published by Jonathan Cape. Used by permission of The Random House Group Limited.   **page 68:** MHV Archiv (Gerd Pfeiffer)   **page 70:** Fremdenverkehrsamt Malta, Frankfurt; extract from "Neither here nor there" by Bill Bryson, Secker&Warburg, The Random House Group Limited

page 71: IFA Bilderteam (Schösser), München   **page 72, 73, 150:** plus 49 (Christoph Keller), Hamburg   **page 74:** 3x MHV Archiv (Erna Friedrich)   **page 75:** Imagine (Horizon), Hamburg   **page 78:** *left:* Myriam Fischer, Großostheim; *middle:* The Stock Market (Jon Feingersh), Düsseldorf; *right & top:* IFA Bilderteam (it-stock & Harris), München   **page 80:** photodisc; extract from The Weekender, Times of Malta   **page 82:** IFA Bilderteam (IPS), München   **page 83:** *2x top right:* IFA Bilderteam (Welsh, Gall), München; *middle:* Imagine (Coleman), Hamburg; *bottom:* IFA Bilderteam (Krahmer), München   **page 84:** IFA Bilderteam, it/tpl, München   **page 88:** Look (Franz Marc Frei), München   **page 91:** photodisc   **page 92:** IFA Bilderteam (LDW), München   **page 93:** photodisc; Spotlight Verlag & Co KG, Planegg   **page 94:** IFA Bilderteam, it-stock, München   **page 96:** *middle:* MHV Archiv (Erna Friedrich); *right:* IFA Bilderteam, direct stock, München   **page 100:** Fallschirmsportverein Känguruh Club, Gauting   **page 102:** IFA Bilderteam, it/tpl, München   **page 104:** extract from "English as a Global Language" by David Crystal, Cambridge University Press)   **page 107:** The Stock Market (Rob Lewine), Düsseldorf   **page 110:** Visum (Steche), Hamburg   **page 115:** MHV Archiv (Erna Friedrich)   **page 117:** photodisc   **page 119:** Holger Latzel, München   **page 121:** Imagine (Horizon), Hamburg   **page 122:** Holger Latzel, München   **page 131:** "Red Nose Day", copyright: Comic Relief   **page 142:** Sony Europe GmbH   **page 143 & 167:** Micro Compact Car smart GmbH (A2000F7031), Renningen   **page 155:** Imagine (Coleman), Hamburg   **page 159:** "There was an Old Man of Berlin" by Edward Lear, published by Reclam   **page 163:** Sue Morris, Schwindegg   **page 186:** "Tom's Diner", M+T: Suzanne Vega, copyright by Waifersongs Ltd. / WB Music Corp. Für D/A/CH: Neue Welt Musikverlag GmbH   **page 189:** "The Modern Day Little Red Riding Hood" by Roald Dahl, from Revolting Rhymes, Puffin Books, Penguin. Used by permission of David Higham Associates.   **pages 192-193:** "If I had a million dollars", M+T: Steven J. Page / Ed Robertson, copyright by Treat Baker Music Inc. / WB Music Corp. Für D/A/CH: Neue Welt Musikverlag GmbH

My notes

My notes